PRAISE FOR
SUCCESSFUL EMPLOYEE COMMUNICATIONS

"It's great to see that Liam and Sue have teamed up again to share their considerable wealth of experience. We have here a manual which practitioners will find practical and actually want to use. The book's organization makes it an easy general read but also to use as a 'Help – what should I do here!' reference. And most of all, the book focuses on what matters most: not what you do, but the meaning you bring in creating patterns in the mess for employees."
Russell Grossman, Head of Profession for Internal Communications, Government Communication Service

"*Successful Employee Communications* is an essential read for any communication professional, whether working in the field of internal communication or not. Succinct, readable and compelling, it presents every topic from a strategic and outcome-focused perspective, supported by a perfect balance of evidence and research. Sue and Liam provide sound advice, recommendations and answers to overcome many barriers, as well as posing some challenging yet critical questions to consider. With an excellent collection of case studies, as well as frameworks and tools, the book offers actionable steps practitioners can take to make sure they bring value and make a difference in their organization. If you only read one book this year, make it this much-needed one."
Lise Michaud, Founder, IC Kollectif

"This book is exactly what the world of internal comms needs right now! A clear, practical guide to successful employee comms, grounded in evidence, and best-practice case-studies to illustrate the points made. It gives the reader plenty of easy to follow guidance on a range of employee comms topics, making it useful for IC pros no matter how long they have been working in the sector. Sue and Liam share their personal experiences and stories, which really help to bring the concepts to life. It's clear that they have been there, done it and got the comms T-shirt, and now they're sharing the secrets of their success with us, distilling many years of experience into an easy to digest book. If you only buy one book on employee comms, make sure it's this one."
Emma Bridger, People Lab MD and author of *Employee Engagement*

"Written by two of the most experienced people in employee communication, what makes this book really special is that it is like having two wise, friendly mentors by your side whom you can consult whenever you need to. Authoritative, easy-to-read, practical and pragmatic, it's packed with great case studies to illustrate the key points."
Hilary Scarlett, international speaker and author of
Neuroscience for Organizational Change

"A very accessible and interesting read – it gives a good overview of the breadth, scope and power of effective employee engagement brought to life through some really powerful and practical case studies. It makes a highly useful reference guide and approach for any company trying to engage better with their people."
Emma Cox, Partner, UK Head of Purpose, PwC

"People are the most important asset organizations have. Crucial to success and growth of any organization is how effective communication across the organization is. As a leader who looks after over 160,000 people, I cannot stress this enough. So delighted to see this book by Sue and Liam focusing on employee communications, and I highly recommend it."
Leena Nair, Chief HR Officer, Unilever

"The role of the internal communicator continues to evolve. Drawing on years of being at the heart of the profession, Liam and Sue clearly articulate how communicators today can play significant and influential roles that deliver business success. They demonstrate how this happens where communicators focus on delivering great outcomes, supported by the insights and data that come from truly listening to, and understanding, their audiences. This book is a valuable addition to the resources available for new and experienced communicators alike."
Howard Krais, President, International Association of Business Communicators (IABC) UK 2019

"In today's social and digital reality, the key to sustainable organizational success is engagement. Leaders, managers, and employees must form an interactive system where information, point of view, feedback, conversation, debate, and interpretation work in concert to result in an experience that furthers growth. From an employee communications standpoint, it's truly all about achieving outcomes; viewing engagement and experience as the result of such a

progressive approach to employee communications. In their ground breaking book, Dewhurst and Fitzpatrick share their expertise in implementing communications inside an organization in an approach and manner reflective of a digital age where information is no longer at the direction of the corporation. Rather, content is now ubiquitous and the company only owns context. This book is a must read for anyone looking to breakthrough and create lasting relationships throughout the organization."
Gary F Grates, Principal, W2O Group, New York

"Employee communications is increasingly central to the job of PR professionals. Dewhurst and FitzPatrick provide a practical and thoughtful approach to many of the issues which a practitioner needs to deal with on a daily basis. As well as providing a discussion of how to create engagement and to build a reputation from the inside out, they share stories from leading specialists from around the world. There is much good practice in this book and I hope it will become a standard for the profession."
Francis Ingham, Chief Executive, ICCO

Successful Employee Communications

A practitioner's guide to tools, models and best practice for internal communication

Sue Dewhurst and Liam FitzPatrick

KoganPage

Publisher's note

Every possible effort has been made to ensure that the information contained in this book is accurate at the time of going to press, and the publishers and authors cannot accept responsibility for any errors or omissions, however caused. No responsibility for loss or damage occasioned to any person acting, or refraining from action, as a result of the material in this publication can be accepted by the editor, the publisher or the authors.

First published in Great Britain and the United States in 2019 by Kogan Page Limited

2nd Floor, 45 Gee Street	122 W 27th St, 10th Floor	4737/23 Ansari Road
London	New York, NY 10001	Daryaganj
EC1V 3RS	USA	New Delhi 110002
United Kingdom		India

www.koganpage.com

ISBNs

Hardback	978 0 7494 9887 0
Paperback	978 0 7494 8452 1
Ebook	978 0 7494 8453 8

British Library Cataloguing-in-Publication Data

A CIP record for this book is available from the British Library.

Library of Congress Cataloging-in-Publication Data

Names: FitzPatrick, Liam, author. | Dewhurst, Sue, author.
Title: Successful employee communications : a practitioner's guide to tools,
    models and best practice for internal communication / Liam FitzPatrick and
    Sue Dewhurst.
Description: 1 Edition. | New York : Kogan Page Ltd, [2019].
Identifiers: LCCN 2019006376 (print) | LCCN 2019007649 (ebook) | ISBN
    9780749484538 (ebook) | ISBN 9780749498870 (hardback) | ISBN 9780749484521
    (pbk.)
Subjects: LCSH: Communication in management. | Communication in
    organizations. | Business communication.
Classification: LCC HD30.3 (ebook) | LCC HD30.3 .F555 2019 (print) | DDC
    658.4/5–dc23
LC record available at https://lccn.loc.gov/2019006376

Typeset by Integra
Print production managed by Jellyfish
Printed and bound by CPI Group (UK) Ltd, Croydon CR0 4YY

CONTENTS

FIGURES AND TABLES

PREFACE: READ THIS FIRST

We have known each other for nearly 20 years. During that time we've shared horror stories, celebrated successes, developed and delivered training for employee communicators and researched and written about many aspects of practice. This book reflects that experience, the great number of brilliant practitioners we've met, and is informed by the increasing body of academic research that is now happening in our field. Reading this book you'll see a number of themes come up again and again, but most of all there is a single red thread that runs through how we see our profession: *we are in the profession of meaning – everything flows from that.*

At its simplest, 'meaning' describes the process of transferring an idea from one person to another. It's the core skill that brings us into contact with some exciting people with interesting things to say. It's our key to meetings with senior leaders who need to break difficult news or share compelling visions. It's our passport into conversations with colleagues who have brought to work their fears, their ambitions, their personality and hopefully their whole selves.

But we are all more than technicians. We work with significance, helping people frame their understanding of why they are at work, and find purpose. This book discusses practice, process and technique as the foundations for building shared context. As communicators we are lucky to be involved in helping to shape how our colleagues see the world and celebrate their achievements.

That's quite special. And we argue that all is only possible if we realize a few important realities about our role.

Employee communications is not just about management's point of view

It is no longer possible to ignore that what people think matters. People who are listened to are engaged, and the evolution of technology presents all sorts of exciting possibilities to create dialogue, foster debate and trigger collaboration. Great internal communication has always been about making connections.

It's about outcomes – mostly

We have a fantastic opportunity to facilitate and support important objectives for our organizations and practitioners are increasingly recognized for the outcomes they deliver. We ensure that business strategy is implemented, that people work safely, look after clients and build creative and innovative organizations, among other things. We sustain cultures, aligning business plans and how people see their world. Outcomes should be our primary focus. But how we deliver them still matters: our outputs are our 'shop window', and our professionalism and knowhow are something that we should defend proudly.

It's all about change

Until recently, change communication was almost a separate specialism within employee communication. Today, it's what we all do. Because we are concerned with outcomes, we approach every situation asking where we need to take people from and where we need to get them to. Even the simplest 'business as usual' message will include an element of improvement or of change. Our role includes helping our internal customers and stakeholders clarify what they really want to happen and connect it to the meaning that our colleagues hold about their work.

Insight – our killer app

If what we do is all about change, a foundational asset for us is an unrivalled understanding of our colleagues. You cannot act as a bridge between groups in your organization if you do not know who they are, what they think, what interests them and what they do. Who do leaders in your organization turn to when they want unbiased guidance and a complete picture?

Your network has the answer

Whatever problem you face, it always comes back to what our colleagues understand. Your informal network is your window on the world of your people. Your network will always help you find the right answer. Why are people unhappy? How can I make a complicated project happen? What do people really care about? Where are the stories of people living our purpose? For the answers to all those questions, ask your network. It's one of the most important investments you will make as a communicator.

Sue and Liam

Making the case for employee communication

CHAPTER OBJECTIVES

Sooner or later most internal or employee communicators get asked *the question*. The very fact that it gets asked suggests that there is still a debate to be had about the answer.

And the question is, 'Why do we bother communicating with our people?'

The question comes up in a number of different forms. It can be asked about the value we bring to our organizations or our clients. It can be posed in terms of return on investment or it might be about our role in delivering things like employee engagement or customer satisfaction.

Although the response is often obvious (what sort of organization could survive without communication?) the specific answer will vary from place to place. The exact reason for internal or employee communication will determine, in large part, how you do the job. If you don't know why communication matters in your workplace or what difference it makes, you run the risk of doing it poorly.

This chapter looks at the value that good employee communication can add to an organization and aims to help you think about the processes and practices you need to follow if you want to make a difference.

We'll start by defining some terms and then look at some of the recent theory surrounding employee communication. After that we'll explore some common approaches to deciding where internal communication (IC) adds value. Our hope is that by the end of this chapter you will know the questions you should be asking yourself as you begin to develop a strategic approach to employee communication and you'll be set up to think about auditing – the subject of Chapter 2.

What exactly is employee communication?

Let's try to get something straight at the start. We're interested in how organizations communicate. This book is about the conversation that takes place between a group of colleagues who are joined together by a common goal or set of goals. That might be to make profits in a company, to help a charity's beneficiaries or to provide government services. And when we say 'conversation', we mean things like messages to staff, listening to employees or how a leader directs and focuses their team.

This book is not about how to improve one-to-one communication or fixing broken individual interpersonal relationships in the workplace. When a pair of colleagues fall out or just can't work together, it is often described as a failure to communicate. And while interpersonal communication has similar components to group communication, they are not the same thing and not the main focus of this book.

People use a range of skills to communicate with each other. As well as our verbal skills, we rely on non-verbal cues (like people leaving the room when someone enters, or fidgeting in a stressful meeting) or on our ability to listen to what is actually being said in a conversation. These skills might be used to share information, indicate respect, negotiate, solve problems and collaborate or influence other people.

It is sometimes useful to pretend that an organization is the same as an individual when it comes to communication. When you need to explain the problems of an organization getting its message over or understanding its people, it can be helpful to use the language of the individual. Perhaps we might say 'The organization needs to listen more carefully' or complain that 'mixed messages are being sent' when what the boss does is in conflict with what she says. But we should always keep in mind that, although organizations are made up of people, they are not people.

An internal communicator is concerned with the conversation within the organization and not automatically the interpersonal skills of regular colleagues in the office or factory. The day-to-day ebb and flow of relationships between co-workers are mostly the realm of organizational communication and not what we're looking at in this book.

Having this clear saves a degree of confusion. From an academic standpoint, it is interesting to connect line management communication, peer-to-peer communication, project communication and internal corporate communication (Welch and Jackson, 2007). When you think about it, they clearly are connected but, for practical reasons, we have to draw some lines around what a communication manager can be expected to achieve in the workplace.

Context matters for employee communication

However, life is rarely simple when it comes to matters of communication. Although we are concentrating on the conversation between staff and the organization, there is naturally some overlap between the individual and the collective. Without a basic understanding of human psychology it is probably difficult to manage corporate communication or advise on messaging.

In particular, as communicators we have an important role in creating a sense of shared context in an organization. When colleagues are agreed on their objectives or the challenges facing them, the scope for misunderstanding decreases. In fact, collaboration becomes far easier when people have a shared view of what they are trying to achieve and can anticipate correctly the needs and intentions of their colleagues. We'll return again and again to this theme in this book, especially when we talk about change and handling bad news.

So, at the most basic level, the value that we add is in fostering shared understanding within a workplace. If we do nothing else well, getting everyone on the same page immediately makes organizations work better and be more effective.

Defining employee communication

People who work in employee communication can find themselves being pulled in several directions. We can be reporters, coaches, change agents, consultants and even organizational strategists (Likely, 2008). Although it is tempting to define internal or employee communication, the range of work that gets done by practitioners can be incredibly broad and subject to some debate (Verčič et al, 2012).

There isn't a clearly agreed definition that tells us what employee communication is, apart from in general terms such as 'the planned use of communication actions to systematically influence the knowledge, attitudes and behaviours of current employees' (Strauss and Hoffman, 2000: 143).

So, in the rest of this book, we'll explore what internal or employee communication is through the lens of what practitioners do and the impact which they have. However, although we're not proposing a new definition we do need to highlight a couple of elements that are worth stressing.

The Strauss and Hoffman definition mentions planning and being systematic; these are surely essential components of a strategically minded management process. As people who have worked with, and trained, professional communicators over many years we can attest to the difference between a professional who works to a plan and a structure, and an amateur who turns up for work every day with no idea of what they are going to do. Real professionals think ahead, consider results and focus on resources.

Current employees are also mentioned in the definition. In this book we do not assume that employees are paid or necessarily current. Charities or non-profit organizations commonly have employees who give their time freely or in return for a benefit such as training or work experience. Noting this point reminds us that a pay cheque is actually only a small part of the reason why people come to work.

Furthermore, ex-employees are important stakeholders for many organizations. They might be important sources of future sales (many consultancies, for example, routinely manage a large alumni network and benefit from the goodwill of ex-staffers) or may return again as workers, bringing valuable experience of how customers use products. A company's pensioners can be a powerful reminder to serving workers of the benefits of loyalty. While we are not planning on looking at alumni communication in this book, we mention it here to illustrate how varied the concerns of an employee communicator can be.

Finally, let's not get the idea that employee communication is a one-way street. Changes of technology to help collaboration and developing expectation mean listening to the 'employee voice' is increasingly important. We're in the 'listening' and 'talking' business more than the 'telling' game.

Where does the employee communicator's value lie?

It would be brilliant if there were a simple formula that said that for every kilo of communication you added to an organization there would be so many tonnes of benefit. There is a temptation to go looking for the killer fact or the brilliant case study that can be worked into a board presentation to explain exactly why we should have the budget and access that we deserve. We would be allowed to get on with the job and probably be paid a lot more!

Of course, life is not like that; in fact, it's far more fun. Organizational behaviours cannot be summed up like a high school chemistry lesson or

Figure 1.1   The value of employee communication

written down like a cake recipe. Communications professionals have to be in command of a subtle universe of creativity, insight and project management.

Explaining where we add value in the organizations we support is therefore challenging and often a very subjective conversation. The subtleties of how we judge the role of communications have to be weighed against the importance or strategic impact that a programme of communication might have on the organization. Figure 1.1 illustrates this idea and suggests that there are four general approaches to understanding the value of workplace communication.

The content producer

Employee communication partly has its roots in corporate journalism (Yaxley and Ruck, 2015). Some of the earliest work on employee communication was done in corporate newspapers, magazines and even film units and reflected the need to get information out to a workforce and give people a degree of pride in where they worked. Today, content production remains an important focus for employee communications teams, not least because we have access to more channels than ever before and there is a belief that workers are hungry for large volumes of lively content.

We will distinguish throughout this book between *outputs* and *outcomes*. Outputs are communication products such as content on a website, a staff conference or a chief executive officer (CEO) webcast. Outcomes are the results that come from those communications taking place.

It is often quite simple to make a subjective judgement about the quality of IC outputs. We can track whether people are looking at it and interacting with it. As well as knowing how people are sharing our internal content, we can make a judgement about whether the material is on message or appropriate. Whether that is useful data, though, is another matter; the communications team might be satisfied that a well-crafted piece of content got colleagues talking, but we do need to be aware that this doesn't mean it has actually moved the organization forward!

We should also not lose sight of the fact that in busy and challenging organizations just managing to create materials and get things done is a major achievement. As we discuss in Chapter 8, we have found that the ability to project manage and 'make things happen' is one of the most prized attributes of internal communicators (Dewhurst and FitzPatrick, 2007). Over time, the challenges facing professionals have not become any easier – being able to generate outputs is important and takes effort and skill.

Yet, there is little point in being busy for its own sake and there is probably little strategic value in just producing material. Unless we can show how the life of the organization is improved by a slick video or user-generated content, we may find ourselves facing some tough questions when next year's budget cuts are mooted. If there are no outcomes following all your excellent work, it amounts to little more than corporate shouting!

Explaining our value is often simpler when we can point to specific changes we have brought about as a result of communication.

Behaviour drivers

The Strauss and Hoffman definition mentioned above indicates that the purpose of planned and systematic communication is to change something; we communicate to share information, influence attitudes and drive actions. Communication is done with a purpose; with an outcome in mind. We actually think that most employee communication is about change.

Like many commentators, Strauss and Hoffman imply that outcomes can be best seen in terms of knowledge, understanding and behaviours. People commonly talk about 'know/feel/do' as the three standard objectives of communication and it is certainly a useful formula when thinking about communication objectives. Obviously, every organization has separate pressures, and seemingly similar operations will have different needs from their workforces. A discount retailer might emphasize the need to keep rails and shelves restocked and a rapid flow of customers though the check-outs, whilst a high-end fashion store may want staff to think about the client experience and protecting brand values.

However, there are some generic behaviours which employers want to promote (FitzPatrick, 2016: 298). These will include encouraging staff to stay (in order to reduce staff turnover and manage employment costs), promoting collaboration between colleagues, helping workers focus on the right things and follow rules, promoting advocacy outside the organization and responding positively to major change.

The list of desired outcomes might be longer, but it is useful to look at the actions that could result from good employee communication. If we know what we want people to *do*, then, in theory, it is easier to ask what they need to *feel* and *know* on the path to promoting that behaviour. Yet communication is rarely the sole driver of a particular behaviour in the workplace. We do things partly because we think they are a good idea, but also because our boss orders us to do so, because it is interesting, because we have the right tools to do the job, or because there's an attractive bonus payment coming if we hit our targets. Communication promotes actions, but it is rarely the only reason why our colleagues do things; Chapter 4 argues that by deeply understanding our audiences we unlock real value for our organizations.

Supporters and facilitators

Increasingly, communicators describe themselves as people who help others achieve their goals. They often talk about being business partners or supporters. This means that instead of the value of our work coming directly from the results of what we do, the benefits come through helping others do their jobs (Zerfass and Franke, 2012). This might involve coaching a manager before they hold a staff meeting or drafting messages for a senior leader.

Communicators are often attached to specific departments or teams who see communication as essential to their mission. Information technology (IT) organizations may need a communicator to ensure that news about service changes gets out and that users know how to make use of new tools. A quality team or a safety function might have someone to drive messages in support of their missions.

Modern managers understand that communication is as much part of the management process as resource planning or data management. We help them run things efficiently by either supporting individuals in their leadership or helping whole functions to explain themselves. We also see opportunities that others have missed. The job is not just about visiting the CEO and taking instruction; it is about bringing ideas that no one has thought about. It may be that we know that customer satisfaction is suffering as a consequence of unhappiness in the factory, so we might want to prompt the CEO to visit for a 'back to the floor' exercise to hear, first hand, what staff are saying. Perhaps we've noticed that staff turnover among younger colleagues is higher than expected, so we could offer some ideas around recognition to the human resources (HR) director.

Our value, therefore, often comes not from the work that we do but from the work that we empower others to do. Quantifying the value of our contribution is challenging, but we can be an ever-more integrated part of the management process and should be integral to helping achieve results.

Asset growing

Focusing on behaviours is a useful place to start when planning employee communication. For specific projects, asking at the beginning what you need people to do is valuable and a powerful guide to the results that are needed. However, is the value in employee communication only to be found in specific behaviours?

When communications leaders are asked about the purpose of their role they actually come up with a more complicated answer (Zerfass and Viertmann, 2017). Certainly, shaping attitudes and behaviours is important, but does it fully account for the creation of intangible assets such as employee engagement or a positive workplace culture (Alfes et al, 2013)? Does the importance of communication lie mainly in promoting defined feelings and actions? And where does building a brand fit into the mix?

Although closely related to behaviour, concepts of engagement or culture are not the same and have an importance that supersedes specific actions. A coffee shop or hotel might want someone to follow specific steps, for example, in delivering customer service, but are employees authentically hospitable because they are told to be so? The genuine compassion that a patient might experience from hospital staff could have less to do with a campaign by management and more with the overall ethos of the institution. Equally, an engineer might decide to falsify emissions test results or bend safety rules because they misunderstand what their organization stands for.

People in healthy organizations think and act in common ways that help it grow and achieve its purpose. In Chapter 12 we'll talk about the role that employee communicators can play in the partly organic processes that nurture intangible assets like brand, goodwill and culture (Zerfass and Viertmann, 2016). We should see it as part of our mission, although it is difficult to assess what impact we are having in practical terms. The difficulty comes in accounting for the size of the intangible asset and the contribution that internal or employee communication makes to that asset. Laying aside for the moment the debates that rage in management circles about quantifying things like brands, there are endless arguments to be had about the importance of employee communication in that mix, or indeed the type of communication that matters.

One example of the complexity is the issue of employee voice. Some writers suggest that having an outlet for employee opinions is massively important (Kang and Sung, 2017) and one of the main drivers of employee engagement (MacLeod and Clarke, 2010). Others will think it is sufficient to listen to workers only to check how much of the core messages have been understood. Undoubtedly, employee communication, listening to workers and creating a shared sense of context and purpose are important, but there is little consensus about how important.

Choosing your own value proposition

You'd be forgiven for shaking your head in despair. How on earth can a communicator show that employee communication is worth doing?

Discussions about the rate of return to be expected from investments in communication can quickly descend into farce. Finding a formula or algorithm which translates inputs into results in a commercial organization will need everyone to agree about the relative importance of factors such as pay, leadership skills, training or the equipment supplied to workers. In non-profits, which look for more complicated results than profits, the equation is bound to be even more complicated. It is almost impossible to say that a budget of X or team of Y people should have benefit Z.

This is not, of course, to suggest that there is no causal relationship between good communication and organization success. Plainly, we all see it with our own eyes and we all know that the absence of communication is a recipe for disaster. The challenge is to understand what benefit we are seeking for our own organization and use that as our guiding compass.

Defining the value you add through employee communication

As a simple guide we find it useful to think about the core value that an IC function can offer to the organization that it supports. Our thinking is that there are probably four main areas – or value spaces – that a communicator needs to consider when thinking about what they should be doing. Figure 1.2 summarizes this. All these value spaces overlap and in some cases are interlinked. In reality we commonly have to deliver across all four areas but need to think about the relative importance of each. The exact proportions of each one will vary depending on what your organization does, the problems it faces and even its history.

We've been partly influenced by the work of people who have tried to define the core components of employee communication (Yates, 2006) and have admired attempts to actually attach specific values to different elements

Figure 1.2   Four value spaces

Get the basics Right	Drive Outcomes	Support others	Build Intangible Assets
• Channels that reach everyone • Ways to listen • Dependability to make things happen • Routines and forward plans • Ability to report back on impact • Creativity and imagination	• Focuses on communications to link knowledge, attitudes and, crucially, behaviours • Understands and speaks up regarding non-communications barriers to focuses actions • Applies audience insights	• Understands audiences better than anyone else • Understands business needs and how communications can support them • Gives persuasive advice: earns respect	• Understands the role of communications in building employee engagement • Connects external reputation or brand with employees understanding and belief • Identifies how communications helps to maintain a positive culture

of the mix. Some of this work has not always been terribly convincing but it seems that writers generally keep returning to four areas:

- *operating effective systems* (to which we will return later in the book);

- *working to deliver outcomes* such as behaviours or positive attitudes;

- *supporting others* to achieve their goals through communication; and

- contributing to the *growth of intangible assets* in the organization (such as employee engagement, positive culture or brand).

So how do you decide which matter most to you and where you should concentrate your efforts?

Before you start worrying too much about which activity sits under which heading we should say that Figure 1.2 is illustrative only. Often, activities will sit within several or all boxes. For example, running an intelligence service that listens to employee views and concerns and shares it with leaders is a foundational role for all of the value spaces in the model. The emphasis and scale of each will vary from situation to situation, but the aim here is to explore the idea that we add value in different ways and so need to adapt our practice accordingly.

Our view is that, for now, it is very hard to tag specific cash values to the results of the work that we do. Whilst it will frequently be evident what impact our work might have, for example, on sales or in reducing accidents in the workplace, defining a return on investment with a high degree of accuracy is challenging and likely to be time-consuming.

The point is that we need to think about what our organization needs from us. Even if you can't reliably quantify the value we add, if you are working on the right things, our usefulness will be plain and the choices we have to make in defining our plans or choosing where to spend time will be clear. How we do our work will be shaped by an understanding of the value we need to add. An app designed to share operational information will look very different to one intended to support individual leaders, for example.

Pause for thought

- Do you understand the main issues that are on the leadership agenda in your organization? What are the subjects that get regularly reported on at board or senior executive meetings, and are they reflected in your communication plan?

- In your organization what are the drivers of employee engagement and where does employee communication fit in? Do you understand how well the organization is performing against the non-communication elements of engagement and are you aware of the steps to improve them?

- What support do your leaders expect from communication and have you asked them lately? When you have a conversation with leaders what can you tell them that they don't already know, for example about current employee attitudes or the effectiveness of their own messaging?

- How many of your communication plans have clearly defined objectives that are about knowledge, understanding or behaviours?

- Who would notice if the employee communication team was axed in your organization and what would they miss most?

Getting the basics right

In later chapters we will explore this area more fully. For now, the main point we want to make is that creating and managing a reliable system for delivering news and information to staff, getting people talking, listening to feedback or supporting collaboration are often the original raison d'être for many employee communication functions. Neglecting the need for essential systems and processes will get you into trouble quite quickly.

It's a message that our peers in service functions like IT understand only too well. The chief information officer (CIO) would not dream of attempting a discussion about the strategic direction of data management while the organization is screaming that their computers don't work and email has been down for a week. There are 'utility' elements to the offer that are expected and will kill off any other conversation if they are underperforming.

For communicators, this likely means ensuring that you should be able to put a message in front of employees in a timely and engaging way, that people can find information when they need it, that you have a process for maintaining a flow of communication and that you have a reliable way to collect and share the sentiment of employees. It will certainly involve having the capability to deliver projects as required by the organization – be that from posting content on the intranet to running the annual leadership conference. A communications team that cannot deliver these essentials will quickly find themselves replaced or disbanded.

So, the question you need to ask is: what are the basics that my organization needs? These will almost certainly involve having a process for delivering current news, spaces for people to find information when they need it, a way for you to gather and report on feedback and hear employees' thoughts, and the capacity to run campaigns.

And when you know the answer, you need to think about whether this is the most important thing in your world. But we'll come back to that in a moment.

Driving outcomes

A focus on the results as well as the process of communication is an important source of value. This calls for a mindset among the team that looks for the point of any activity and thinks about the attitudinal or behavioural outcome that is needed.

It is our experience that even just asking the question 'What do we want people to do?' is often usefully provocative and forces colleagues to reconsider their plans and objectives. And naturally, once you start asking the question, you need to have the ability to provide alternative answers. Our value will not lie in telling the HR director that her planned all-staff email is a waste of time; suggesting alternative and more useful approaches will more surely win us friends than saying no all the time.

In order to deliver value in this box you will need processes for taking briefs, for developing plans linked to defined results and probably the skills and resources that enable you to turn business problems into impactful communications plans.

Supporting others

Later on we'll explore the role of the employee communicator as an adviser and an involved team player. Importantly, this role requires the communicator to think wider than messaging practice. We need to understand how our organization works, where revenue comes from, what makes our organization successful, how costs are managed, what risks we face and anything else that is the strategic concern of leaders.

The role that we fulfil is about acting as a partner and adviser rather than an order-taker. We can be most useful when we can anticipate the communication needs of a team or of leaders and bring solutions, rather than waiting for people who are not specialists in our area to define their communication needs and turn it into a brief for us.

In Chapter 3 when we talk about objectives we look at the questions to ask when planning, as we want to suggest that our role is not just about taking orders or responding to requests but also about proposing solutions. Sometimes those solutions will go beyond pure communication advice. As well as being knowledgeable about the business and audiences we also have to be skilled as coaches and advocates for our solutions.

If this is a value space that is significant for you, your focus will extend to being a business leader in your own right and not simply a member of a team of technicians who translate defined results into communication plans.

Asset builders

Employee communicators have a role in shaping the strategic assets – brand, culture and ethos – of their businesses. It is a role that requires us to think far beyond the basic mechanics of email lists, social media content and forward editorial schedules. It requires owning one's own professionalism around communication but also being ready, as a senior player, to input on other areas of the business and not just on communication issues. Drawing on a deep knowledge of employees, of the business and of the overall strategy empowers you to contribute to the very heart of the organization. This can mean being occasionally courageous and often challenging. Our backgrounds, experiences and insights into the audience win us admission to the conversations about brands or employee engagement; it is our attitude as business leaders that equips us to contribute in ways that go beyond being corporate reporters.

If you decide that this is a space where your organization needs you to have an impact, you will undoubtedly be investing in systems that enable you to understand how communication is part of the asset-building process. You will need to understand, for example, what makes engaged employees in your workplace and where you fit into that mix. It could result in you developing the capacity to build relationships, gather feedback and intelligence and to be a respected commentator within the organization.

It's not one or the other

The four value spaces are not mutually exclusive. You can't support leaders or build intangible assets if your basic systems are not in order. Your basics will inevitably involve having platforms for leadership communication or include a brief-taking process that looks at know/feel/do.

The point is that you have to decide in what proportion they matter to your organization and build your employee communication effort accordingly. An entrepreneur-led small business might need systems for supporting leaders more than brand building. A large multi-site organization that is heavily concerned with safety or production quality might have a stronger need for an outcome-driven operation. But whatever the lead priority, all four value spaces are likely to be present to a greater or lesser extent. The role of the strategically minded employee communicator is to look at these four areas and decide where their efforts are best focused.

Conclusion

When you are thinking about the type of communications operation you should be running, everything comes back to the point of why you do the job at all. What does your organization need from communications – is it to have a process for sharing information, gathering intelligence and community building, is it about having a team who can translate business problems into business solutions, could it rely on a function that helps the organization communicate or is it mostly concerned with building an intangible asset? Of course, for most of us, it will be a combination of all four; the challenge is to decide in which proportion they are needed and where you should be putting your effort.

However, we don't get to decide our usefulness all by ourselves. Other people in our organization will have a view about the value that we need to bring and what we bring in practice. There is no point investing tonnes of energy in providing leaders with advice or worrying about culture when your CEO thinks that a neat app does everything that is needed. You have to reflect what the organization thinks it wants, as much as what you know it needs. And that means you need to be close to the decision-makers and the corporate conversations that are taking place around you.

And there is one other sense in which value matters. Are you actually doing a good job? Are you as good as you could be at what you set out to do? If you can't deliver on the basics, are a poor adviser or just can't make things happen, it is unlikely that anyone will ever see the added value that internal communication can bring. Our daily challenge is to be as good as we can be; otherwise, any of the discussion about added value is pointless. When you are effective, when people around you know that they will get a great service when they ask you for help and when leaders trust you to tell them what is going on the organization, you start to win the space to offer ever greater value.

In later chapters we will explore what good looks like. However, every organization needs a unique blend of communication and so our approach will be to pose questions as much as suggest answers. We have always agreed with Bill Quirke, one of the greatest writers on IC matters, who said that you can't take someone else's medicine. This book is about helping you draw up your own prescription.

References

Alfes, K, Shantz, AD, Truss, C and Soane, EC (2013) The link between perceived human resource management practices, engagement and employee behaviour: A moderated mediation model, *The International Journal of Human Resource Management*, 24(2), pp 330–51

Dewhurst, S and FitzPatrick, L (2007) *How to Develop Outstanding Internal Communicators*, Melcrum

FitzPatrick, L (2016) Internal communication, in *The Public Relations Handbook*, A Theaker, Routledge

Kang, M and Sung, M (2017) How symmetrical employee communication leads to employee engagement and positive employee communication behaviors: The mediation of employee–organization relationships, *Journal of Communication Management*, 21(1), pp 82–10

Likely, F (2008) Securing the function: The greatest protection, *Strategic Communication Management*, 12(3), p 15

MacLeod, D and Clarke, N (2010) Leadership and employee engagement: Passing fad or a new way of doing business? *International Journal of Leadership in Public Services*, 6(4), pp 26–30

Stauss, B and Hoffmann, F (2000) Minimizing internal communication gaps by using business television, in *Internal Marketing: Directions for management*, ed B Lewis and R Varey, pp 141–59, Taylor & Francis

Verčič, AT, Verčič, D and Sriramesh, K (2012) Internal communication: Definition, parameters, and the future, *Public Relations Review*, **38**(2), pp 223–30

Welch, M and Jackson, PR (2007) Rethinking internal communication: A stakeholder approach, *Corporate Communications: An international journal*, **12**(2), pp 177–98

Yates, K (2006) Internal communication effectiveness enhances bottom-line results, *Global Business and Organizational Excellence*, **25**(3), pp 71–79

Yaxley, H and Ruck, K (2015) Tracking the rise and rise of internal communication, in *Exploring Internal Communication: Towards informed employee voice*, 3rd edn, ed K Ruck, pp 3–14, Routledge

Zerfass, A and Franke, N (2012) Enabling, advising, supporting, executing: a theoretical framework for internal communication consulting within organizations, Institute for Public Relations Top Three Papers Award, presented at the Fifteenth Annual International Public Relations Research Conference

Zerfass, A and Viertmann, C (2016) The communication value circle: How communication contributes to corporate success, *Communication Director*, **2**, pp 50–53

Zerfass, A and Viertmann, C (2017) Creating business value through corporate communication: A theory-based framework and its practical application, *Journal of Communication Management*, **21**(1), pp 68–81

Conducting your own employee communication audit 02

CHAPTER OBJECTIVES

We all find ourselves wondering from time to time if we are doing a good job. Everyone questions whether their team is focused on the right things or whether they could be doing things better. This chapter offers a framework for asking questions about the effectiveness and efficiency of an IC or employee communications (EC) function. We are not looking at whether your organization is communicative or where the blockages are in the flow of information around the organization; our focus is on whether the communications function is working on the right things and getting the right results for the organization,

Here we will look at the overall operation and ask whether it has the right goals and whether it is set up to achieve them. Of course, goals, resources and results are closely linked but we will deal mainly with the first two in this chapter; Chapter 11 looks more closely at whether individual communications are landing.

We suggest a list of areas that matter in the running of a communication department and so should be of interest in an audit. We'll look at how you assess how well you are setting objectives for the EC function and for making judgements about how well it is working. Importantly, we believe that collecting information on its own is of little value; it only matters when you apply that data to make a difference to your organization and to help leaders make better communication decisions.

As with the rest of this book, we're not looking at the detail of interpersonal interactions between colleagues or teams – there are some great resources that cover this topic in the right detail[1] – our aim is to think about the value that is to be had from general communication.

Why bother reviewing your employee communication?

In Chapter 1 we argued that EC can make a difference in retaining great people, explaining to them their objectives, helping them collaborate, encouraging them to be powerful advocates and facilitating change. If we claim we can add value, we should at least check that we've got the plans, people and processes in place to make sure we can deliver it!

From day one, when creating a department from scratch, you will want to know where to start. Whether you are an experienced communications leader or entirely new to the discipline, you can benefit from taking a systematic look at the job to be done and how it can be achieved. When things are up and running, a good manager will also periodically wonder if they are putting effort and resources into the right places. Organizations and their priorities change, so from time to time we all need to step back and take stock.

Organizations like Novo Nordisk in our case study (page 30) also include auditing as a continuing process for helping local leaders improve their own communications operations. And every communications manager will, one day, have the experience that things have stopped working. Suddenly we'll notice that we don't seem to be getting results any more and we may have no idea why. Could it be a change in the team that has caught us out? Maybe it's a shift in the audience demographics or a need for change in the range of channels that could be the problem. Without taking a look under the car's bonnet it is hard to know what to tune up. We take our cars (or bicycle in Liam's case) in for a service; we should do the same with our communications set-up.

A few pitfalls with auditing employee communication

The value of conducting some sort of review from time to time seems obvious. However, audits are not without their pitfalls; traps that, if not avoided, could have very negative consequences.

Before setting out to audit or review keep in mind:

- **What you measure can dictate what you end up doing.** Choose carefully where you focus, as you can find yourself doing the wrong things just because they fit on a dashboard or people expect you to report on them. Do email open rates tell you if people understand? Does producing a quarterly newsletter on time ensure that staff are excited by company strategy? If we don't identify the things that do matter, we can create self-fulfilling prophecies or confound ourselves with misleading data (Carnall and By, 2014: 221).

- **Don't ignore what's working.** It's easy to concentrate on what is broken. Successes are your opportunities to develop and, properly analysed, can keep you on track (Bridger, 2014: 121).

- **Listen to employees.** Writers who talk about 'employee voice' warn against ignoring staff perspective on communication (Ruck and Welch, 2012). When we don't ask colleagues what they want to say or hear, we miss out on data about a vital driver of engagement.

- **Don't get hung up on what other people are doing.** EC pioneer Bill Quirke said that making comparisons was like trying to take a dose of another patient's medicine – what is useful in one place could be meaningless, or even confusing, in another.

- **Keep it simple and know when to stop digging.** We live in a complex world and oversimplifying things can lead to problems. However, we need to be practical and delve into the right level of detail. Knowing the minutiae of the preferences of audience segments might be fascinating, but is the effort involved in researching it worth it? We can all learn from the UK's Government Communication Service, which has developed a simple methodology for 'capability reviews' (Government Communication Service, no date). These explore whether communications teams have clear plans, the right resources and are able to implement programmes effectively. The approach involves a team of senior practitioners from other government departments and from outside government who work through a structured set of questions in interviews and site visits.

- **Finally, expect to hear things you would rather not know.** Auditing communication could tell you that no one, except the CEO, likes the CEO's quarterly video, that your best friend in the team is actually redundant or that you are making no difference whatsoever to the organization's performance. Before you start, be ready for some tough news and be prepared to deal with it.

The audit wheel – a simple guide to what to look at

However you approach your review, you will probably want to include some common topics. For example, work among universities in the UK highlighted the need for a clear organizational vision and leadership involvement in the process (Simpson and Taylor, 2009), while other writers will mention resourcing, competencies in the communications team and ensuring that line managers have a defined and supported role.

The most common components of an employee communications audit are set out in Figure 2.1 and include:

- Effectiveness shapers – are we doing the right things?
  - o clarity about business goals;
  - o authentic involvement of senior leaders;
  - o having an agreed communication strategy.
- Efficiency drivers – are we doing them in the right way?
  - o appropriate resources;
  - o range of channels;
  - o supporting managers;
  - o data and insight.

Communication effectiveness – are we doing the right things?

Any review process should ideally begin by understanding what the EC operation is expected to achieve. If you can't say what the job is, you won't be able to judge the efficiency of the team. Assessing if you have the right tools, process and resources in place relies on being clear about what effectiveness looks like.

Figure 2.1   The audit wheel

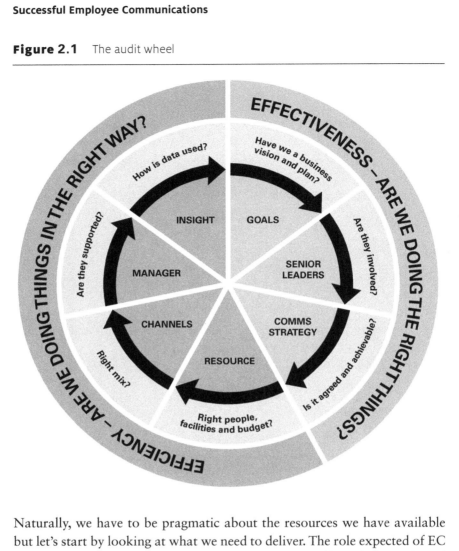

Naturally, we have to be pragmatic about the resources we have available but let's start by looking at what we need to deliver. The role expected of EC shapes every other consideration about things like staffing, skills, tools and processes.

And the best place to begin is to ask senior leaders two simple questions:

- If we were starting from scratch, what would be the single most important thing that a new employee communications department could do to improve our performance or profitability?[2]

- What does that mean for the things that communications do?

These questions focus the conversation on corporate value rather than getting into an immediate discussion of channels or tactics; it means that it is then much easier to trace findings back to the strategic needs of the organization.

The follow-up question about activities needs careful handling, as very often stakeholders can jump straight into using their favourite tactics without making the connection back to their potential impact on results. If, for example, a leader says that supporting employee retention is a priority, it might be necessary to question their view that an app is the most important deliverable. Likewise, running the staff summer party might not obviously deliver on their vision of a communications operation that drives environmental compliance.

Conversations about value will give you an insight into the focus of the communications team and the basis for more detailed assessments. Leaders often disagree amongst themselves but that shouldn't be a worry as it is part of our role to guide their understanding and expectations. The point is that we have begun the task of connecting organizational success to communication; this is essential in planning the EC function and in shaping leaders' understanding of what we can deliver.

We say much more about this in Chapter 3 and make a number of suggestions about the conversations a communicator needs to have with their stakeholders.

Communication goals

Often, the basic value we deliver is to explain the vision or strategy to our colleagues, although this does assume that your organization actually has a vision or a strategy that can be explained. If nothing exists or the plans only make sense to those who created them, how can we communicate them? Just because the CEO says there is a strategy, it doesn't actually mean that there is one!

Some years ago, we worked with a communications team that inadvertently discovered it was the strategy department by default. At a leadership conference, the CEO had been challenged about the lack of a strategy for the business and he had responded by pointing at the conference slogan and exclaiming that 'Creating Impact' was the perfect expression of what they were trying to achieve. In fact, the slogan had been invented during a late-night conference planning session in the events team and so they and their communications colleagues spent the next 12 months trying to turn the slogan into something that looked and felt like a long-term business philosophy. Unsurprisingly, they failed and had to live with repeated feedback that staff felt the business lacked direction and had no idea how their roles supported success. If there isn't a plan, no amount of communication will make one magically appear.

When a strategy or plan does exist, it will need to align with what staff think the purpose and values of the organization are. No matter how skilful the communications team, staff will always be confused when they see the organization drift away from what they believe it exists for. A university that shuts down research programmes is likely to find itself in conflict with its workforce. A bank that deliberately overcharges customers whilst claiming to be trustworthy presents its employee communications team with a real headache.

So your review starts by establishing whether there is a credible strategy that communication can be shaped to support. The crucial areas to explore are typically:

- Do we have a clear purpose and set of values that inform decision-making at the top of the organization?
- Does the purpose of the organization align to what is morally and culturally appropriate for its workforce?
- Are the business strategy and related plans credible and will employees be able to see their roles in them?

Senior leaders shaping communication

Senior management involvement is a deciding factor in whether communication is credible and effective (Ni, 2007; Men, 2014). If leaders are not part of the process, communication is bound to be seriously hampered.

That means we need to ask whether the communications function is actually seen as important for the success of the organization (Falkheimer *et al*, 2017). In the past, EC and even public relations (PR) were treated as support functions that focused on process and producing content but, as relationships and access to resources are increasingly seen as corporate assets, we need to be clear whether our senior leaders give communication the attention it needs. And we need to check how the communications function supports the leadership culture of the organization.

Academics draw a distinction between *task-oriented* leadership and *transformational* leadership (Men, 2014). Simplistically, task-oriented leaders are mostly concerned with giving clear instructions to get a job done, whilst a leader who adopts a transformational approach will ask team members to go beyond personal interest in the pursuit of a common goal.

Naturally, most leaders and their organizations use a mix of approaches. Perhaps when talking about safety or ethics an organization might want to be mostly task-oriented – setting out clear expectations and orders. A transformational approach might be more relevant when promoting innovation or collaboration. We will want to understand how and when these approaches are at play[3] and whether communications can support them accordingly. Although there will be no cut and dried approach, transformational leadership will probably need a lot of face-to-face communication and a strong interest in feedback and listening. A task-oriented style might favour channels that are effective at delivering detailed information.

Although it may be very obvious whether or not senior leaders are involved in shaping and driving communication, it is useful to think about the exact nature of involvement by asking:

- How are executives engaged in defining the communication strategy? Is it something that they debate at length (and are committed to) or do they just sign off a paper (which they later ignore)?

- How are executives involved in shaping and agreeing essential messages, in general and on specific occasions?

- Do leaders think about how major decisions are to be communicated at the time when those decisions are made, or is it an afterthought?

- What feedback do senior managers receive from communication and do they respond to it?

- Is face-to-face communication a regular habit for upper managers?

- Does being a good communicator matter when people are considered for top posts?

- Do executives actually care about the communication strategy?

Leaders need to be authentic in how they communicate. People should see that they genuinely care about the message getting through, that they are interested in the response and that leaders' actions match their words. The above questions should help establish some of the components of authenticity, but the big question is whether communication truly matters to leaders.

Communication strategy

There are two issues to think about here – is there a defined and agreed communication strategy, and is that EC strategy aligned to the overall needs of the organization?

We shouldn't assume that a communication strategy or plan exists in the first place; a newly created team will need to develop one from scratch, and big changes in an organization might make the old approach obsolete. If a plan doesn't exist then this book should help you formulate one. And if the plan exists, does it directly address the big issues in the organization? For example, if holding on to talented staff is a strategic challenge, how will communication help to persuade people to stay? If the survival of the organization depends on innovation, where does communication support the development of new ideas? Will communication make the organization a safer place to work if safety is the organization's first priority?

We don't claim that there is a perfect format or structure for a communication strategy as every organization has different needs; an approach that is right in one place is not necessarily going to work in another. However, the strategy and plan should meet some of the following criteria:

- Is it written down? Is its existence known to anyone who has a responsibility for implementing it or approving elements of it?
- Does the plan specifically address corporate strategic challenges? Does it say how communication is going to deliver value for the organization?
- Does the plan enjoy the support of the most senior managers? Are they clear about their role in its delivery?
- Is the plan actually realistic or sensible, given the size and complexity of the organization?
- How often is the strategy reviewed? Is it keeping pace with corporate strategy?
- Does it dovetail with plans for relevant departments such as external communications or HR?
- Does it set out audiences and how they are to be approached?
- Are general messages defined and clear?
- Is there a detailed timeline and pipeline for future activities (that reflects organizational priorities)?
- What is the governance process for ensuring that senior leaders are involved, that peers are informed and that messages and tactics are aligned?

Resourcing communications

After exploring objectives, we can look at resources. There is little point in having a beautifully defined plan if you haven't the funds, organization and resources to bring it to life. An audit needs to ask whether the communications function has the right structure, right people and right budget to get the job done. However, as we said above, the resources should ideally reflect the objectives, and not the other way around.

People approach budgeting in many different ways and it would be wrong to suggest that there is a perfect approach that works for everyone. You might start by thinking about the value that leaders expect their communicators to deliver; if they expect a lot they may be more willing to invest. But, generally, there are no common standards or rules of thumb that suggest an organization with X number of people should spend Y on its employee communication. Looking for benchmarks based on things like organizational complexity, location, sector or financial turnover does not seem to help much; people just budget and organize differently for a very diverse range of reasons. The reviewer can only really ask whether the budget available is sufficient for the tasks to be done, and that is normally a subjective judgement based on experience and the expectation of senior leaders.

Just as it is hard to prescribe the right budget, defining the shape and structure of the communications function is equally challenging. Research over the years, including a recent study for the IABC (Moss *et al*, 2017), suggests that there are no typical ways to organize a team. Debates about how the team should align with other functions like PR, HR or operations have been common for decades but structure and organization should be an attempt to balance efficacy, control, standardization of practice, the needs of business areas and the culture of the organization.

In the past we investigated the competencies (the mix of skills, knowledge and experiences) needed in a communications function (Dewhurst and FitzPatrick, 2007).[4] Our research among 860 practitioners highlighted that there is no such thing as a standard internal communicator. We found, depending on myriad factors such as history, sector, culture, organization challenges or role, that practitioners could be expected to display up to 12 different competencies and each competency could be practised at three different levels. In practice, a review needs to look at the job to be done and the skills that will be needed to do it rather than assuming that all communicators are interchangeable.

This part of the review should also consider the ability and performance of the head of the communications function. Are they up to the job, do they build strong relationships, do they have access to senior leaders?

We should also think of relationships as a resource in the context of a communication function. In order to do their job, a communicator needs to be respected by stakeholders and have relationships around the organization. Reviewers need to ask whether the team can persuade reluctant colleagues to help with projects, can use influence (as we rarely have power) and are welcome at any level in the organization. And the team does need to be systematic and organized; it needs processes and practices that enable it to be reliable and efficient.

In short, an audit needs to consider:

- Are the financial resources commensurate with the value that EC is expected to deliver for the organization?
- Can the communications function balance the demands of the organization as a whole, of different business areas and service functions?
- Does the communications function have working processes for gathering intelligence, predicting and managing demand, planning content, making things happen and tracking impact?
- Does the communications team have rich relationships with colleagues at all levels of the organization?
- Are communicators trusted and valued by the most senior managers in the organization?
- How well do all members of the communication team understand the business, its challenges and priorities and are they reflected in their work?
- Does the team have access to relevant skills (eg writing, digital, design) at an acceptable standard?
- Does the communications team follow and promote corporate brand and identity standards?
- Are the team's processes and people adaptable and able to respond to changing demands?

Right channels?

We look at channels in Chapter 6 so will not repeat ourselves greatly here. Rather, as a simple guide to understanding the tools and processes that need developing, we suggest auditors think about the following questions:

- Are the roles and rules for each channel or tactic defined and shared inside and outside the communications team?

- Are there tools for 'pushing' information or news out to staff regardless of location or IT access?

- How do staff find or 'pull' information or news when they need it?

- Are there formal and informal channels for collecting feedback or reactions from staff?

- What channels exist for briefing line managers that allow them to explore issues in a safe place?

- Do staff have regular team discussions about work and organizational issues?

- What opportunities are there for staff to socialize, collaborate or debate among themselves?

- Are there formats in place for senior leaders to talk with staff face-to-face both in large groups and in more informal settings?

- Are multiple channels used to ensure that different audience groups can be reached?

Manager roles

As every communicator knows, managers are central to effective employee communication. They have a vital part to play in converting corporate messages into terms that make sense to their teams and it is they who should understand better than anyone how regular colleagues think.

We explore these issues in more detail in Chapter 7, but for now we suggest that an audit thinks about some simple questions:

- Are managers clear about their role in the communication process in general and on a day-to-day basis?

- Are managers given proper briefings on a regular basis and a chance to debate issues to ensure that they understand them before discussing them with their teams?

- What training in communication and facilitation skills is given to managers?

- What materials are given to help managers explain messages to their teams?

- Is there an established process for sharing manager feedback with senior leaders?

Insight

A slogan we repeat often is 'Come with data – leave with respect.' It's born out of the realization that most executive team members live and die by spreadsheets, and they expect their peers to bring evidence to meetings. Employee communicators can't afford to be different.

Broadly speaking, communicators need to know:

- who works here: the population of the organization broken down by location, function, grade and any other relevant social demographic;
- what they think or feel: the current attitudes and sentiment of the workforce (refreshed on a regular if not continual basis);
- what they are hearing and how they are reacting: as far as possible we need to be able to say which messages are getting through. And, if at all possible, how that is reflected in behaviours and business performance.

We go into this in more detail throughout the book, but you need to know whether the communications team gathers data at an appropriate level and draws insight from it. Importantly, communicators need a mechanism for sharing that data with senior leaders and using it to shape plans and policies (rather than simply to justify their existence).

CASE STUDY   A structured approach at Novo Nordisk

Global pharmaceutical leader Novo Nordisk takes employee communication very seriously and has developed a structured approach to assessing communication practice. Its communication effectiveness review (CER) methodology has evolved to be a cornerstone of a business strategy that sees communication and engagement as drivers in creating a high-performing organization.

Novo Nordisk's central communications function has a dual role. It has a professional operation for managing news and dialogue alongside a wider brief to advise business leaders on how to engage colleagues, explain company strategy, shape change and build the core culture of the firm.

Supporting leaders is a continual process for the Copenhagen-based communications team. The CER is a standard process that helps local leaders and their communications function to have more impact. Run in close collaboration not just with the local communications team, it also directly involves the local general manager, HR and the wider local leadership team.

'The aim is to engage managers with the idea of what communications should be doing for their business rather than talking about what individual channels are doing or how often they should be sending out emails,' explains Mats Bark, Senior Adviser, Leadership Communication. 'It's about the outcomes, rather than the act of communication.'

Over time, the structure of the CER has been refined and today follows a proven sequence that culminates in an intensive site visit over two to three days. Experience has taught the communications function to concentrate on six main areas. As well as touching on the communication behaviours that are prescribed by the Novo Nordisk Way (the statement of the company's core values), the CER explores to what extent:

- leaders at all levels set clear direction, and explain relevant context;
- employees have easy access to relevant information;
- leaders and employees contribute to a climate of openness and trust;
- employees receive timely feedback and recognition of their role;
- employees have the opportunity to provide input and influence;
- employees are enabled to connect and share with colleagues.

'Our experience tells us that these issues are the ones that matter most often in high-performing organizations,' says Bark. 'Naturally, there are other concerns that come up from time to time, but these seem to be the topics with the most impact for our businesses.'

Pre-work for the CER process includes a broad survey, phone interviews with local senior management and a desk review of local strategies and plans. The results of the pre-survey allow the CER team to anticipate, before arriving on site, what topics are likely to arise and, indeed, give thought to the structure of the final presentation.

Once on site, the communications advisers follow a standard process, including meetings with HR, the general manager and the local communications experts. The visit will include focus groups with office employees, field employees and managers to get a deeper understanding of survey results. Whilst on site, the findings of the pre-survey and the discussions in the interviews and focus groups are swiftly analysed and presented at a concluding management meeting that looks at the key findings, explores current gaps and plans essential actions to strengthen communication.

'This final workshop is so important,' explains Bark. 'Here, senior management sees the clear link between meeting communication challenges and achieving business goals. And we see their commitments and action plans. It's very rewarding for everyone involved.'

'With many CERs we find that organizations can benefit by looking at how they involve or equip managers to live up the expectations placed on them,' reflects Bark. 'If you want them to have a real conversation with their teams there's an investment to be made in terms of time and detailed briefing to ensure they get the *why*. Then there's a chance they can make the message their own and turn it into a story that resonates with their teams locally.'

The CER process is effective because it has a consistent and detailed agenda. Over several years and many reviews, the team has learned to plan stakeholder engagement and how best to structure topic guides for interviews and focus groups. The review process follows a list of actions that cover everything from basic logistics to the content of meetings with internal clients.

Underpinning the CER process is a focus on the goals of the business and the impact that good communication and engagement can have. 'At Novo Nordisk it is understood that you cannot achieve strategy and plans if people do not understand them or get how they fit in; CER is our tool for exploring with senior leaders what they need communication to do for them and their role in building employee engagement,' concludes Mats Bark.

Constructing the audit: Research methods

Once you have decided which issues matter in your organization you need to think about how to understand them in a systematic way.

Although many of the answers to your questions will be obvious from a five-minute conversation, an organized approach is important. It might be plain that no one has any idea why they need a forward plan or what staff think, but if you want to improve things you will need some insight. And people respond better to arguments for change when they feel that there is a body of evidence behind it; and when the proposed change is difficult or challenging, we owe people some care in how we decided it is needed.

A reviewer also needs to think about timing. There will naturally be times when an audit or a review is unhelpful and can lead to things dragging on. The best reviews are often the swiftest; planned in advance and executed with the minimum disruption to the team.

Research will typically involve four components:

- desk review;
- quantitative research;

- qualitative research;
- reporting.

We will go into some of the methodologies for evaluating communication in Chapter 11. For now, it is worth thinking through how all of these approaches work together to build up a picture of the effectiveness and efficiency of the team and where improvement is needed.

Desk research

Desk research involves the process of reviewing materials and is often best done before the face-to-face stages of the audit. Looking at documents will help define the questions to ask and focus your effort. Typically, we would ask to see as much information as possible, covering (and expect that not all of it will be readily available):

- the overall business strategy;
- the communication strategy, budget and plan;
- an organization chart for the whole organization;
- examples of all channels (this might include videos as well as printed materials and often we make arrangements to view digital channels that are closed to external people) and, if possible, notes on how they are produced and distributed;
- any data on employee attitudes and understanding (such as the full report of the employee survey);
- data on channel usage;
- example campaigns;
- an organization chart for the communications function, role descriptions and resumés for team members;
- examples of any reports on communication matters.

The term 'desk research' also probably extends to visiting a site and taking a look around. The work environment – how people interact in the workplace, whether signs and posters are up to date and relevant, for example – says much about the context in which communication takes place.

As external reviewers we normally find that other material is also relevant, or the information we want does not exist in the format we requested. You have to be flexible about the list and you may also need to ask politely multiple times for information. Failing to hand over material is a great way to sabotage an audit or undermine its findings. Always remember that just asking for some of this material can stir up issues and raise concerns in the team; it has to be done with sensitivity, care and tenacity.

Quantitative research

Quantitative research involves gathering data such as employee attitudes or channel performance. Often, reports of the annual survey, for example, may already exist in a useful form and will be part of the desk research phase. If time permits, it can be a good idea to conduct a short survey to address communication issues and, if you can, try to collect data in a way that enables you to compare senior attitudes to communication with those of their staff.

A number of approaches exist for looking at channel preferences. Research expert Susan Walker warns against asking questions about issues that an experienced editor or professional should be able to make judgements on anyway (Walker, 2012: 98). Regular employees might not need to be asked about things like font types in the magazine or writing styles for digital content; we should know what good practice looks like. This is not to question the value of user experience research, but rather to say we should focus employee research on things which we cannot find out about in other, more effective ways.

Hargie and Tourish (2009) suggest a very comprehensive survey approach to asking staff what channels they like or value. Their suggested questionnaire includes questions about the information received (respondents are asked how much they currently receive and how much they need). The questionnaire also asks, among other things, how people feel about the volume of information they receive and would like to receive from different sources and the different types of information they send or would like to send.

Practitioners may find the approach complex, but they say some helpful things about usefulness and volume when it comes to talking about information received. Remember, though, that purely numerical data may not actually give much of a clue as to what improvement is possible. Sometimes a qualitative approach may be more helpful.

Qualitative research

Qualitative approaches involve interviews and focus groups and provide a depth of understanding about what can be improved in a way that survey data cannot. For fact-finding sessions, discussion or focus groups, a clear topic guide is always advisable and we talk about these in more detail in

Chapter 11. Never go into a meeting without preparing the questions you need to address; not only is it rude, it risks missing some vital information.

Earlier in this chapter we mentioned an approach for asking stakeholders what they valued. Collecting information on the same topic from multiple respondents can provoke a powerful discussion in a final presentation of findings. For employee groups, we have found it useful to ask people to think about their information needs and whether these are met. We do this by asking them to write on separate sticky notes the types of information they need or want and then we ask them to position these along a line drawn on a flipchart labelled at one end 'I get too much of this' and at the other 'I would like more of this'. When everyone has added multiple notes, a discussion of their views can then explore where people find the main types of information they have listed.

This is a simplified version of a pattern analysis, an approach advocated by measurement expert Angela Sinickas (2005). It's a methodology that can be used both quantitatively and qualitatively, and her approach stresses the importance of predefining the topics about which employees might want to know (rather than leaving them to generate the list, as in the process described above).

There are many ways to gather employee feedback in discussion groups, and a communications team always benefits by having a couple of members who are skilled at running research sessions. External facilitators are especially helpful when there is a fear that staff might be nervous about being totally honest in front of the communications team. We have experienced groups where participants were worried about upsetting the editor of the house magazine who was present in the room and so told us virtually nothing useful about the improvements they wanted!

Reporting your audit findings

A review should find improvements and not be destructive; explaining findings skilfully ensures that people focus on the way forward rather than become defensive or offended that their hard work is undervalued. The reporting process should consider how best to present findings and then engage people in a discussion of next steps.

It can be interesting to see how other organizations deal with similar issues and, we have found, employee communicators are naturally generous with their time and experience in benchmarking conversations. Finding benchmarking partners can be supported by an external consultant or through professional networks.

The results of a benchmarking exercise are always useful to include in a reporting session as this can bring a note of reality and some comfort that other people have similar issues – subject, of course, to the caveat above about taking someone else's medicine!

A typical reporting meeting might include an agenda that covers:

- the reasons for conducting the review;
- how the review was conducted (including who was involved, what materials were seen, what else relevant might have been happening whilst the audit was in progress);
- the headline findings;
- discussion and prioritization of improvement areas;
- next steps.

Conclusion

Time spent understanding what is working and what can be improved is never time wasted, in our experience. In this chapter we have included a comprehensive range of issues to consider but you can make a real difference to the performance of your team just by concentrating on a few of them. However, we want to stress that the best results come when the process starts by asking what value employee communication can bring. For the rest of this book, this is an issue that underlines our approach; great EC is about making a difference to the organizations we support. If we keep that in mind, we will rarely go far wrong.

Notes

1 Cal Downs and Allyson Adrian's *Assessing Organizational Communication* (2004) and Owen Hargie and Dennis Tourish's *Auditing Organizational Communication* (2009) are good starting points if you want to look at how organizational effectiveness can be improved through better communications at the individual or team level.

2 We first came across this approach in an article in the magazine *Strategic Communications Management* profiling the work of the then Director of Corporate Communications at Owens Corning, Kristen Kelley.

3 Hargie and Tourish (2009) are very helpful here and they have produced a robust and academically credible approach to exploring the issue of management culture and communications.

4 A summary of the competencies work can also be found in Wright (2016).

References

Bridger, E (2014) *Employee Engagement*, Kogan Page

Carnall, C and By, RT (2014) *Managing Change in Organizations*, 6th edn, Pearson Higher Education

Dewhurst, S and FitzPatrick, L (2007) *How to Develop Outstanding Internal Communicators*, Melcrum Publishing

Downs, C and Adrian, A (2004) *Assessing Organizational Communication*, Guilford Press

Falkheimer, J, Heide, M, Nothhaft, H, von Platen, S, Simonsson, C and Andersson, R (2017) Is strategic communication too important to be left to communication professionals? Managers' and coworkers' attitudes towards strategic communication and communication professionals, *Public Relations Review*, 43(1), pp 91–101

Government Communication Service (no date) Capability reviews. [Online] https://gcs.civilservice.gov.uk/about-us/capabilityreviews/#

Hargie, O and Tourish, D (eds) (2009) *Auditing Organizational Communication: A handbook of research, theory and practice*, Routledge

Men, LR (2014) Strategic internal communication: Transformational leadership, communication channels, and employee satisfaction, *Management Communication Quarterly*, 28(2), pp 264–84

Moss, D, Likely, F, Sriramesh, K and Ferrari, MA (2017) Structure of the public relations/communication department: Key findings from a global study, *Public Relations Review*, 43(1), pp 80–90

Ni, L (2007) Refined understanding of perspectives on employee–organization relationships: Themes and variations, *Journal of Communication Management*, 11(1), pp 53–70

Ruck, K and Welch, M (2012) Valuing internal communication: Management and employee perspectives, *Public Relations Review*, 38(2), pp 294–302

Simpson, L and Taylor, R (2009) *HELiX: Higher education – leading internal communications. Case studies of good communication*, University of Leicester.

[Online] http://www.theknowledgepartnership.com/media/1065/helix-case-studies1.pdf

Sinickas, A (2005) Conducting a comms channel analysis. [Online] https://www.sinicom.com/resources/publications/communication-channel-analysis/?cn-reloaded=1

Walker, S (2012) *Employee Engagement and Communication Research: Measurement, strategy and action*, Kogan Page

Wright, M (ed) (2016) *Gower Handbook of Internal Communication*, CRC Press

Setting objectives for employee communication plans
03

Considerations, frameworks and examples

CHAPTER OBJECTIVES

In Chapter 1 we described good employee communication as outcome-focused. To be perceived as valuable, a professional communicator must *add* value to their organization by helping to fulfil its purpose and achieve its strategy. We also introduced a distinction between outputs (communication products) and outcomes (the results that come from those communications taking place).

This chapter will explore how to establish and agree target outcomes with stakeholders and articulate them clearly. We'll look at how to link communication to a business or organizational need and set measurable objectives.

Whilst this might sound a simple and straightforward task, we've probably all experienced times when it's quite the opposite. We've certainly both met our fair share of stakeholders who just wanted a video, their profile raising, or to tick the 'communication' box on their project plan, preferably by tomorrow. And sometimes it's not easy to really nail down what constitutes a successful outcome.

However, there are ways to guide stakeholders into different ways of thinking and make life easier for ourselves. This chapter will provide some simple frameworks to do just that.

Wants, needs and problems

A few years ago, Sue woke up one Sunday morning to find her hand red and swollen. Puzzled about what had caused it, she took a photograph, posted it on Facebook, and sought opinions. Consensus was that she'd been bitten by a spider in the night. By the next morning, her hand looked considerably worse and she was about to head overseas for a week of workshops. Feeling panic-stricken about the time of her impending flight, she made an emergency doctor's appointment and opened the conversation by saying 'Sorry, I'm in quite a hurry. I've been bitten by a spider. Can you please give me a prescription for some antibiotics?'

What she *wanted* was for the doctor to say 'Yes, of course. Here's the prescription. Safe travels!' Or something along those lines.

What actually happened was this. The doctor said, 'I understand you're in a hurry. I can help you, but I need to take some time to have a look at things and ask a few questions first.' After a little while, he concluded that Sue had indeed been bitten. However, he explained that since the bite wasn't infected, antibiotics would make no difference. The *problem* was that she was suffering an allergic reaction. What she *needed* to resolve the problem was a different prescription – for antihistamines.

Sometimes, what people *want* and what they *need* are different things. And sometimes they don't really understand the *problem* they need to solve... even if they think they do.

Do you see some parallels here for communicators?

Giving stakeholders what they want

Often, when someone asks a communicator for help, they come with a 'want'. They want a communication output, whether it is a video, an infographic, a series of roadshows or whatever. They're busy and time-pressured. The last thing they want is for you to start asking questions. They just want you to give them what they asked for.

The easiest route is just to do as they ask, isn't it? Make the video, do a fantastic job of it, one happy stakeholder. And yet, how helpful is that, really? Not only is it possible the video will make little difference, it will also cost money that may have been better spent elsewhere.

How might communicators be contributing?

In general, we find communicators like and agree with the concept of moving from a focus on outputs to outcomes. Often their perception is that they would *like* to focus on outcomes, if only their stakeholders would let them. However, frequently, when we watch conversations play out, it's communicators who unwittingly lead them into the territory of communication outputs.

In training workshops, we put communicators into an imaginary initial stakeholder meeting and invite them to spend a short time asking questions to understand the business outcomes the stakeholder needs to achieve. We specifically direct them not to talk about communication outputs.

Time and time again, communicators turn the conversation to outputs. Many participants can't resist moving into solution mode. Sometimes, they believe they know what's needed within the first few minutes, and begin sharing examples of tactics they've tried before. Once the suggestions start coming, the conversational dynamics shift. The stakeholder stops talking and the communicators take over.

If you truly want outcome-focused communication, there's only one place to start. Get *really clear* about the outcome that's needed. Lurking somewhere beneath the opening request made by your stakeholder is the actual reason why your help is needed. Help them find it. Invest time in helping the stakeholder define the problem they need to solve.

This sounds eminently sensible in theory. But for a communicator who has developed a habit of getting quickly into a conversation about tactical solutions, it can feel uncomfortable in practice. The customer isn't getting what they wanted, and they don't yet have an alternative solution either! How is the communicator helping? Yet public relations professor Anne Gregory goes so far as to say this could be the most important thing a communicator does in the whole project (Gregory and Willis, 2013). In working with the stakeholder to think through the problem, we *are* helping them. Just not in the way we (or they) might be used to.

Everything in the communication plan should be guided by what's identified here. All conversations should ultimately lead back to it. If the problem to be solved is collaboratively defined, it will bring a shared focus, guide you towards certain messages and strategies and act as a destination to return to whenever you are questioned, challenged, or need to take stock of how to spend your time most wisely. Time invested here is always time well spent.

CASE STUDY   Telia: Finding the pain points

Communication planning starts with a 'pain point', according to Vija Valentukonyte-Urbanaviciene, Lithuania's Head of Internal Communication for telephone company Telia. However, communicators need to dig deeper to understand what needs fixing and be ready to talk about things that may not be strictly communication issues.

In her organization, Vija sees pain points typically falling into three categories:

1   business targets and objectives (what the organization needs to achieve);

2   culture and values (how people in the organization work together);

3   issues arising from the company engagement survey.

In the first category, she gives an example of a lead generation programme, and explains, 'Sometimes the link between communication and business goals is clearer than others. In this case it was very clear. The sales team set an objective that a percentage of sales should be made through leads, of which a proportion should be employee leads. Successful new sales leads could earn staff members a bonus.'

The communication team was initially asked to repackage an old scheme to look new and interesting, but, by digging deeper, they found they also needed to break misconceptions about how the scheme worked. 'Previously, people had to go into a complicated sales system. They found it so complex, they didn't bother. We had to show this had changed. We also got the sales team to alter the bonus attached to the scheme, to divide the budget up in a different way. If it wasn't attractive, we could sing and dance as much as we liked, but people wouldn't be interested.'

Sometimes, things may be less clear-cut. In 2017 Telia merged two of its companies, and the customer experience team came forward with a pain point. Whilst both companies shared Telia's group purpose and values, they had distinct ways of working and identified strongly with their individual legacy brands. The team was concerned these very different cultures would be reflected in an inconsistent customer experience from the newly merged company, which would operate under the core Telia brand.

The customer experience team worked collaboratively with communications and HR to work out how to address the problem. Vija comments, 'We weren't clear exactly what we were aiming for – we started with a pain point and found our direction.'

The group decided to unite the two companies through something that was already shared: the group-wide values of dare, care and simplify. From here, they identified what needed to be fixed: people didn't feel ownership of the values, found them too vague to put in to practice, and managers didn't know how to talk about them in performance conversations. This insight led to the values being translated into nine simple behaviours. Experiential training and communication were used to help people get to know the behaviours, try them out through personal reflection, and understand how to use them in daily work and performance conversations.

Through discussion, the group also identified how they would measure results. Ultimately their work would be reflected in the net promoter score (NPS), although other things would also affect this measure. They tracked value-based behaviours by observing actions people took after attending workshops, such as simplifying customer communication. And they used employee engagement survey results, since the survey is structured around the three values.

The employee engagement survey is in itself the third source of pain points identified by Vija. In this case, employees highlight the problem areas. 'For example,' she recalls, 'the survey showed a need for more collaboration. We ran focus groups to ask, "What does better collaboration mean? What do we need to fix?"'

A key frustration identified was the length of the sales-to-implementation cycle. Vija comments, 'We've learned that when you dig down to understand what's underlying the pain point, you can't just think about communication. You gather whatever information will address the issue, and come back to the management team or other departments if you need to. Part of our role and competence is to bring insights.'

Vija says being brought early into conversations has been an 'earned position', which she partly attributes to the focus on business-critical pain points and gaining insights into what's driving them. 'Our team would often spot issues before they come up. We're open to all feedback and we work cross-functionally. We could say "Well, this is not our area, it's HR," but if you're blocking yourself from these things, you're not able to influence them either.'

Adopting a consultant mindset

Block (2011) defines a consultant as someone who has influence but no direct power to make things happen. In this sense, communicators perhaps spend more time than they realize taking a consultant role. In these initial conversations, we can't *force* our stakeholders to change their mind about what they want from us. But we can guide, influence and coach.

Block suggests those stepping into a consultant role set themselves a goal to establish a collaborative relationship with their stakeholders – something we see clearly in the Telia case study – so the specialized expertise of the consultant is brought together with the stakeholder's business knowledge. His rationale is that collaboration makes the best use of resources and skills, shares the responsibility for success and failure, and quite simply is a pleasant way to work.

A key assumption of the collaborative relationship is that the communicator doesn't solve the problem *for* the stakeholder. They help them think it through for themselves. If we approach these conversations skilfully, we start to coach stakeholders to think about communication differently and, over time, we make our lives easier. People should start coming to us less often with an 'I want', and be more open to discussing the problem they need our help to solve.

CHECKLIST   What you can do in practice

- Reframe the way you think about the initial stakeholder conversation. Maister (1997) suggests envisaging it as a think tank, focused on exploring the problem to be solved.

- Ask questions, especially open questions beginning with the words 'how' or 'what'. (You might have heard of the useful 'five whys' technique, originally developed by Sakichi Toyoda and used within the Toyota Motor Corporation. The idea is that if you keep asking 'why?' you will eventually reach the root cause behind a request. (We suggest taking special care with 'why' questions, though. Used with a friendly smile and an attitude of genuine curiosity, they are useful. However, asked in an accusatory tone and accompanied by a hard stare, whilst inwardly bemoaning 'Why are you asking me for yet another newsletter, for goodness' sake? Why? Why?' such questions can cause stakeholders to feel rather defensive!)

- Listen with curiosity and without judgement.
- Allow the stakeholder to do most of the talking.
- Respect your stakeholder as an equal. Whether they are more or less senior than you, each of you brings knowledge and expertise to this conversation.
- Keep the conversation focused on the business/organization/your stakeholder's issue. Don't offer communication solutions yet.
- Stay open-minded. Avoid going into the conversation assuming you already know the answers.
- Cultivate empathy. People are busy and time-pressured. They don't always know the answers to questions. They're not always aware of the problem they need to solve and their problems are actually often not easy *to* solve. Stakeholders are not just being difficult, and this is not only happening in your organization.

Setting out the route: The ARROW framework

The ARROW framework, set out in Table 3.1, offers a series of questions to guide you and your stakeholder along a conversational route to explore the problem to be solved.

- **Aim.** It begins by guiding you to ask about the destination to be reached, in business terms. What should be different, and how does this translate into behaviours and targets?

- **Reality.** Next, it prompts you to explore the current state. What is happening now, and how is this problematic? What are the current behaviours, and what's driving them? How do we know – is research needed?

- **Roadblocks.** The framework then examines the journey between the current state and the destination. What might stand in the way? Have changes like this been made before? What happened? Are there lessons to be learned?

- **Opportunities.** This section invites you to explore where time is best invested. Of everything that needs to be achieved, what matters most of all?

- **Who and when.** Finally, it prompts you to ask who is affected, or needs to make changes; when targets should be achieved or changes need to be made.

Questions don't necessarily need to be asked in this order. They are simply prompts to make sure each area is covered.

Table 3.1   The ARROW framework

ARROW focus	Sample questions
Aim Where do we want to be at the end of the road?	• Six months from now, in business terms, what do you want to be different? • What do you want people to be doing differently? • How would you like people to feel? • What do you need people to know? • What business targets should be achieved?
Reality Where are we now?	• What's happening now? • What are people doing? • How are people feeling? • What do people know at this point? • What's driving these behaviours/feelings? How do we know? • Where do we stand against the targets?
Roadblocks What could get in the way of reaching the aim?	• What could stop the project being successful? • What obstacles might we expect to encounter? • When we've made changes like this in the past, what got in the way? • What's the worst thing that could happen?

(continued)

Table 3.1 (*Continued*)

ARROW focus	Sample questions
Opportunities What could have the biggest, quickest impact on reaching the aim?	• What's the one thing that matters most over the next six months? • If we could just get people to take one action, what should it be? • What's the easiest step we can help people take first?
Who and when Who's affected? When does it need to happen?	• Who is directly affected by this? • Who exactly needs to do something differently? • When does this project need to be completed? • When do the targets need to be achieved?

SOURCE Sue Dewhurst, 2009, reproduced with permission

Managing concerns

Of course, changing working habits takes practice and persistence. Initially, there might be concerns like these:

- **I don't have time.** Investing time here should avoid wasting time later, working on communication outputs that are not really needed, or won't work (or both).

- **My stakeholders don't have time.** Start with a 'killer question'. One communicator we know was asked into a meeting to be talked through an email the group wanted her to send. She started by saying, 'Just before we go through the email, I have one question. What are you hoping people will do, feel and know, after they read it?' Someone said 'That's a good question.' A discussion followed. After a while, one of the group turned to her and said, 'An email isn't going to achieve any of this, is it? What should we really be doing?'

- **People are used to me giving them what they want.** Then that's what they will keep asking for. If that's what you want, and it gets results, there's no reason to try anything different. If it isn't, and it doesn't, something needs to change.

- **They won't like me asking questions.** In our workshops, people taking the role of stakeholder are often surprised at how useful it is to have someone help them think things through. They also enjoy the opportunity to talk about a project that's important to them.

- **This is completely different to the way I usually work. I don't know where to start.** Practise with a communications colleague first. Then seek out your most accessible and easy-going stakeholder and ask if they'd be willing to give it a try.

CASE STUDY   Centrica: Changing the stakeholder conversation

International energy and services company Centrica has faced a demanding operating environment as it responds to the three macro-changes of decentralization, digitalization and more choice and power for its customers. But whilst the company's internal communicators were ready to talk about how to help the business transform, they were faced with stakeholders focused on communication outputs.

Enter the 'tablemat'. Devised by Head of Group Internal Communications Geoff Timblick, it started life as an A3 pad of paper taken into stakeholder meetings, to help communicators steer the conversation in a different direction. Timblick explains, 'Our starting point was to think about the conversation we *wanted* to have – to show the value we can bring to the organization. We wanted to help our stakeholders, instead of having them tell us what to do. So, we looked for tools we could put in place to facilitate that conversation.'

The tablemat gives communicators set questions to ask, and helps them begin writing the communication plan as they go through the conversation. 'The team had just gone through Sue's training, and her ARROW framework was top of people's minds,' says Timblick. 'So I led a small "hit-squad" to put together a similar framework tailored for our business. We're a very process- and form-driven organization, so we deliberately designed something that outlined our process and thinking and put that onto an A3 sheet. Every communicator was given an A3 pad of tablemats, and everyone would walk into their meetings carrying their pad.'

The tablemat has brought three benefits to the team. First, it has changed the conversations with stakeholders, as they wanted. Second, it showed the value communicators could bring as advisers rather than just deliverers. Third, it has given stakeholders a consistent experience when working with the communications team. The conversation is the same, whoever they speak to.

Timblick comments, 'It has helped stakeholders to change the way they think about communication. We've found that what starts out as "I've got x budget and I want a video…" often ends up with the person saying "Actually, I don't need that at all."'

It's been an education process for communicators, too. Timblick explains, 'It helped people change their conversations at a time when either they might not have realized they needed to, or they didn't feel comfortable about doing it.'

Initially, things were helped on their way by a competition to post a selfie on Yammer with a completed tablemat. 'Communicators embraced the tool because it helped them with stakeholder conversations,' says Timblick. 'But some people were worried leaders would ignore the questions and just push for the video they wanted in the first place. The selfie competition was a bit of fun and the early adopters raved about the tablemat, so everyone said they'd give it a try.'

As for ignoring the questions and pushing for the video, 'The very first question on the mat is "What is the business issue you are trying to solve?" We're linking everything back to helping stakeholders solve business problems and help customers. I don't think I've ever had anyone say "I still want."'

Eighteen months on, the conversation has changed and the tablemats are not always needed. Timblick comments, 'I took a tablemat with me last month because I wanted to be prepared for a tough stakeholder meeting. But it's become a tool in our arsenal, rather than a process we go through every single time.'

And whilst the A3 pads still exist, the tablemat has also moved online. Thanks to a purpose-built microsite, communicators can type their notes directly onto any device, which auto-populates sections of a communication plan, as well as a Centrica-wide planner.

Timblick comments, 'We had been using an Excel spreadsheet to compile our business-wide plans. We produced a weekly report, which two people manually analysed to produce forward sentiment plans for the next month, three months and one year ahead. Now I can fill in my tablemat in the meeting, and it auto-populates anything that translates directly across to a communication plan template, for example communication objectives, audiences, key stakeholders, dates and budget. Meanwhile, as I'm walking out of the meeting, if I know something will happen on a set date, I can drop it into the business-wide planner.'

It's a slick technical solution. But Timblick's advice to others is to start with the conversation. 'Look at the stakeholder conversation you're having today. Think about the conversation you'd like to be having. Then look what needs to happen to facilitate the change.'

So, you've helped your stakeholder explore the problem to be solved. Now what?

We hope you made good notes during the conversation, because now you'll use the information you gathered to start putting together a communication plan. If you've explored the issues thoroughly, you should be armed with useful insights about what this plan really needs to achieve, what needs to change, and where your efforts can most usefully be focused. Just as with the Centrica case, you'll now take these insights and drop them into your plan.

Gregory highlights flaws that commonly arise in the planning process (Gregory and Willis, 2013). We've suggested some solutions:

- **Many plans are written in siloed pieces, which seem disconnected.** Imagine your aim is to run a unifying 'red thread' through the whole plan, each step providing the insight to help you develop the next, everything ultimately connecting back towards achieving the core aim. To check if you've succeeded, ask a colleague to question what you've set out. A plan with a solid red thread is difficult to challenge, because the connecting rationale is strong.

- **Objectives are often unrealistic.** When we ask communicators to set SMART objectives in workshops, there are always people arguing for targets of 100 per cent understanding, or suggesting that every employee should change their behaviour or believe in the benefits of an unpopular change. Ask yourself whether you'd be prepared to stake your annual bonus on attaining the targets you set. It's a good way of focusing your mind on what's really achievable.

- **Few communicators link objectives to measurement criteria.** Instead of thinking about measurement at the end of your plan, why not consider it now? Develop your objectives and decide how you'll measure them, right up front. (See Chapter 11 for ideas about evaluation.)

The core business/organizational aim

Start your plan by setting out the core business or organizational aim it should achieve. This should come from the stakeholder you're seeking to help and will probably rely on more than just good communication to be achieved. Examples of core aims could be reducing accident rates, improving quality or increasing sales.

If you find yourself setting an aim relating to something people should do, feel or know, ask yourself why these things are needed. Keep asking 'why' until you reach a business or organizational target or statement. For example, if you want people to better understand the safety processes for their area, presumably that's because you want them to follow the processes more consistently. The reason for this is probably because you want people to be safer at work, that is, you want fewer accidents to happen. There's the core aim: reduce accident rates. (By how many, by when?)

Don't go too far with the 'why' questions. Many aims can ultimately be related back to reducing costs or increasing sales, but keep things focused on the problem your customer actually wants to solve. That's what this plan is all about.

If this is the core aim of the plan, you'll want to track how things are going – for example, are accident rates reducing or increasing? Since this is a business/organizational aim, someone should probably be measuring it already. All you'll need to do is keep an eye on the figures.

The communication objectives: Do, feel, know

Here come the outcomes you will focus on achieving. Since we're focusing on employee communication, we're now interested in the part employees can play in helping to achieve the core aim of this plan.

Organizations perform, customers are satisfied (or not), costs increase or decrease and accidents happen through employee behaviours. When we say 'employees', we mean anyone carrying out work in the organization, from volunteers, to people on the front line, to the most senior leaders.

What behaviours are needed in order to help achieve the core business/organizational aim? Who needs to do these things? What's driving the behaviours people are adopting today? Is it something to do with feelings/beliefs/attitudes? Something connected to a lack of knowledge or understanding? Or both? These are all questions you will have explored with your stakeholder in your 'think tank' conversation.

Employee behaviours: What do you need people to *do*? Who needs to do it?

Set out the 'do' first. Keeping in mind the idea of the red thread, work backwards from the core business/organizational aim. What did you discover in your stakeholder conversation? For example, if there's a problem with safety today, what behaviours are driving it? Is this a general issue with accidents across the organization, or does it apply to a specific group of people, in a particular situation?

Be as specific as you can about *what* behaviour is needed, by *whom*, and, if appropriate, *in what situation*. Six months from now, what should be different? Is this about stopping a current behaviour, starting a new one, or changing something about the way things are done? Your plan might not necessarily include 'behaviour change', but if a business activity impacts people, there may well be something you would like them to do in response, such as completing a preference exercise during a restructure.

Check that you really are talking about behaviours. Sometimes we hear people say, 'What I want people to do is understand how this affects them.' (Sometimes it also pops up under feel – 'I want people to feel they understand why we've taken this decision.') Remember, understanding relates to what people *know*. Keep it in its place!

Employee perceptions/mindsets/attitudes/values/beliefs: How would you like people to *feel*?

Ask anyone how they would like employees to feel in relation to a topic, and it's likely a string of words will emerge along the lines of 'engaged, motivated and excited'. Closely followed by 'empowered, involved and responsible.' However, we'd like to challenge you to dig deeper. Look again at the 'do' objective. Keep in mind the idea of the red thread, everything connected. In what ways are people's perceptions, mindsets or beliefs driving their behaviours today? Is there an unhelpful or inaccurate perception you'd like to shift? And/or is there a feeling you can evoke, to inspire people to make a change?

In his spare time, Liam can often be found cycling around the UK. Sue, on the other hand, is a couch potato! She has an unhelpful core belief that she is 'not a sporty person', fuelled by less than positive memories of school sports lessons. However, one summer she was challenged to complete the 'Couch to 5k' running programme. Accompanying the programme was a social media forum. Reading the posts, Sue found they were full of similarly 'non-sporty' types feeling astonished and proud of themselves that they were managing to complete the increasingly longer runs. Thanks to the forum, Sue formed a belief that 'If people like me can do it, I can probably do it too.' She read the forum posts every single day for inspiration, and successfully completed the Couch to 5k. We can only imagine that this is exactly what the forum was designed to achieve.

Employee knowledge and understanding: What would you like people to *know*?

This is most people's communication comfort zone. We're used to focusing on 'getting messages across'. But we're going to hold onto the red thread, and invite you to look once again at the 'do' and 'feel' objectives you've now set. Is there a gap in people's current knowledge or understanding that needs to be closed, to contribute towards the feel and do?

In the Telia case earlier in this chapter, the communications team aimed to have employees take the action of generating and submitting sales leads. They discovered that one thing putting people off, due to previous experience, was a belief that the sales system used for submitting the leads was too complicated. The communications team needed colleagues to *know* this system had now changed, and its replacement was far easier to use. In this way, they could challenge an outdated *belief*, which in turn led more people to *take action*.

Using research to fill the gaps

Sometimes the 'think tank' conversation will help you and your stakeholder discover that you're not clear about the concrete behaviour to be changed. Perhaps you might know what you'd like people to do differently, but have no idea about what's driving their current behaviours. Or, it could be that your stakeholder starts the conversation thinking they understand the problem to be solved, but when you start digging a different picture emerges.

In these cases you might suggest doing some research to close the gaps. Look back to the Telia case about sales leads – the stakeholder request was to repackage the sales lead scheme to make it look new and interesting. But the communications team also dug deeper, to find insights into what obstacles might stand in the way of employees submitting leads. It was their research that uncovered people's reluctance to use a sales system they mistakenly believed was old and complex.

You'll need to invest a little time to undertake research, but it doesn't need to be large-scale or complicated. Sometimes a quick ring around will get you all the insight you need. And this is another time investment that pays off. You can see in this case the impact of *not* doing it. Had the team focused only on repackaging the scheme, employees may well not have used it, and the core aim of the plan, to generate sales leads, would not have been achieved.

Making communication objectives SMART

We review a lot of communication objectives. Some are vague ('raise awareness of safety'); others are long and complicated; some seem simple but don't stand up well to questioning. Wanting people to feel 'engaged' is a common 'feel' objective; but how many questions does your organization have in its engagement survey? What exactly does it mean to feel 'engaged'? How would you measure it? What about a do objective of 'embrace change'? What would we see people doing, if they were embracing change? What does it mean to 'be an ambassador'?

Making objectives SMART forces you to work with these types of questions. As a reminder, SMART stands for:

- specific;
- measureable;
- achievable;
- realistic;
- timely.

For instance, let's take the example of a communication plan to promote an organization's new 'refer a friend' scheme, with a core business aim of recruiting 50 new employees in time for the peak summer holiday season.

- A vague *do* goal to 'be an ambassador' could translate into *20 per cent of employees successfully encourage a friend or family member to submit an employment enquiry via the dedicated HR recruitment hub, by 31 June*, measured via the number of HR hub submissions.

- A *feel* objective might be *70 per cent of employees would recommend X company as a place to work, by 30 May*, measured via an employee engagement survey question.

- A *know* objective could be *80 per cent of employees know how to direct friends and family to the new dedicated HR recruitment hub, by 31 March*, measured via a single 'quick poll' question on the organization's news app or intranet.

So, where are we now?

Whether this stakeholder arrived with a 'want' for communication outputs, or a more open-minded 'need' for a support with a project, you should have:

- helped them to think through and clarify the problem they need to solve;

- enabled them to take stock of the current situation, and brought insight into what might be driving it;

- identified the gap between where people are today, and where they need to be;

- set clear, measurable communication objectives, and potentially identified how you'll measure them.

We've provided a simple worksheet (see Table 3.2) to set out the core business aim and how you'll track it, together with the current state and wanted position for each employee group you need to impact. Use an additional worksheet for each key group that shares a distinct set of communication objectives. The core business aim will stay the same.

Your task from this point is to work out how to close the gaps you've identified and meet the measurable objectives set. Each communication plan is a new opportunity for creative problem solving! Identify how far gaps can be closed through communication, and recommend if there are other actions the stakeholder needs to take, or issues they will need to resolve. For example, the Telia communications team encouraged their stakeholder to re-think the bonus arrangements relating to employee leads generated.

Table 3.2   Worksheet: Defining communication plan outcomes

Core business/organizational aim		Tracking method
Key audience 1		
What are people doing now?	SMART goal: What do we want people to do in the future?	Research need?
How do people feel now?	SMART goal: How do we want people to feel in the future?	Research need?
What do people know now?	SMART goal: What do we want people to know in the future?	Research need?

A final word on flexibility

It feels important to say that, whilst we advocate a planned approach, communicators need to be flexible and responsive. Plans help us to share intentions, and guide the way forward, but they can't be set in stone – business plans change, people are unpredictable and behaviours are complex. So:

- Watch, listen and measure. Know what's happening 'on the ground'. Look for opportunities and notice if something needs to be addressed. Respond to what's happening and adapt.

- Be open to experimenting and learning. The strategies you propose might work out, and they might not. If they don't, no problem. Learn from it, then try something else.

- Keep collaborating. Maintain a good dialogue with your key stakeholders. The insights you gather will be valuable to them, too. Plus, you'll want to keep up to date with changes to the business or project plans – things can change quickly and unexpectedly. Agree what's a realistic timescale to plan ahead, and when you should regroup, take stock and get ready for the next phase.

Conclusion

Most communicators we meet have a good idea of how to produce content or tactics in response to customer requests, and there can be real satisfaction in writing powerful copy, commissioning a video or prompting a great debate on Yammer. But the process of planning gives us a powerful toolkit for making a bigger difference.

When we work collaboratively to think through problems and agree objectives, we start a journey in which each person brings their unique perspectives and skills to solving those problems. With our skills, we can contribute insights and suggest communication strategies that deliver results for our colleagues and avoid wasted time.

Outputs, or outcomes? Service providers, known for our skill in writing, editing and designing? Or business enablers, known for helping colleagues use communication to solve problems? In this first step of the planning process, we choose our path. Through the way we respond to an initial request for help, our approach to conversation, the objectives we set, and the insights we provide, we shape how our colleagues see us and are likely to respond to us. We shape how we will spend our time working on this plan, what direction it will take, and how its success will be defined. Which path will you choose, this time?

References and further reading

Block, P (2011) *Flawless Consulting*, Jossey-Bass
Gregory, A and Willis, P (2013) *Strategic Public Relations Leadership*, Routledge
Maister, DH (1997) *Managing the Professional Services Firm*, The Free Press
Maister, D, Green, C and Galford, R (2002) *The Trusted Adviser*, Simon & Schuster (Contains good, practical advice relating to the type of stakeholder conversations we've described here.)

Understanding your audiences

04

What practitioners do in practice

CHAPTER OBJECTIVES

Shouting into the darkness isn't communicating. A conversation needs at least two sides, and a communicator knows that the best discussions begin by understanding the people you're are talking with. Sadly, in the rush to get the day-to-day job done, many of us can neglect thinking about our audiences or make assumptions about who they are and what they think. And that is a shame because what we know and believe about our audiences shapes a great deal of every other aspect of our communication; misjudge your audience and your communication plan could be built on shaky foundations.

In this chapter we'll recap on why understanding audiences matters, and highlight a number of things that we all should know about the people we work with. We'll also take a look at the main ways in which you can segment your audiences. We are therefore addressing three central issues:

- How well do you really know your audiences?
- Why you need to know them.
- How you can find out who your audiences are and how they think.

The main message of this chapter is that deep audience understanding is one of the most useful things we can bring to our organizations. Other professionals might have some insight into the shape and sentiment of our workforce, but it is our job to translate that understanding into communication that satisfies everyone (or most of them!). That overarching awareness is one of the reasons why leaders seek out our opinion.

Let's start with a quick test

Let's take a moment to see if you can answer a few questions about where you work; your options are *yes, no* or *sort of*. No one's watching and we won't tell anyone your answers.

- Can you say how many people are employed by your organization?
- Do you know how many people work at different sites and in different departments?
- Do you know the average length of service of your colleagues across your organization?
- Would you be able to say what the average salary is in your workplace?
- Are you aware of the proportions of your workforce that are men and women?
- Can you tell us what percentage of your colleagues does not normally work in front of a screen or computer?
- Do you know how many of your colleagues would recommend your organization as a place to work?
- Do you know what percentage of the workforce knows their departmental objectives for the coming year?
- Can you say how many colleagues are positive about the direction of your organization?
- Do you know how many middle managers in your workplace would consider themselves well informed?

So, how did you do?

If your answers were mostly yes, then we'd say that you were doing unusually well. Our experience is that most of your answers will be sort of, with a few guilty no answers in there as well. You might feel that these questions are not really relevant to your organization, and perhaps we could have picked different ones. However, our point is that many of us often skip the details of who our audiences are and what they think.

Audience understanding, like evaluation and checking the tyre pressure on our cars, is one of those things that we all mean to do more often but somehow never get around to. It is so easy to be locked into the day-to-day challenges of producing content, advising on plans, explaining to the latest project team that a newsletter isn't the answer to their dreams and trying to stay on top of everything else. For much of the time, we think we have a 'good enough' idea of who our people are and what they think; nailing audience data is a problem that we can put off to next week, next month or next year. And it's a shame, because there is so much we can achieve if we had a deeper insight into the people with whom we communicate at work.

In our case study from Cisco, we see how one team values the importance of deep audience understanding and uses it to help leaders be better communicators.

CASE STUDY Cisco

When change really is a constant, what is a communicator's most important competency? According to Cisco's Lisa Atherfold, 'In a world where companies will not exist in their current form sooner than you can imagine, because of the pace of technology change, keeping employees engaged is a critical priority for everyone. Being in tune with the audience matters most.'

Cisco, the 74,000 strong technology leader, has change and innovation written into its DNA. 'The business is always evolving and developing new technologies. To work here you have to be comfortable with change, and it's communications' job to keep people engaged with the direction of the company and make the strategy personal for them,' explains the Director of Communications for Europe, the Middle East, Africa and Russia (EMEAR).

Her 27-strong team in EMEAR rely heavily on data and insight in order to go beyond listening. 'Just using channels that match preferences of the audience or using attention-getting data and stories might mean a message is understood, but it doesn't shape perceptions or drive behaviour. Unless you are really "in tune" with what people are thinking, how can you produce communications that make a real difference?' asks Atherfold. 'You have to deeply understand how people see things and their situations if you want to draw together the cognitive threads for them and engage them in thinking and talking about the things that matter.'

As well as being out and about building personal connections, the team is a heavy consumer of data. As part of a broader communication approach, Cisco holds monthly global and quarterly EMEAR employee get-togethers, designed to be more of an experience than an event, where employees bring a flavour of their local culture to the meeting, and where they can ask the toughest questions. After the CEO's monthly Cisco Beat or the EMEARin60, employees are invited to give open feedback.

Specifically, employees are asked, 'If you could say something to leaders what would you say?' or 'Is the work I do important for our customers?' – these questions are aligned to the company's surveying in support of the three core pillars of the Cisco culture – The People Deal. Responses are analysed using natural language processing – a technology that identifies the range of topics being raised and, importantly, the sentiment behind the language being used. Atherfold says that this approach provides important guidance on the emotion behind topics. 'Being "in tune" goes deeper than just being a good listener, it's using data to find out what is really going on across a large audience. It's a powerful influence on our planning.'

This data supplements the quantitative information coming from the company-wide culture survey that goes to all employees. This explores how aligned people's work is to business goals (Connecting Everything); how they create an environment where they can be bold (Innovate Everywhere) and whether people feel supported and able to make a meaningful difference (Benefit Everyone).

In such a large organization, the communications team works hard to be sensitive to the diversity of people who work for the company and the views they may hold. 'Like many big organizations, we get asked what stance the company will take on geopolitical dynamics, for example,' explains Atherfold. 'Communications' role is to help executives be "in tune" with the real emotion and sentiment behind issues and respond with sensitivity so that the organization remains aligned whilst people can have different views on a topic. We are able to brief our leaders on the strength of feeling and advise on how to explain the response that the company is going to make. Whilst we try to steer clear of public controversy and respect the mix of, often conflicting, opinions that might exist inside the company, people do tell us that they feel listened to by the CEO and senior executives.'

Having that emotional sensitivity matters in a world of change and uncertainty. 'Part of our challenge is to show people that they can look to senior executives as people they can trust in a world where things are unclear.'

Data gathering also includes a continuing process of focus groups across the region. 'At least twice a year we ask volunteers to come and tell us what they think. We're especially interested in issues such as pride in the company, understanding of the company direction and feeling their work matters. Over time we have found that discussing these areas helps us build a narrative and helps us localize our messages.' Communications team members facilitate the focus groups, as Atherfold sees this an essential skill for practitioners. And there are never any shortages of volunteers to participate. 'The last time we put the call out, 500 people put themselves forward.'

Atherfold points out that information coming back from surveys, focus groups and other listening exercises shouldn't be used to justify the existence of the communications function. Although leaders have different ways of responding to the data, it is the job of communications to help them understand what it is telling them.

'The data is best received when it's part of a conversation about the scope for improvement. Executives will always have a feel for what works or doesn't work for them; and there's always more interest in finding fresh ways to get a message over and, indeed, what could be dropped.'

Know your place

It is incredibly difficult to craft communication for people we have never met and every communicator has a story to tell of working with two seemingly identical companies and how they had completely different cultures and ways of working. You can't hope to capture and keep the attention of your audience if you don't know how they think. Planning content, developing story angles, crafting messages, organizing channels all require an awareness of what interests people and what will stimulate a reaction.

But the need to really understand the people you work with goes deeper than being able to produce compelling or interesting content. Perhaps most importantly, senior leaders need someone on hand to tell them what their people are thinking and feeling. As you progress up the corporate ladder, you find that your old colleagues tell you less and less of what is really happening and more and more of what they think you need to know. The boss needs help to keep a finger on the pulse.

The EC team is in the privileged position of having access to their own sources and methods that are not automatically available to anyone else. HR colleagues will have a good feel for the organization, but as self-service and business partnering models of people management develop, HR's position as the sounding board can suffer. Whilst other functions may have a partial view of what's being said around the organization, it's the communications team who are most likely to have an ear to the most ground.

If we can't say what people are thinking and saying, we are neglecting a big opportunity to add value to our leaders. And when we can add that value we find that we are trusted to help and advise on an ever-widening range of issues. Audience insight is one of the foundations of influence for an EC professional and it is foolish to neglect it.

And leaders expect us to know how to apply that knowledge and advise on what channels or tactics will reach specific audiences. Executives are grateful when we can explain how to connect with different teams and they'll listen more closely to our recommendations if they respect that we have access to special knowledge. Communicators with insight are asked their opinion.

We have said many times that the crucial role of a communicator is to act as a bridge between an organization and its audiences (FitzPatrick, 2016: 305). If our job is to make sure that both sides of the bridge listen to each other, we have to have the best possible awareness of everyone's ideas, experiences and communication practices. It's a necessary role because, as we said in Chapter 1, workplaces with a voice are more engaged and, by extension, perform better (MacLeod and Clarke, 2010).

Our approach is that the role of communications leaders is wider than the delivery of messages and the management of channels; it's about the essential impact we have on the workplace and on business efficiency, change and success (Waters *et al*, 2013). If that's a mission you accept, it requires you to be the expert on the defining element of your realm – the employees. As our case study from Hydro shows, with audiences front and centre in your thinking, project success is much more likely.

CASE STUDY   Hydro: Understanding the difference between change and transformation

The IT team at global industrial group Hydro understand that things change and people transform. That's why they appointed a specialist to drive digital adoption and ensure investment in new IT tools leads to better collaboration, engagement and performance.

Oslo-based Gro Elin Hansen, who leads the company's Digital Collaboration Team, explains, 'In 2015 a modernization of IT set out to make the most of a range of new cloud technologies. We wanted to avoid the classic trap of the "launch and leave" approach that has been so typical for many IT investments, where all the effort goes into development and there's little thought given to what happens next.'

Her challenge was how to get people to take the tools and find fresh ways of working and collaborating across a company that is now **35,000** strong. 'Sure, you can force people to use stuff by doing things like turning off their old tools,' says the former IC leader, 'but how do you give people some sense of how a new tool can make a difference? How do you make them curious about the potential?'

She used her communications background to help her IT colleagues think about the demographics of their users. 'We looked at how the needs of a 25-year company veteran line manager in a staff function are different to those of a young engineer working at a plant a long way from head office.' The team developed a series of 'types' or personas that described their different approaches and tastes. They also took account of national and cultural characteristics, which can bring big differences in how people feel about technology, personal data and privacy. 'You have to be mindful of these things if you want to change behaviours and practices.'

Detailed understanding of stakeholders underpins their work to promote adoption. Drawing on online surveys, focus groups, workshops and one-to-one interviews, the team spend a lot of time out and about talking to colleagues in the business. Around two-thirds of Hydro people do not spend their day at a desk, and interesting factory colleagues in the potential for greater collaboration was a pressing concern. Hansen gives the example of a recent pilot to increase usage of an Office 365-based digital tool set among workers in an aluminium plant The aim was to introduce a digital tool for shift scheduling, task sharing, team communication (eg incident reporting and knowledge-sharing) and personal administration (eg reporting absence).

'We spent a lot of time talking to shift managers and unions. These conversations and our surveys told us that people had a number of needs and highlighted a concern among supervisors who often felt trapped in long meetings when they wanted to be out on the shop floor talking to their teams.'

Subsequently, the team held on-site demonstrations to address the issues raised, such as showing people how to use the new digital tool to share operational information. They also talked to managers about how the tools could keep communication flowing even when they were away from the plant, helping them remain present for their teams. Hansen comments, 'It's a truism that you need to get line managers on board, but you can really see the importance when you are out there talking to them. How they respond to things can be so varied depending on how they see their role as a leader.'

Results have been positive, with staff using the tool actively including, unusually for blue-collar workers, when they are at home. Managers say they can respond to things faster and their teams confirm they are more visible.

HR colleagues also report more involvement, including participation in the employee satisfaction survey and use of the HR portal for self-service transactions. 'We also see faster feedback on health and safety incidents; people are hearing about issues quickly rather than waiting several weeks for the next safety meeting,' she adds.

Hansen's central message is clear: 'When you're closely oriented to the business you recognize that much of what comes out of head office doesn't always seem relevant. Time spent talking to local managers always pays off. Understanding their experience and helping them see how they can do their job better is a continual process – not just when you do a kick off but showing them how to communicate and keep walking the talk.'

The essentials we all need to know

We should acknowledge a reality faced by even the smallest organizations. Most organizations have an imperfect understanding of whom they employ. Records will lack things you might assume were essentials, like birthday, qualifications, disabilities and gender. Even payroll and tax records can be incorrect and you can't assume that IT actually have a reliable list of real people with real IT accounts. It is also possible that in some countries certain data is deliberately not collected or stored centrally for legal or privacy reasons. No wonder many communicators decide that they would rather get on with dealing with the immediate demands of their jobs than do battle extracting information from IT, HR and payroll systems! However, if we do want to get some core facts we may have to make the best of what's available.

So what will a practitioner want to know? On day one, as far as it is possible to find out, we should understand:

- the number of people who work for the organization;
- at what locations they work;
- any patterns to their work (such as whether people work shifts or are based away from an office or depot);
- how the organization is broken up in to departments and divisions (and their relative sizes);
- what people actually do;

- the languages that are spoken and the channels that reach them;
- the age and length of service profile of the workforce;
- the gender breakdown.

We also think that employment status is becoming of increasing importance for a number of reasons. Traditional relationships between employers and employees are changing, with evolving expectations on both sides in terms of security, reward and longevity. Some people no longer look for a job (or even career) that will last them a lifetime, and whole sectors of the economy have developed because technology enables work to be parcelled up into tiny units. Understanding how people are employed matters not least so that methods of communicating with them can be developed.

In the non-profit sector we also need to be aware that employment doesn't necessarily mean that someone is paid a salary. People who work as 'volunteers' may have a very clear transaction in mind; they may give their time and labour in return for training, work experience or a chance to make a social difference. In a very real sense they are employees (Garner and Garner, 2011; Kang 2016) and so need to be factored into the communicator's thinking.

Other demographic information will matter in your organization. The aim is to understand the main characteristics of the workforce in so far as they might affect how things are explained, the detail and context provided and the method by which they are communicated. And, most importantly, to help you decide how to earn and keep their attention.

Segmentation

Of course, one size does not fit all when it comes to communication. Just take a look around your family. You're all related but you react differently to the same information, you're interested in different things and your grandparents keep comparing everything to the past. If it's hard enough to get a group of relatives to understand each other, it's amazing that organizations made up of different departments, jobs, locations and a myriad other differences ever manage to share the simplest of messages!

But that's exactly our job. We have to get diverse groups of people to talk and listen to each other, and it can only be done if we understand the different groups or clusters of employees to be found in their workplace.

All the time, or just for projects?

It can be quite time-consuming to think through all the segments you need for your communication; we discuss below a few of the general approaches but it's hardly surprising that many communicators say they haven't the time. A common approach is not to go into too much detail for regular or 'business as usual' communication but rather look at segmentation on a project-by-project basis.

One reason for not having a hard and fast approach is that some groupings and their relevance are actually determined by specific situations or issues. Situational theory (Kim 2011) attempts to explain that audiences become active or interested at different times depending on how pressing an issue seems to them. People who drive to work might not perceive they have a common connection until a review of parking at the factory is announced, or managers' interest in sales information may change significantly as the year-end bonus deadline approaches. Our case study from the Coventry Building Society (page 73) illustrates how one communicator went about defining audiences for a change programme.

Our aim should be to understand how groups with common communication needs or characteristics are formed and what implications it has for how we do our job.

What is a useful segment?

You need to know how far to take 'slicing and dicing' your audiences. There's a useful limit to the depth of segmentation as you could get carried away and try to personalize communication for every single individual! Whilst some tools, like email software linked to your HR database, can target people by a combination of location, grade, skill set and shoe size, you need to use your judgement about where to stop. You want to find groupings of colleagues where there is some distinctive similarity between them and which might affect the information that they need, how they receive it or how they might interpret it.

The UK's Government Communication Service has a useful public website for EC professionals, which suggests segmenting audiences according to demography, management status, career stage, role, attitudinal and channel access (Government Communication Service, no date). Which factors you use may depend on the communication situation under consideration. For example, if supporting a workplace diversity programme, it might be useful to have a way of specifically reaching black and minority ethic colleagues. Before announcing major changes to HR policies, we might want particularly to target briefings at people who manage large groups of staff.

As well as demographic information, some communicators are also working with psychographic data and segmenting people according to their attitude.

Think about 'Generation Whatever'

People often talk about our society being divided up into different generations, and there is some debate about whether workplace communication should be tailored to meet the specific needs of these groups. There is a suggestion that generations have distinctive expectations about the information they should receive at work and the ways in which they are involved in conversations. Millennial workers are thought to be more interested in messages about purpose, and workers from the Baby Boomer generation are said to be more relaxed about being involved in strategy discussions (Lyons and Kuron, 2014).

However, how far can we make generalizations about large swathes of the population that are useful for communicators? To what extent is there agreement about the characteristics of each generation, and how reliable is the evidence that predicts how best to communicate with them? Can we generalize about attitudes across societies – do Millennials in Miami see life in the same way as their contemporaries in Munich, Madrid, Mumbai and Melbourne? Lyons and Kuron (2014) ask how useful generational models of segmentation really are.

Think about organizations you know. For what sort of communication are generational factors a useful guide to targeting?

Let them decide

A common approach is to develop communication content that appeals to people with different levels of engagement. The beauty of doing things this way is that you don't need to identify people individually. As we mentioned above, they will be attracted to the content that interests them and so will be self-selecting.

The challenge is that people will not automatically agree that whatever the CEO wants to talk about is interesting; it's our job to translate messages into terms that will be interesting and relevant to our audience. We have to understand what our colleagues believe and not just see things through the eyes of people at head office or uncritically accept the project team's beautifully produced PowerPoint. Our audience will decide if they are engaged or interested, they will decide if something seems relevant or not, and we have to come to them and not the other way around.

It is theoretically possible to segment people according to predefined personality types, and we have come across people who have attempted to apply models like Myers-Briggs to their communication strategizing, but with mixed results. Planning and execution of communication can be challenging if you want to address all of the multiple groupings that these tools offer, but it can be worthwhile in situations where personality type is likely to be a bigger driver of communication engagement than other factors such as location, age, status or situation.

It could be that a campaign around flexible rewards needs to address groups whose interests vary between pension planning, personal development or maximizing leave time to go surfing. Knowing how to appeal to diverse mindsets would be valuable in that case, but of less use when planning communication about a cost reduction programme or better sales processes.

Who matters around here: Social influence

Another approach that is worthy of some attention is looking for influencers. Malcolm Gladwell's book *The Tipping Point* (2004) is still one of the best and most readable explanations of the mix of social and psychological factors needed to create trends or change within a population. His point is that people perform a variety of different roles in a group, ranging from being subject matter experts to super-social connectors, and that they all work together to make change happen.

The message is that official status or hierarchy are not reliable guides to who is influential. A manager might matter less than the person who always organizes the charity appeal; the CEO could actually have less social clout than a junior supervisor. And modern technology makes it easier to work with the individuals who have better personal networks and get listened to internally. Platforms like Yammer and Workplace by Facebook are among some of the better-known tools used by communicators to discover who are the best-connected and influential people in their organization and work with them. Leveraging these well-networked people might involve directly asking them for feedback on a specific issue, inviting them to briefings or giving them access to senior leaders to talk about current concerns or developments.

Segments with personality

One very useful approach for communication planning is to develop some simplified stereotypes or audience personas. It's a tactic that people are copying from our colleagues in consumer marketing and from IT.

A persona represents a recognizable audience type. A car manufacturer will target groups such as young men who want a sporty car, families who value safety, seniors who want reliability and economy from their ride. A tax authority might communicate different messages to people who want to pay their taxes as easily as possible compared to other taxpayers who are more concerned about paying the right amount or others who may be active evaders who will break the law if possible.

Our case study from Hydro (page 64) mentions how IT colleagues might have detailed models of how different colleagues consume IT services; they might need to think through how they support the day-to-day desktop user as well as finance managers who need bespoke applications or the researcher who wants unlimited processing power. The car maker, the tax collector or the IT project manager will give these types a name such as 'safety first drivers', 'accurate compliers' or 'superuser Steve' and list their main characteristics. These are stereotypes, and inevitably simplistic, but they help define messages and target support. In the workplace, it helps to draw up some simple personas to represent typical groups of colleagues; in fact, it works well to involve staff themselves in shaping the stereotypes through workshops.

In practice: Creating a set of personas

A persona is a simple stereotypical guide to a common audience grouping in your organization. Use them to help you think through how to make your content gripping when working with stakeholders on drafting their messages. Develop a handful of personas to illustrate the main audience groups in your organization and include information about their age, typical grade, likes and dislikes and channel preferences.

To be useful, a persona needs to be quite simple; resist the temptation to cram too much information in (otherwise people will be distracted by the detail rather than let the stereotype prompt useful thoughts about communication).

A good way to start is to hold a team workshop to propose a number of different types, or alternatively invite a group of colleagues from across the business to help you. We have found it useful to just ask people to work with words at first; ask them to think of a single type of person they meet regularly and describe:

- a name (calling them Miguel or Mairead brings them to life and helps the group visualize the person they are discussing);
- the type of role they might do;
- how long they have been in your organization;
- where they see their job taking them;
- what they like about working for your organization;
- what drives them mad;
- what communications particularly interest them;
- what communications bore them.

Listen carefully when people are discussing their character as they may suggest other important dimensions you had not considered such as location, department or even how they get to work! Sometimes asking people to draw a picture works better than getting them to write things out.

Validate your personas with a few people and gather some facts that illustrate the image you are developing. Use data to keep the examples real; if 75 per cent of your workforce is female, then three-quarters of your personas should be female. Email shouldn't be anyone's preferred channel if you know hardly anyone opens corporate email. Customers will need to appear as a key concern for your personas if your engagement survey tells you that they matter to the workforce.

Produce illustrations or infographics that you can keep on the office wall or take to stakeholder meetings. And get in to the habit of asking, when you are considering any plans or content, 'What would Mairead think of this and how can we get Miguel interested?'

Having your persona model on hand aids thinking about plans and angles for your content and informs stakeholder discussions about messages or the perceived benefits that a particular project might bring. The conversation can transform the attitude of a programme leader who assumes that a single message will be enough to convince everyone.

CASE STUDY Coventry Building Society: Understanding
the details that matter

In 2015, UK financial institution Coventry Building Society embarked on Project
ATOM: an assignment of two halves. 'A' stood for accommodation, focused on
acquiring more head office space, due to business growth. 'TOM' concerned
changes to the target operating model for the organization's mortgage processes.

The project impacted 75 per cent of the company's 1,800 head-office staff. For
some, it meant a change to their office location. For others, it brought changes to
their role. And for others, it meant both.

Internal Communications Manager Kirsty Bowen explains, 'There was a lot of
complexity. I spent time understanding the detail of what the changes would
mean for people and segmenting them into groups which shared common
characteristics.'

Bowen identified 19 different audience groups. She started by asking herself,
'How is this group affected differently to another?' Then, she put together a crib
sheet to help her understand and record the answers for each audience.

Title of audience

Number involved

Line manager

Proposed host of face-to-face briefings for impacted staff

Proposed host of face-to-face briefings for non-impacted staff

Proposed host of conference call briefing (remote teams)

Logistical and other considerations (eg fragmented teams, customer-facing
teams who couldn't all be taken off the phones at once, which section of the
project impacted them, etc)

Key messages (of particular relevance to this team, such as how they are
impacted, how they might feel about different changes according to their
context, etc)

Delivery (how the briefings will be run, including any mop-up sessions)

Supporting information from intranet repository (which particular documents/
information would be relevant for this team, amongst everything we would
make available on our intranet site for the programme)

Bowen comments, 'It was the practical details that concerned people. Some people were moving to a different office that wasn't too far away, but there wasn't much onsite parking, and there was an issue with bus routes. This meant a walk to the office, which they didn't have before. It also disrupted people's routines for taking their children to and from school.

'I had to be careful not to make assumptions. Some employees were moving from a city centre office. I'd assumed they would view the move as a positive change to their working environment and had expected it to be a good news story for them. But when I actually spoke to people who knew the audience well, I realized some people had worked there for a long time, and really liked being in the city centre.'

Through careful research and planning, Bowen was able to identify details and practicalities that would make the changes easier for people. Concerns about changes to roles could be addressed through thoughtful messaging, and giving people choices about the roles they moved into. Employees were concerned about a loss of variety in their work. So, communication focused on how people could develop more in-depth expertise in the new model. A preference exercise for some meant staff didn't feel forced into a future role.

Meanwhile, concerns about transport relating to office moves were addressed through the property team talking to the Council about local bus routes, and putting on a new shuttle bus service. Home comforts and traditions were also important – getting a much-loved table-tennis table brought over to the new office was appreciated.

Bowen used her crib sheets to plan initial face-to-face briefings about the changes, taking account of people's working patterns and shifts; and working with contact centre resourcing teams to plan how many people could be taken away from answering calls at any one time. She also identified what supporting information would be needed for each group, depending on how they were affected by the changes.

Her advice to other communicators facing similar projects is to 'plan, plan, plan. Get involved with programme teams early, so you have the time to understand how people are impacted by changes. Segment your audiences, so you can tailor communication. And keep good relationships with senior stakeholders, so they can help address non-communication issues that matter to people, which are equally important to positive engagement.'

Where to get your audience data

As we said above, the data you want about your audiences is not always easy to find. Perhaps because data is often incomplete, not consistently collected or plain wrong, many communicators don't try looking too hard. After all, if your organization is data incompetent you can probably find more pressing things to do than go fact-hunting!

If you are willing to compromise a little, though, there is often quite a lot within easy reach. Our colleagues in HR will have a good idea of numbers and where people are based, and will probably produce a regular report that includes information about employment status and perhaps length of service. The compensation and benefit team might have some useful insights about things like average salary and age profiles.

It is worth talking though other information that HR hold. Data and anecdote about things like sickness and absence, staff turnover, discipline and disputes will tell a story, especially if you can make comparisons between teams. You do not need to probe very deeply and need to respect privacy rules. All you want is an insight into differences in outlook and culture that could shape how you plan and deliver communication.

Other colleagues in teams like finance could be a good back-up as well. If there is any debate about the size of the workforce, payroll should be able to tell you how many people get paid. IT can tell you how many people have a computer and could be sitting on a ton of other information they have used for planning services. Facilities may have a sustainability plan that will tell you things like how people travel to your site. A bit of lateral thinking and a little patience should uncover a fair amount of information to supplement your own knowledge of the organization. If you or your predecessors have never collected or collated the data before, expect a few puzzled looks but persevere. You're the professional who needs to know who you're talking with.

Attitudinal data will come from a number of sources. The employee survey is an obvious starting point, and if you can get access to the base data you can commission your own reports, which is especially useful. If your organization is more than a couple of thousand strong consider asking a data scientist to see if there is additional business intelligence that can be extracted. Depending on how the survey was managed and the questions asked, you could possibly identify statistically significant clusters of workers who can be defined by their attitudes or communication preferences.

Working with data doesn't need to end with the staff survey. Inspired by the possibilities of big data, some research is starting to explore how behaviours like how quickly we respond to emails can give a clue to attitudes and employee engagement (Watts, 2016).

It's not just the numbers

Data and facts are our friends and we have mentioned elsewhere that we are often surrounded by managers who live and die by their spreadsheets; if we want to get their ear we should be prepared to bring evidence to our conversations. However, evidence does not just come in columns of figures and in neatly drawn graphs. Our personal insight gained from talking to people around the organization makes us valuable and so should not be neglected.

We have touched on this point in several other places, and we make no apologies for repeating it here. Great communicators, in our experience, always take the opportunity to listen and actively put themselves in the way of intelligence. That means getting away from the desk at lunchtime, having contacts around the organization we can sound out from time to time and creating networks on our social platforms that we can contact for advice and reaction. The better our network, the more useful we are to leaders and project teams who want an honest appraisal of whether their message is landing or how people might react to a new initiative.

Developing these networks takes time and perseverance. Think about the following tactics to start building your network:

- Run some simple focus groups, and afterwards ask the more helpful participants if you can stay in touch with them.

- Watch Yammer or your other social platforms, follow well-connected people and strike up a relationship – look for people who are not commenting all the time but, when they do, they're the ones who start conversations.

- When visiting other locations make a point of joining a local contact for lunch or coffee and chat to anyone they introduce you to.

- Always, always, always find time to chat to security staff, receptionists, assistants and administrators – they will know who the local influencers are and will have a good feel for the mood of the people around them.

- Rediscover the telephone – time spent talking is always better invested than an email.

- Consider once a month emailing or messaging everyone you met in the previous few weeks and asking them a communication-related question. It ensures that you don't forget your new contacts and it keeps your knowledge of your audiences fresh.

Not everyone is sociable, and many of us dread large-scale meetings with new people. The trick is to find ways of building up contacts that work for you, and where you can be authentic; people only relax with relaxed people, and this should be fun for you and for your colleagues. And remember, building intelligence is a team effort; everyone in the EC department should be chatting and listening so you can all play to your respective strengths.

Conclusion

We add the most value when we can escape the day-to-day routine. Investing time in understanding our audiences provides a key to unlocking the support of senior colleagues and offering advice that they can listen to. But there is a more fundamental reason why we need to understand our audiences. If we do not know what interests them, grabs their attention or provides their motivation, our attempts to engage them and hold a meaningful conversation are going to be based on unreliable guesswork. And there are plenty of amateurs around in our organizations who can speculate about how best to communicate; audience insight is one of the foundations of professionalism.

References

FitzPatrick, L (2016) Internal communications, in *The Public Relations Handbook*, 4th edn, ed A Theaker, pp 273–310, Routledge

Garner, JT and Garner, LT (2011) Volunteering an opinion: Organizational voice and volunteer retention in nonprofit organizations, *Nonprofit and Voluntary Sector Quarterly*, 40(5), pp 813–28

Gladwell, M (2004) *The Tipping Point: How little things can make a big difference*, Abacus

Government Communication Service (no date) How do you segment your audience? [Online] https://communication.cabinetoffice.gov.uk/ic-space/audience-segmentation-and-insight/how-do-you-segment-your-audiences/

Kang, M (2016) Moderating effects of identification on volunteer engagement: An exploratory study of a faith-based charity organization, *Journal of Communication Management*, 20(2), pp 102–17

Kim, JN (2011) Public segmentation using situational theory of problem solving: Illustrating summation method and testing segmented public profiles, *PRism*, 8(2), pp 1–12

Lyons, S and Kuron, L (2014) Generational differences in the workplace: A review of the evidence and directions for future research, *Journal of Organizational Behavior*, 35(S1), pp S139–57

MacLeod, D and Clarke, N (2010) Leadership and employee engagement: Passing fad or a new way of doing business? *International Journal of Leadership in Public Services*, 6(4), pp 26–30

Waters, R, Sevick Bortree, D and Tindall, NTJ (2013) Can public relations improve the workplace? Measuring the impact of stewardship on the employer–employee relationship, *Employee Relations*, 35(6), pp 613–29

Watts, D (2016) The organizational spectroscope. [Online] https://medium.com/@duncanjwatts/the-organizational-spectroscope-7f9f239a897c

Messaging

Managing meaning

05

CHAPTER OBJECTIVES

At its most basic, communication is about the sharing of meaning between people or groups. When we say something, we'd like other people to understand. But, ideally, we'd like them to agree with us as well. For a professional communicator, the job is about explaining and getting our colleagues to see that it's a good idea to do the things we'd like them to do. We work in the realm of sharing and shaping meaning.

This chapter looks at how people's fundamental opinions about the world shape how they will react to information and events. And, we'll think about how the stories and messages we share can help shift those opinions to help support our organizations. We'll look at how to set out those stories and messages so that they are impactful.

This is the world of messaging. It involves understanding other people's points of view and how to go about influencing them for the good of the organization. And, like everything else in this book, we come at it from the position that expert communicators don't just create content or outputs. We're in the business of delivering results or outcomes.

Frame, narrative, message

A while back, a public housing association that specialized in homes for older people had a safety issue. Its highly skilled and experienced maintenance staff were having a lot of small injuries at work. Luckily nothing terrible had happened but the association was concerned about the long list of trips, grazes, bruises and scrapes that were being reported. The safety manager was particularly worried that no one was actually reporting any near misses; he was terrified something big would happen and no one would see it coming.

When the safety manager spoke to staff they just didn't see the issue. As skilled craftsmen and women, they expected that they'd bang their knees or get a small cut occasionally. Stopping to do risk assessments was just a waste of time; it was better to get on with the job and look after residents; many of the safety procedures, such as calling a colleague from another job to hold a ladder steady for 30 seconds, were plain nonsense. The housing organization had done all the right things with posters and safety training days but they were not having any impact. A fundamental shift in attitude was needed.

In the end, the solution was actually quite simple. The safety manager worked with the fact that maintenance workers saw themselves as experts. He started talking about the dangerous things people did in their own homes and the maintenance staff were quick to supply examples of things that they saw every day in residents' homes. Fire alarms without batteries, electric lamps perched on the side of baths, stair carpet that was loose and multiple plugs attached to a single power socket were just the tip of the domestic health and safety iceberg!

So, maintenance crew were encouraged to start mentioning to residents safer ways to do things, and, in some cases, nail down a trip hazard here or fit a smoke alarm battery there. They were encouraged to hand out a stock of home-safety leaflets when they made calls. After all, a crafts person was a safe person and took the care of residents seriously. If maintenance workers started helping residents to be safer, the HSE manager reasoned, they'd have to model safe behaviour themselves. It took a while, but gradually minor incidents involving staff declined and reports of near misses started to come in. The association was becoming safer because it had started talking about safety in terms that made sense to staff.

We're telling you this tale (which has a few details changed to make the point) because it demonstrates the three different aspects of the communicator's craft.

First, it concerns what we call *frame* – the way we see the world and how this decides how we'll react to a piece of information. The maintenance men and women had seen all the posters and videos about safety but they thought safety just got in the way of doing what was important for the people who really mattered – the residents. Lee Bolman and Terrence Deal have written extensively over the years about organizations and the importance of aligning leadership with how organizations see themselves (Bolman and Deal, 2017). Either you work with the existing frame or mindset or you set out to shift it.

Figure 5.1 Frame, narrative and message

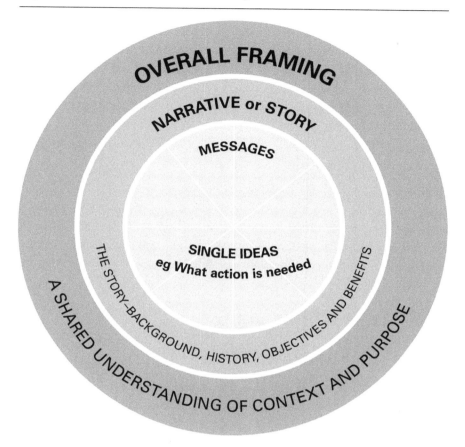

OVERALL FRAMING

NARRATIVE or STORY

MESSAGES

SINGLE IDEAS
eg What action is needed

THE STORY—BACKGROUND, HISTORY, OBJECTIVES AND BENEFITS

A SHARED UNDERSTANDING OF CONTEXT AND PURPOSE

Second, there was a *narrative* used in the housing association. It acknowledged that staff were skilled professionals who wanted to help tenants. And it used the stories they told about domestic hazards to highlight that safety was worth talking about.

And last, staff received specific *messages* about helping residents, offering safety advice and reporting concerns. The messages on their own may not have worked if they had landed in a hostile environment where the audience's frame or point of view was completely at odds with the idea and instructions contained in the messages.

And so, we have just told you a story to draw out the three levels of meaning with which we work as communicators (Theaker, 2016: 41–46), which we refer to collectively as messaging and which we have illustrated in Figure 5.1:

- **Frame:** The perspective through which people interpret facts. In the case of the housing association, employees thought that safety got in the way of skilled people doing their job.

- **Narrative:** The more detailed explanation of how things are, which draws out the situation, the journey and the benefit, and possibly ties it all together with some history or a story. In this case the safety manager got maintenance staff to think about residents' hazards and suggested they could do something about it.

- **Message:** The point of the communication. Here, it was specific suggestions about helping tenants and reporting concerns.

Of course, there is overlap between these concepts in the strictest sense, because the process of shaping meaning, or messaging, is not a series of steps; when thinking about them we go backwards and forwards several times. They all feed off each other, but we have broken them out here because we think it helps to show how meaning can be managed in a practical way.

It all starts with framing

Frames shape what people hear

Imagine your staff are tired of abuse from customers. Every day they get phone calls from people who are rude, demanding and possibly (in their view) a bit stupid. How will they react when the CEO starts talking about going an extra mile for customers? Or imagine that your workers believe senior management are always looking for ways to make them work harder for less money. News of a new pay structure and shift patterns may be met with suspicion.

People interpret what they hear or see according to their frame; information only means something within a wider worldview (Fairhurst, 2005). If you understand that worldview, you can make sure that what you say fits within it and is easier to understand and accept.[1]

We hear from neuroscientists (Scarlett, 2016: 119–25) that people's set beliefs can be powerful causes of misunderstanding. What we actually notice, and how we decide who we are going to agree or disagree with, might have no basis in logic and effectively be hardwired in our brains. Scientists call these reasons to hold fast to a set of views or a frame 'biases'.

What we say isn't the only thing that matters. What people see, feel or remember makes powerful evidence to confirm or create a frame. Once, in a highly conservative company, we produced a new style of video with senior leaders discussing a new strategy in a relaxed and informal way. When asked what message they had received, many staff only noticed what they thought was a change to the dress code so that men no longer needed to wear neckties.

The point is that frames can be deeply embedded and can block even the most exciting and powerful communications. Our skill involves seeing things the way our audiences do and applying that knowledge to the communication we produce.

Communicators suggest frames

As well as needing to understand audiences and their frames, we also have to suggest the frame that should be applied to new information or work out how to adjust a deeply held set of beliefs. In our housing association example, we talked about changing fundamental attitudes towards safety in order to get people to avoid and report hazards. New rules about customer service could be seen as added bureaucracy or they could be seen as a great way to make customers happy. Our job is not just to pump information out; we help people interpret it as well.

We do that by providing context, bringing in the opinion of people who are respected by our audiences and showing the benefits we hope to achieve or the problems we are trying to avoid. We have to avoid 'spinning' a workforce because they will only accept what is credible and can ultimately be shown to be true. Only an idiot hopes to get away with lying to their workforce. Even if it wasn't unethical, internal audiences will always find you out sooner or later and they rarely forgive you.

We also have to be aware that what you do is as important as what you say in setting context and creating frames. No amount of talking about cost saving will wash if the executives still fly business class or have obvious perks. A safety culture is unlikely to thrive in a world where leaders demand relentless quarter-on-quarter financial performance as the number one priority.

Narratives connect

Throughout the 1970s and 1980s, Southwest Airlines, flying in the US, virtually created the concept of the challenger low-cost airline. Unlike its bigger,

more established and dearer competitors, it relished its culture of rebellious-
ness and fun. Legends abound about pranks played by its cabin crew and its
irreverent approach to the mores of the aviation industry.

On the walls of its headquarters in Dallas is a mural that depicts a
defining moment in the history of the business. In 1992, Southwest found
itself in dispute with another small carrier over the use of an advertising
slogan, but rather than spend hundreds of thousands of dollars on legal
fees and wait years for the courts to resolve the argument, the CEOs of
the two companies chose a novel way to settle the matter. They arm-
wrestled each other.

Who won doesn't really matter now. Rather, Southwest cemented its status as the airline that did things differently, that didn't take itself too seriously, wasn't bound by convention and was willing to innovate. It's a story
that everyone at Southwest knows.

The Southwest tale is an extreme example, but stories stick and take
on a life of their own. In order to tell a story you need to explain context
and a dilemma or challenge, an objective or destination, a description of
the events or the journey and a conclusion. When you use a story, your
audience understands and remembers; the telling creates an actual experience that they can own and relate to (O'Murchu, 2015). Done well,
stories provide a step-by-step sharing of information that can build
awareness, lay out a sequence of events, help people connect their own
situation to the organization, help build trust and reinforce values
(Gill, 2011).

What's a narrative?

Very simply, we are going to use *narrative* to mean the wider context and
story into which a message fits. We'll explain these in more detail below but
there are a couple of points we should flag up about the features of a narrative. Narratives need to:

- make sense to people as a coherent explanation of what is happening;
- reflect what people currently believe, or certainly not ask them to make
  too big a leap away from what they understand or hold to be true;
- be true (even if they include opinion and interpretation).

Constructing a narrative

The process of building a series of ideas or incidents on top of each other is well known to us, and in fact theorists believe that there are actually a limited number of story structures or narratives. Some argue that we can follow the same base structures used in tales like *The Lord of the Rings* or *Die Hard* to engage people with the idea that we're facing a challenge but that after many trials and tribulations we will triumph (Kent, 2015).

Perhaps you are not quite ready yet to embark on an elaborate storytelling process. However, a narrative that explores our situation, a destination to be reached, a journey to get there and a prize at the end is recognizable and compelling. We use a simple format to help draw out the components of the narrative; they are summarized in Figure 5.2.

The four components are a useful aide memoire to make sure the main elements are covered. They explore:

- Our challenge: The current and future environment, and what stakeholders such as customers or regulators expect now and tomorrow. It can include a significant danger or an opportunity to be grasped.

- Our destination: The end state to which the organization is headed and a sense of the commitment of leaders or decision-makers to that goal.

- The journey: The steps and milestones toward the destination. It should refer also to the resources (material and emotional) that will be needed and where they will come from.

- The prize: A statement of what reaching the destination will bring.

Once you have defined the key elements you can decide how to bring them to life. Perhaps there are examples of conversations with customers that a leader can bring to bear, or a supervisor could be encouraged to think of the moment when they realized a core element of the story. It might be that the narrator reports hearing the CEO describe a personal experience.

The narrative also works at the beginning of a change or through the life of the transformation. Whilst the essential facts may evolve as milestones are passed or the course is adjusted, the underlying rationale and values remain the same.

Figure 5.2 The narrative framework

OUR CHALLENGE

A description of the world we're in – customers, competitors, stakeholders and what they expect of us

What is coming – the **factual** and **emotional** reasons why we can't stand still and the potential opportunity to be grasped

OUR DESTINATION

What our future looks like – a factual description of where we need to get to

Evidence of the our **commitment** to the destination

THE JOURNEY

The steps we will have to take and the **staging posts** along the way

The **support we** will have along the way and the **strengths** we will draw upon

The **risks we face** if we waver or weaken

THE PRIZE

What will the final destination **feel** like and what **material benefits** will it bring to us, to the people we care about and the world which we serve?

Why we should have **faith** that we will reach our goal

EXERCISE 5.1

Helping leaders to develop their own framework

Leaders are often more likely to embrace a narrative if they've created it themselves. Try this simple facilitation with a management group to get the narrative agreed. This exercise needs at least four people to work but is most effective if there are 12 or more participants.

1 Set up four flip charts around a room, labelled individually *Our challenge, Our destination, The journey* and *The prize*. Include the descriptions in Figure 5.2 as prompts.

2 Explain the idea of the narrative model and give each participant an ample supply of sticky notes. Give the group 15 minutes to circulate on their own between the flip charts and to write on individual sticky notes ideas or facts that seem appropriate to attach to each flip chart. This stage of the exercise is done solo and no discussion is needed.

3 Be sure to encourage the participants to visit each flip chart more than once so that they are prompted by the thoughts left by other people.

4 After 15 minutes, or when the charts are full, split the group into four teams and allocate them to one of the charts. Now ask them to spend 10 minutes discussing the ideas on the chart in front of them. They can add to the notes or donate notes to other groups if they feel they belong elsewhere. Their task is to come up with a statement that describes the principal issues on their own chart.

5 When you are ready, ask the group working on the *Our challenge* chart to debrief the room on what they have agreed. Listen carefully and make sure a detailed note is made of what is said and the language used. When the debrief is finished, ask any points of clarification that you may have and invite the rest of the participants to do the same.

6 If the description lacks facts or emotion, prompt the whole group to supply them by asking questions like 'Why is that the case?',

'How do you think people will feel about that?' or 'Why should anyone believe you?'

7 You want to achieve consensus about what should be included in this element of the narrative.

8 Next, turn to the group who worked on *Our destination* and repeat the exercise, before moving on to *The journey* and *The prize*.

9 Summarize by reading back from your notes what you have been told by each group in turn. They should now be hearing a narrative that they can all recognize and support.

10 Write up the narrative as quickly as possible to make sure you don't forget anything, and supply it to the group.

Figure 5.3 is a worked example of the narrative model for a semi-fictional international relief and development agency introducing a new HR model that includes leadership training and a more consistent approach to performance management.

Importantly, we have to be mindful of factual and emotional evidence. A compelling reason for change might be to increase revenues or to respond to a new regulation, or it might be to transform the lives of our stakeholders. The prize for reaching our destination could be a more manageable cost base or it could the continuance of our brand for another 20 years. We need both the hard data and the softer human elements.

The role of the communicator is to help develop the story and think about the personal experiences that bring it to life. Few people are by nature talking spreadsheets, but many managers are initially fearful of being over-personal; some discussion should help them find a level of comfort in adding details that make their telling of narrative authentic and compelling. Remember what we said before about discussing an encounter with a customer; or perhaps they can recall a time when they witnessed something like an empty warehouse or dealing with an angry colleague.

Figure 5.3 Worked example of a narrative model for a fictionalized relief agency introducing new leadership training and performance management tools

OUR CHALLENGE

The work we do matters more than it has ever done. Today we support five crises of the highest severity – more than ever before in our history. At the same time, funding for what we do isn't growing; the world deserves better.

To reach the people we are missing today will need different approaches and different skills; we need to unlock the creativity of our people, retain the best and grow their skills to deliver in innovative ways.

OUR DESTINATION

We can do more for more people, but that means we need to change how we think and how we work. Our mindset has to be relentlessly focused on results.

Our goals need the best leaders in the sector. We are investing in leadership and will have the skills, processes and tools to empower our people to be great. People will work here because they are supported to deliver more for our beneficiaries and have the chance to be the best that they can be.

THE JOURNEY

Leaders at every level will have a development plan for the first time; we'll apply a common mindset to motivating and growing the teams around us. We'll set ourselves goals for getting more from our people and become consistent in how we support their performance.

We're learning new ways to solve old problems and the courage to face fresh challenges.

THE PRIZE

We'll make even more of a difference when we give people clarity about their roles, support to develop and leadership to innovate. We'll make it possible to reach the people being left behind and we'll become the benchmark of how agencies can perform.

Our jobs will be more satisfying: taking personal control allows us to develop and for the organization to deploy the best people where they can make the most impact.

CASE STUDY   Keeping the message personal at KPMG

At global business advisory firm KPMG, technology is transforming the firm and how clients are served. It's the job of Marta Van Ranst to explain it to colleagues.

Working across 165 countries is not an easy job, not least because of the volume of information in circulation. 'I have to think about how we catch people's attention – who wants to get another email or another newsletter? Video is becoming increasingly ubiquitous and it's quite broad brush in what it can say. And new interesting tools like apps only work if staff actually want to look at them,' explains Marta.

Her approach has been to apply some of the lessons she learned as a journalist before entering corporate life. 'You have to think about writing content for the intranet and emails that's quick and attractive to read. We were taught that you have to be able to write gripping headlines, and that's what I still try to do.'

It's a discipline made all the more important by the finite resources available to her. 'When we look at material that explains complex issues, like infographics produced by media organizations, I know that dozens of people worked on it. Internally, we have to work with smaller teams and manage competing demands.' She therefore thinks carefully about the message and how to make it impactful. By simplifying and understanding her audiences, she knows she can make a difference.

Talking about a simple project to get an ISO security accreditation she explains, 'Certification matters, as major clients trust us with their data. Passing an ISO audit isn't just about having the right processes and rules; we have to show that staff understand and apply them.'

She began by asking what specific behaviours were needed from staff at their three main hubs in London, Amsterdam and New Jersey. It was plain that knowing about rules and getting staff to apply them were different things. 'It's one thing to say "You have to do this..." and another thing to actually change disciplines around stuff like card swiping, desk clearing, laptop locking and that sort of thing,' she reflects.

The team took into account a number of factors, including cultural difference between their three sites and their specific physical layout and history. Tactics that worked in one place would not necessarily work elsewhere, so giving managers a strong set of messages to cascade was important. Underlying everything, they looked for a way to make the message powerful. 'We set out to explain the value to the business of having certification and what it would mean if we didn't come up to ISO standards,' says Marta.

In order to highlight important behaviours, the programme developed a simple mnemonic – CLIP – which stood for:

- Clear desk.
- Lock your laptop.
- ID at all times.
- Prepare to answer questions about the policy.

'And we kicked off with a message from the chief information officer – it's not a tactic we use a lot. It felt a more authentic way to get people to adopt the rules, and we reinforced it by another one from the chief of staff the day before the audit began.'

They maintained a drumbeat of communication, including red and green cards left on desks overnight to highlight model behaviours, and handed out free desk locks for laptops. Events like lunch-and-learn sessions proved popular and there was a drive to talk in the language that people used.

Throughout, there was an emphasis on peer communication. Working with local champions created a sense that everyone bought into the campaign. 'Although we were working through managers, people don't want to be the teacher's pet, so peer pressure matters,' says Marta. 'So in New Jersey we looked for people on each pod [a cluster of desks] who could influence the rest and reinforce the message that we're in this together.'

The programme proved to be a success, with few non-conformers, and they passed the audit with only a couple of minor comments from the assessors.

Marta doesn't have a set process for messaging, but she always starts by exploring with a project team what they want to achieve. She reflects on the need to apply a dose of healthy scepticism. 'You learn to boil things down to what is actually important and see how to make it compelling and understandable. That is only possible if you have a feel for the audience and how they talk and think.' So, most importantly in a busy world, she asks, 'Is this message a good use of people's time – if there is no value to the reader, are they going to even look?'

Getting your message straight

So, you know how your audience thinks and you've provided an explanation that covers why and how things are happening. Now you need to focus in on the central idea that you need to get over in order to get results. That's what we mean by a message.

We think that great messages need to be:

- simple;
- energizing and interesting;
- relevant to the audience and not just the sender;
- interpretation as well as information;
- true;
- able to fit within the narrative;
- actionable.

The case study from KPMG is a great example of making the messages work simply and being actionable.

Your message recipe

Messages supply detail and clarity, but we have found that they work best when they contain:

- **A single memorable idea:** Try not to cram too much into a single message. You may need a supporting message or two but start with a headline of just a few words.

- **A sense of why the audience should care:** Be careful of the 'What's in for me?' trap! You do not need to have a benefit for every single message, and we've seen some awful communications created in order to find an upside to every initiative. One HR team we knew wanted to talk of 'careers of horizonal richness' as an exciting alternative to job promotions (the prospect of which they were removing with a new restructuring initiative). It's enough to be clear about why the audience should care or be interested. If it's bad news, explain the mitigations by all means but don't try to con your staff; they will very probably see straight through it.

- **Information compatible with current beliefs:** If people believe the sky is blue, telling them that it's really green is going to be a challenge. Ideally, as communicators we want to avoid too many surprises that shock our colleagues; some things can only be done in small steps. In the 1980s smoking at your desk was entirely acceptable in most workplaces, but now smokers have to stand in the street when they want to light up; the change happened in many small steps over 30 years. Whilst there will of course be times when we need to dramatically reframe beliefs, we will normally take people in small steps unless the stakes are high.

- **A proof point:** Insisting on evidence is one of the communicator's defences against the dark arts of spin and manipulation. If we're claiming to be committed to developing our workforce we should be able to point to how it proposes to train or upskill people. If there is a transformation programme designed to reshape a company and make it more effective, we should be ready to share the details of workstreams beyond the one that cuts headcount. What counts as a proof point will vary from situation to situation; they may include simple facts, links to external sources or statements or details of plans but the main test is whether it is true and credible. Writers Chip and Dan Heath talk very engagingly about making a message sticky and highlight the importance of being credible and concrete (Heath and Heath, 2008).

- **As little corporate waffle as possible:** When was the last time you decided to take the bus to work because you were 'optimizing your logistics options for cost and operational viability'? Would it be more likely that the car park had put its prices up and you couldn't afford to drive any more? For some reason, organizations seem to hate plain language, especially when there is a difficult message to put over. We might try to keep it simple but by the time a committee of nervous managers have finished with our message no one will have a clue what it was trying to say. Of course, a message is never meant to be used as a verbatim script but if you start out with something in corporate waffle, imagine what it will be like by the time it is delivered! And there's a danger that managers deep in the organization will just forward your beautiful obscured message in a suitably sarcastic email to their teams. A plain message is a trusted message.

- **A call to action:** People notice when you give them an action. A clear message will say what needs to be done in practical terms; the more direct the better. It might be interesting to ask staff to 'spend the company's money as if it were their own' but perhaps it's better to direct the message at people who make purchasing decisions and tell them what rules they need to apply or how to manage their budgets. Safety might be 'everyone's first concern' but would the message be more potent if you also asked office staff to hold the handrail when going up stairs?

Putting it together

Setting out a message helps you think through the elements to ensure it make sense and provides a consistent basis for briefing colleagues and leaders on the message they need to deliver. When you are writing down a message it is best not to treat it as a rigid script to be repeated without variation; the aim is to lay out an idea that leaders and communication colleagues can put in their own words or adapt to suit the media or channels though which it will be shared. Messages are not slogans (although slogans can be powerful expressions of messages).

Messages are more than words; we all know that *how* something is said is as much part of the message as the well-crafted phrases that have been agreed with lawyers and regulators. A redundancy notice sent by email, a CEO who refuses to answer legitimate press questions or an executive who comes in person to listen to an employee's views will all tell us something without saying a word.

When discussing potential messages with leaders, they can worry about the exact meaning of individual words being used and, with a language like English with its rich and subtle vocabulary, that can be a painful and pointless experience. Even native speakers of English will not always understand the nuance of carefully chosen words; it is better to concentrate on the essential idea.

The exact components of a message document are often a matter of personal taste or reflect what works for your leaders at any given time. Figure 5.4 suggests a template for laying out the key elements of your message but typically, you will want to spell out:

- the overall communications objective you have set yourself, possibly broken down according to what you want people to:

    do – the actions you need taken;

    feel or believe – the emotional impetus that will motivate people;

    know – the facts and logical reasoning;

- a simple, memorable statement of the idea you want to get over;
- why the audience should care;
- a maximum of three or four supporting ideas;
- proof points or 'killer facts' that support the 'why' and the 'how' of your message.

Figure 5.5 is a worked example of a message deck from a fictional university that wants to engage its academic staff in more cross-disciplinary research projects.

Figure 5.4 Sample template for a message palette

THE OVERALL COMMUNICATIONS OBJECTIVE

For the specific audience group
The outcome we want to achieve

THE SINGLE MEMORABLE POINT

The idea that we want to get over – expressed as simply as possible

DO	FEEL	KNOW	
		WHY FACTS	**HOW FACTS**
What is the specific action we need people to take?	What feeling will encourage them to do the right thing?	Data that explains the reasoning behing the message	Data or evidence that shows there is a credible plan or that the goal has been reached

SUPPORTING MESSAGES

Limited to three or four

Reflects WHY SHOULD I CARE | RATIONALE | WHAT HAPPENS NEXT

SUPPORTING MESSAGE Simple additional information	**SUPPORTING MESSAGE** Simple additional information	**SUPPORTING MESSAGE** Simple additional information

WHERE YOU CAN FIND OUT MORE

Figure 5.5 Worked example from a fictional university

Supporting the univerity's objective to build greater collaboration between departments to promote cross-disciplinary research and original discoveries by breaking down silos			THE OVERALL COMMS OBJECTIVE
Our greatest achievements happen when we connect we're a powerful force in research because we value collaboration and find fresh inspiration when we step outside our departments			THE SINGLE MEMORABLE POINT
DO	**FEEL**	**KNOW**	DO – FEEL – KNOW
• Join one of the five interdisciplinary networks for active researchers • Commit to sharing a current research issue this year • Attend the internal network launch event	• The university supports my research for active researchers • I can benefit from connecting with other active researchers outside my field • This could be exciting	• % of current 4* work that crosses disciplines • Nobel prizes • Uni target	• Collaboration fund • Set up 5 networks with senior leadership • Time allowance for participation
SUPPORTING MESSAGE Research funding increasingly cross-disciplinary and we punch below our weight in the five key areas	**SUPPORTING MESSAGE** Collaborative projects should provide more opportunities and stability for early career researchers	**SUPPORTING MESSAGE** We attract great minds and have the raw material to outperform our peers domestically and internationally	SUPPORTING MESSAGE
Come to the launch reception and sign up on the Wicked Problems Portal			FIND OUT MORE

Using your message palette

The secret to an effective message is to keep it as simple as possible. Simplicity doesn't just aid understanding; it focuses your efforts and stops you getting distracted.

Your first task is to ensure that the message reflects and informs leaders. You and they need to be saying the same thing. So, draft the message with them and run face-to-face briefings on the message and the supporting facts. Working through the sorts of questions that might arise helps you anticipate what clarification might be needed. With your own work, the message palette should help you think through content that you want to use in your channels and other tactics that might reinforce the message.

Other writers recommend talking to employees about the external world and how stakeholders are experiencing the organization; people with experience of quality and business improvement will be very familiar with the idea of using the 'voice of the customer', and author (and ex-Communications Director) Kevin Murray talks about 'bringing the outside in' as one of the hallmarks of compelling messaging (Murray, 2013).

Whatever approach you use, begin with the audience and have the outcome in mind. The aim of messaging is to share meaning for a purpose. That is always going to be easiest if you bring a deep appreciation of how your audience sees things, what motivates them and where you need to get them to.

CASE STUDY   Making messages work globally at Schneider Electric

Strong processes and disciplines are key to ensuring that messages are relevant and understood at global giant Schneider Electric. Carmel Bawa, Senior Internal Communications Business Partner at the 140,000-strong industrial group, explains, 'As IC professionals it's our job to think through the angles and not just repeat technical information from subject matter experts; we have to explain without oversimplifying.' It's a challenge that matters to Carmel, whose role includes overseeing global articles and other content that is shared with the worldwide workforce.

'We start the year with a clear idea across the whole IC function of our 12-month calendar, setting out a monthly schedule of themes and major internal and external events,' she explains. Carmel and the team convene a monthly editorial committee meeting made up of colleagues from IC, marketing, HR and other interested functions 'We look at the calendar and think about the content we can use to bring the themes to life.'

However, the committee has to be disciplined. 'We're talking to a global audience, so we need to ask whether the stories we want to tell are useful to people at a global level.' When they have agreed a schedule of content the calendar is shared for local IC leads to see and build upon with their relevant content.

Carmel and her colleagues are helped by the training that they have organized for communicators around the world: 'It covers more than writing skills, but at its heart is the question "What makes this interesting and relevant for our varied audiences?"'

She explains that the focus on relevance also appears in the work Schneider Electric's IC community does with projects: 'We're working with brilliant subject matter experts who know their topic inside out and we have to connect them with people who are less knowledgeable or are perhaps new to the subject.'

As an example, she talks about a project where she asked basic questions about how the project team knew they were having an impact or how they might explain their work to someone with a very different experience to their own. Because the project team had not really looked at its work through the eyes of someone with no context, Carmel was able to highlight the value of simplification.

Her desire to make things easy to grasp paradoxically means that a business partner has to really understand the detail of what they are working on. 'I need to analyse everything in front of me – I'll Google stuff, read up on key facts, and research trends. I want to understand the *what – why – how* of a project and look for a juicy angle'. Doing this has a real benefit for Carmel, who explains, 'You need to both show a stakeholder that you're respectful of their expertise and own your own expertise as a communicator.' That communications expertise involves exploring what we need audiences to feel and do and what could potentially motivate them. This is done alongside stakeholder mapping and then thinking through what messages will work with each group.

The messaging process also involves thinking about which channels will work best for delivering different elements of the message. Developing the concepts behind messages might involve, for larger campaigns, input from colleagues in design and discussions with her network in countries and business units who will help her test ideas.

Carmel is also grateful for the support she gets from a new member of the team who specializes in insight. This helps her get a deeper understanding of the audiences around the globe.

'I worry about how you make a message stick and make it relevant to people; having evidence about what works and what doesn't means you can't pretend that because something has been posted on the intranet it's been understood,' she says, 'and in a heavily matrixed 140,000-strong organization you have to know your audiences and how they respond to our channels.'

In order to match message, audience and channel, Carmel explains, 'On our employee portal we have two or three top stories per week for all employees, which will be different from what we add to the pages for a specific topic or project; our social enterprise network is not good for heavy reports but is perfect for celebrations and peer debate. We discuss the more strategic messages in our regular digital team sessions.'

And specific content platforms may need developing. For one programme, Carmel created content focused on personal stories of delivering a better customer experience that worked over a number of channels.

Carmel's advice to other practitioners is to own their professionalism. 'We have to be clear about where we are experts; that's in understanding the audiences and how you explain *what – why – how*. And it's OK to question everything; if you are seeing things from the viewpoint of someone who knows nothing you can't afford to worry about looking stupid.'

Conclusion

Communicators tend to have their own intuitive sense of what makes a great message, and that awareness gets stronger with experience and as we learn more about our audiences. However, we find that messaging is one of the commonest areas of difficulty for the stakeholders we work with. They wish there was a magic word that would convince people to see things their way, believe that a tidal wave of information will change hearts and minds or dream of a knockout slogan that will solve all their problems. Getting communication right is not always that easy and it's the job of a professional to explain the process and help stakeholders make good choices.

The processes we have described above may not always be right for every situation or organization, but we hope that it serves as a useful reminder of the elements you need in order to make your messaging work for you.

Note

1 Framing has received a lot of attention in academic circles in the context of media relations and political communications. Employee communicators might find it interesting to read Robert Entman's work and see the parallels that can be drawn with internal audiences; a good place to start is: Entman, RM, 2007. Framing bias: Media in the distribution of power. *Journal of communication*, *57*(1), pp 163–173.

References

Bolman, LG and Deal, TE (2017) *Reframing Organizations: Artistry, choice, and leadership*, John Wiley & Sons

Fairhurst, GT (2005) Reframing the art of framing: Problems and prospects for leadership, *Leadership*, **1**(2), pp 165–85

Gill, R (2011) Using storytelling to maintain employee loyalty during change, *International Journal of Business and Social Science*, **2**(15), pp 23–32

Heath, C and Heath, D (2008) *Made to Stick: Why some ideas take hold and others come unstuck*, Random House

Kent, ML (2015) The power of storytelling in public relations: Introducing the 20 master plots, *Public Relations Review*, **41**(4), pp 480–89

Murray, K (2013) *The Language of Leaders: How top CEOs communicate to inspire, influence and achieve results*, Kogan Page

O'Murchu, L (2015) Storytelling is serious business, in *Exploring Internal Communication: Towards informed employee voice*, 3rd edn, ed K Ruck, pp 65–70, Routledge

Scarlett, H (2016) *Neuroscience for Organizational Change: An evidence-based practical guide to managing change*, Kogan Page

Theaker, A (2016) *The Public Relations Handbook*, Routledge

Choosing channels for employee communication

06

Finding inspiration from others

CHAPTER OBJECTIVES

Communications pioneer Bill Quirke (1995) was talking about the importance of outcomes over outputs over twenty years ago. It goes to show that many aspects of good communication practice stand the test of time.

What *has* changed is the channels landscape. Thanks to technology, we're working in a golden age of possibilities. We can cross geographies and time zones, reach people working remotely, and invite anyone and everyone to create content, join conversations, form communities and collaborate.

The question we're most often asked in this area is 'What are other people doing?' So, we've focused this chapter largely on case studies. We don't suggest you 'copy' someone else's channels mix – their organization is not your organization. But, we've drawn out the underlying thinking in the cases, and highlighted some key points and questions along the way.

Throughout this book we've emphasized 'outcomes, not outputs'. 'Are channels not outputs?' we hear you ask. Indeed they are. And very important they are, too. Channels are your shop window, the visible face of the communication team for most people in the organization. Our point is that outputs are a means to an end, not an end in themselves. Communicators shouldn't just have great channels. They should deliver results *through* great channels.

Why every organization needs a good toolbox

When Liam was growing up, the only tools in the family home were a hammer, a screwdriver and a funny pointy thing to make holes in leather. His parents were not interested in DIY so every job had to be done with the hammer, the screwdriver or the funny pointy thing. There were a lot of badly done jobs in the FitzPatrick household. As a result, he now has a well-equipped toolbox, as whenever there's a task to be done around the house, he has to have the right tool for the job.

Getting the right tool for the communication job was the point of Quirke's classic framework, the 'channels escalator' (Quirke, 1995:128). At the bottom was awareness, achieved through one-way 'push' information channels. The further the escalator rose through understanding, through support to commitment, the more the recommended tools involved conversations and working things through.

We've met plenty of stakeholders (and communicators!) who hoped to persuade people to 'get on board and take action' by pushing out more and more information. It's the communications equivalent of using a hammer, a screwdriver and a funny pointy thing, over and over. If you want to get buy-in and behaviour change, don't use methods that will only raise awareness.

Like case study company SEAT, every organization needs a channels toolbox that's sufficiently well-equipped for its communications tasks.[1] Otherwise, the solutions you propose will always be the same, because you've only got three channels to choose from. Or, you'll find yourself making up something new every time, because none of the tools you've got are quite right.

CASE STUDY   Channels and experiences: Getting the mix right
at SEAT

Carmaker SEAT uses a mix of channels and experiences to provide its
almost 15,000 strong workforce in Spain with information and inspiration.
Communications at SEAT aim to support growth whilst placing a strong emphasis
on employee engagement. 'We have much to talk about, including our new
Strategy 2025, expansion into new markets, the introduction of innovative new
technology, and between 2018 and 2020 we are going to launch a new model
every six months,' explains María Antonia Fontiverio García-Izquierdo, Head of
Internal Communications at SEAT. 'And we have to do that whilst keeping it
relevant to our employees.'

And, fundamentally, the company wants to be an employer of whom staff are
willing to speak proudly.

Spread over three main sites in Catalonia, SEAT's workforce includes
production workers, software developers, innovation and design engineers and
logistical and office-based staff. It's a team that includes Generation Z and
Millennials working alongside people with over 35–40 years' service.

The company's quarterly magazine *mundoSEAT* (available in print and online)
helps push stories out to this diverse community. The 84-page colour publication
has been in print for over 50 years and has high journalistic standards. María
Antonia explains that the recently redesigned magazine is well received because
of its focus on employees: 'We try to avoid too much "corporate" content, so we
tell stories about the people who work here, and share their point of view in their
own voices.'

SEAT hoy is a weekly newsletter that provides a more immediate news
channel.

On factory floors, the company has communication stations – places where
information about assembly-line performance and quality data is displayed,
mostly for supervisors. Screens on the assembly lines share additional
information, and tend to be mostly used by blue-collar workers.

In 2015 the company launched its *mundoSEAT* app, which draws together
information about the company, products and life in SEAT. The app doesn't need
a password, making it easier for factory staff, who are not normally online, to
use. As well as holding sharable content, the app acts as a hub for the internal
channels and other company platforms, such as the employee portal, payroll and
benefits information.

A pilot project with Facebook's Workplace has shown the potential for greater self-management of services like training or benefits statements and the appetite for more collaboration and sharing. Another platform that offers better integration with the rest of the secure company environment will be rolled out shortly.

However, it is with face-to-face communication that María Antonia is most pleased. 'Each month we host a *Charlando con...*, a discussion with the CEO,' she explains. 'It's very informal and open. We know that employees who attend, report that they have been listened to.'

It's a lesson that is being adopted by some senior managers across the company. Site directors host breakfast with around 15 production colleagues chosen to reflect the mix of ages, roles and seniority in the workforce. After a five-or ten-minute update on current issues, staff are given the floor to talk about their concerns and points of view. The messages that are shared there are complemented occasionally during 'spokespeople' meetings. Internal communications take advantage of this forum in order to spread strategic messages to blue-collar workers. There is one spokesperson for every 15 blue-collar workers and they are provided with simple materials to help them share information. However, time has shown that they are most effective in their role where local supervisors are supportive and encouraging.

Although the company works hard to provide multiple places for information to be shared, such as on assembly-line digital screens or a platform for accessing payroll information, Fontiverio García-Izquierdo is keen to stress the limitations of traditional channels for delivering information. 'We try not to get overexcited about the technology; the impact you get when humans meet humans is so much greater,' she says. 'This is especially true when people have a chance to express themselves and share ideas. It is experiences that really interest employees; what matters is when our people have a chance to "live" the company.'

SEAT is therefore increasingly looking at ways to involve staff in events such as new product launches. 'When we unveiled our new Tarraco SUV we selected six colleagues to attend the launch as citizen journalists and report on what they saw. For example, the videos they produced gave their workmates a powerful sense of the occasion and what it means to the company.

'For a new model we'll often take advantage of the international press presentations to organize an exclusive programme for some employees and their relatives. Additionally we'll give people the opportunity to have a car for a weekend, and we might arrange, for factory colleagues, exhibitions of the new models and create different activities around them like, for example, "micro plays" where the features and benefits of the new car are explained,' she adds.

In the past, the company has held open days at its factory where staff could show their families where they work. 'It all builds a company of which people can be proud and for which they are willing to be brand ambassadors in their communities. We have to explain to people what is happening, but perhaps what matters more is to give them a chance to feel a part of something exciting.'

Fontiverio García-Izquierdo argues that communicators who focus too much on regular tools can miss out on the power of experiences. 'We can all develop beautiful tools, but if they are not meeting the needs of employees what is the point?' she asks. 'Our job is to balance the big corporate message with the desire for employees to be involved and listened to; experiences let you do that.'

First steps in reviewing your channels infrastructure: Five questions from our case studies

Building on the practical prompts in Chapter 2 to guide your thinking, our case studies highlight five fundamental questions to consider:

1 **What should your channels achieve?** If you have an internal communication strategy, start there. In the case of Scottish Water, the internal communications team was inspired by one of the strategic aims of the senior leadership team to achieve high levels of 'sustainable engagement', something Willis Towers Watson suggest is achieved through helping employees to be 'engaged, enabled and energized' (Willis Towers Watson, 2016). They built their channels infrastructure around these three categories.

2 **What kind of organization are you?** For example, Vodafone is a mobile company, which made it 'an obvious thing to do' to launch a mobile app.

3 **Who will you communicate with?** Different people will have different needs, interests and constraints. For example, SEAT needed to appeal to a range of groups, from office workers to production staff.

4 **What's the right balance of face-to-face and technology?** Technology offers great possibilities. But both SEAT and Scottish Water highlight the importance of face-to-face communication and real-life experiences, too. We've dedicated a chapter to supporting leaders – because they're important. Much of their communication with teams will be (or should be) face-to-face.

5 Who's talking? Who needs a share of voice, through what methods, and how will you support them? Think about the communications team, senior leaders, local line managers, peer-to-peer conversation and user-generated content.

CASE STUDY   Scottish Water: Building a new channels strategy

From 2016 to 2018, the communications team at utility company Scottish Water implemented a new suite of channels, and won awards for how they did it. In this case study, Head of Internal Communications Ruth Findlay explains what worked so well about their approach.

We did our homework. We sought feedback from hundreds of employees through focus groups, telephone interviews and a comprehensive online survey. Employees were largely satisfied with our channels, but wanted more opportunities to collaborate, form communities and have conversations. We also benchmarked with other organizations, and explored external ideas.

We seized opportunities. We took advantage of investment projects in IT infrastructure, including a new intranet and the rollout of smartphones. We made very good friends with IT. I was on the intranet steering groups and got heavily involved from the start, to make sure the intranet was an effective communication platform. We can now show animation, blogs, vlogs, video and we're moving towards full adoption of SharePoint and team sites.

We were guided by our communications strategic purpose: 'to engage, enable and energize employees, by providing the guidance, context and tools for good communication to flourish.' We analysed our research through this lens, and aligned our channels accordingly (see Figure 6.1):

- *Enabling channels* give employees the information to do their job well and help them understand how their role contributes to the success of Scottish Water.

- *Engaging channels* help employees to have a rational and emotional connection with Scottish Water. This is about bringing your whole self to work, feeling part of something and being recognized.

- *Energizing channels* provide a sense of community, support and well-being and drive sustainable engagement.

We still have more in the *Enable* category and less in *Energize*, but we're starting to redress the balance, whilst acknowledging that some channels can help us achieve one or more of these three goals.

Figure 6.1   Scottish Water channels mix

Enabled	Engaged	Energized
Push	**Two-way**	**Involved**
IC managed • Scotty – features • Scotty – news • Scotty – breaking news • Scotty – video • Scotty – online campaigns • Podcasts programme • Blogs/vlogs programme • SW wide print mag twice yearly • SW One events • Huddles (including LM briefings) • All company email	**IC managed** • Change communication • Scotty – comments • Scotty – user generated content • Yammer • SW One events • SL events	**IC managed** • Vision awards – new categories • Yammer convos, eg yamjams • All employee events
Shared management • Re-induction programme • On-boarding/induction	**Shared management** • Leadership team site	
Locally 'owned' • Huddle delivery • Time with line manager • Email • Work environment • Digital screens • Directorate/team events • Tailored FAQs • Storytelling • Webinars	**Locally 'owned'** • Huddle delivery • Yammer • Team sites • Time with line manager • Directorate/team events • Storytelling • Aspire and development • Health, safety and well-being • Workshops	**Locally 'owned'** • Huddle delivery • Yammer conversations • Team sites • Directorate/team events • Storytelling • Gem/igem awards

SOURCE Reproduced with kind permission of Scottish Water 2018

We gave our new intranet a personality. It's called Scotty. Scotty is a little dog wearing a Scottish Water hard hat and high-visibility jacket. We built a campaign around the dog – paw prints in the canteen, T-shirts, badges, videos and so on. It helped us gain a lot of momentum and interest.

We coaxed people beyond their comfort zone. Employees wanted more online tools, but also liked traditional print channels. We've tried to position our channels a bit ahead of current demand, without going too far. People liked the monthly print magazine, although they said the content was quickly outdated. We stopped it and introduced a twice-yearly publication with a different focus. Much of the former magazine content is now on the intranet, as our research showed that most of our employees regularly consumed news online.

We tried not to over-regulate our new collaboration tools. We introduced Yammer to build communities of practice and interest. We provided guidelines and how-tos, but overall we've let it grow organically – allowing employees to discover benefits for themselves and also have some fun in the process. The week we launched, someone was carrying out a nature site survey and posted rare footage of a family of badgers. Suddenly there were hundreds of people liking and commenting. Then they realized, 'I can share interesting things in my job, too. I have the communication means at my fingertips.' Our operational employees use Yammer quite a bit to get direct, quick responses from colleagues, sometimes across huge geographical areas. One of the most popular Yammer groups is 'Dogs of Scottish Water'. People share photos of their dogs and puppies, which gets a lot of discussion. I'm all for it.

We spent a lot of time explaining 'how to'. We thought about possible preconceptions and worries. It's easy to make assumptions about things being obvious. A lot of people didn't know what hashtags were or how to use them. Some people had never had a smart device, and found them a challenge. So we had a network of enthusiastic early adopters that we capitalized on, and encouraged community help across Yammer.

We've balanced push and pull. We've given up much of our control and allowed people to pull content and share and curate content for themselves. But we also need to ensure people stay connected to the whole business. So, we have a careful balance of push and pull channels, and of corporate and user-generated content.

We use our new channels to feed each other. We'll use Yammer to recommend content on Scotty, helping the right people have the right conversations. We watch to see what people are interested in. One day, people were discussing wind farms on Yammer. We took it up to do a debate of pros and cons in our print publication.

We found opportunities to increase face-to-face conversations, too. We invested in smaller and more focused all-employee events, delivered in an 'in the round' format. It's meant more investment of time from directors, but the quality of conversation is so much better and we've had an upsurge in energy and engagement as a result.

Changing channels and introducing new ones: Five tips from our case studies

1 **Find out what people want.** Talk to people. See what your engagement survey is saying. If you're looking at your channel mix as a whole, consider an audit. Find out what frustrates people about existing channels, what they'd like more or less of, what they're interested in.

2 **Make it easy.** The Scottish Water case describes the importance of simple 'how tos' and having people on hand to help use new tools, whilst not being too prescriptive about how to use them. Removing barriers makes it more likely people will try things out.

3 **Make it social – use the power of the network.** Many of these cases involve user-generated content. People are making videos, taking photographs and writing content they know their colleagues will be interested in. And they're telling people about it. Early adopters can also enthuse about new channels and help others use them.

4 **Just try it.** Put things out there, maybe with a small group to start with, and see what happens. After a small pilot, Vodafone's news app grew to 2,000 users without them even telling anyone about it.

5 **Look for opportunities.** Scottish Water took advantage of IT changes; as we will see shortly, AXA piggybacked on a brand refresh. Seize timely openings to give your new channels a head start.

CASE STUDY Vodafone: Introducing a mobile news app

In 2017, multinational telecoms conglomerate Vodafone introduced a mobile news app, enabling the company for the first time to reach all 100,000+ employees on their mobile devices. At the same time, out went some old communication channels and in came a less corporate, more authentic style of writing.

Chief of Staff/Head of Internal Communications Erica Lockhart answers our questions.

Why make the change?
We're a mobile company, so it was an obvious thing to do. But people should be able to access most things on mobile now anyway, that's what they expect. I also think that even if you have the best quality of writing, if you have to go into a clunky intranet, it takes ten seconds to upload, it has bad imagery – it's never going to feel journalistic. And for a comms person uploading onto a tool like that, it's not an inspiring way to work.

How did you choose the app?
We looked at the pros and cons of asking an app developer to create something bespoke, or buying something off the shelf. We went for the second option. It looks and works similarly to the BBC News app. The company we chose sell their mobile news app to multiple clients, so they're informed by data from millions of users and know what works. I'm a huge believer in data, not opinion.

How did you launch?

We did a soft launch of a pilot at a conference for 200 senior managers, then it grew organically to 2,000 users, without us telling anyone about it. We then rolled out officially over six months. At that point, we shut down news on the intranet. So, people didn't have the option to use the old. You can access content through your laptop if you need to, but we direct people to the app. The reaction has been really positive. Within a year, 85,000 people had registered and 70 per cent of them are actively using it every month.

What else did you stop?

We killed all email newsletters and stopped our text message service. We had a tool that sent an alert to people's computers; colleagues found it invasive, so we stopped that too. We rarely use mass email, and we do very little print.

How did content and style change?

Previously content was dry, corporate and driven by functional demand. We wanted it to be more about what people want to read. We monitor Workplace, to see what people are talking about. If people don't want to read it, what's the point in writing it?

I asked a couple of national journalists and a digital editor to talk to the team about how to write for the modern age. For example, 20 per cent of content is inspiring/hero stories, 50 per cent is news/updates and 30 per cent is fun stuff to grab attention. We also look for more emotive, inspirational long reads.

Senior executives often want dry messages. You have to look for interesting angles – the stories behind the corporate fluff, the inspiration in the message, and also be willing to talk frankly about things that aren't going well. The tone is more honest and authentic now. And we commissioned really nice photography and started using gifs.

There's *nothing* dull? Honestly?

We have a channel called 'boring but important'. It's about being authentic – occasionally you've just got to call a spade a spade. The thing here is, if there's something dry but need-to-know, people want to hear about it in five words, not ten paragraphs.

What about pushback?

Some teams got upset when we tagged their content in "boring but important" – they thought it was not at all boring! If they really couldn't be convinced by our approach, we took it out and looked for interesting angles instead. For example, some people may find compliance dry, but there are some fascinating stories about when people have broken laws and the consequences. That gets people's attention and makes them think about the topic in a different way.

I operate on the principle that it's easier to ask for forgiveness than permission. Mostly we've done things without asking. We're obsessive about data, and that's useful if we're challenged. The open rate on newsletters was terrible, for example, so we had back-up for why we killed those. We review the most and least read content in our weekly team meetings and send a quarterly report to our key executive stakeholders setting out what we've published, what's worked well, and what people are interested in or not.

Overall this is a progressive place, most people are open-minded, and if they see people are reading their content, they're quite buoyed by that. If they want colleagues to read about their issues, there's no point in writing about them in a way that people aren't interested in reading.

Tone, content and earning attention: Five lessons from our case studies

1 **Less corporate, more human.** Most organizations are fluent in the language of business buzzwords and corporate-eze. Especially when it's written down. Champion the cause of writing in everyday language. Employee journalists will do it anyway, like AXA's employee reporters. Or think about training for your team, as Vodafone did.

2 **Let channels feed channels.** Use one channel to signpost another. Keep an eye on what people are talking about in your social networking tools. It will show you what people are interested in, and spark ideas to follow through into other channels.

3 **Find the right mix.** Let business and 'life' walk together. Vodafone learned to find the right mix of inspiration, news and fun. Scottish Water found Yammer grew hugely after someone posted footage of a family of badgers, and one of their most popular communities is about pet dogs. SEAT brought people's families into their factories. Draw people in. Make your channels interesting and relevant enough that people will stay a while and discover how else they can use them.

4 **Find the angle.** Find the curious, unexpected, interesting or human slant behind corporate issues. Find the hook that will make people want to get involved. The BBC spotted that turning over its flagship channel to employees gives people the chance to get valuable career experience, and harnessed the enthusiasm of new employees by building a slot into their induction.

5 **Use signposting.** Vodafone's 'boring but important' is a good example. Make it easy for people to understand how to use channels, and what they can find, where.

CASE STUDY   The BBC: Reinventing an 80-year-old staff newspaper

Created in 1922, the BBC is the world's leading public service broadcaster and one of Britain's most well-known institutions. For the BBC's 22,000 employees and many more freelancers and contractors, the corporation's internal newspaper, *Ariel*, is another well-established institution. From June 1936 until December 2011 it was printed every week, with a remit to report on life at the BBC and developments in the broadcasting industry. It had an external subscription service and in the past was even printed and given out at underground stations.

In 2012, the print runs stopped. *Ariel* moved online, its newsroom was disbanded, and responsibility for editorial was brought into the internal communications team. And in 2015, with Heather Wagoner appointed Director of Internal Communication and Engagement, there were more changes to come: '*Ariel* needed to be reinvented for a new generation of employees and reflect a fresher, more modern BBC. Reimagining our flagship employee channel was going to be a symbol of broader changes to the organization, with diversity and inclusion as a key editorial priority.'

She recruited Matt Eastley to take on the challenge of breathing new life into the brand. Eastley reviewed anecdotal feedback and employee survey results. People said they found *Ariel* hard to navigate and they weren't sure how it fitted in to the overarching strategy of the BBC – it felt like a lot of ad hoc, unrelated stories. They wanted an easy-to-use, interactive channel they could trust, with features that would give them a voice.

He reflected on the team's new IC objectives to amplify employee voice, to turn managers and leaders into the communicators and storytellers in the organization and, to prevent risk and build trust. And he and the team thought about *Ariel*'s audience, which included some of the finest broadcast journalists and programme-makers in the world. There was a wide employee demographic: a global, young, digitally-savvy workforce working alongside people with 50 years' service – and everyone needed to 'see themselves' in *Ariel*.

What would distinguish this from all other BBC channels was that stories should be told, and policies articulated, through the eyes of employees, and in their own words. Employees would be invited to contribute content they themselves wanted to read, and the channel would be open for people to share the stories of themselves and their teams.

At the start of 2017, the IC team launched the Ariel Network. Eastley explains: 'It was a way of engaging staff in a very visible and immediate way, tapping into their creativity, amplifying their voice and entrusting them with our content. And it was a way that everyone could contribute to Ariel, not just those in content-producing roles.'

Within two weeks of an initial poster campaign, intranet news article, and roadshows across the UK, almost 100 people had signed up. Each provided a photograph and biography to appear on an Ariel Networkers page. Induction sessions were held at various locations and an Ariel guide was produced.

The inductions introduced Ariel Network members to the new, interactive online Ariel news hub, launched at the same time. Features included *The Big Interview*, *Overheard at the BBC* and *The 30-Second Challenge*. The Ariel brand was expanded to include peer recognition schemes *Ariel Unsung Heroes* and *Ariel Unsung Teams*, as well as the Ariel podcast, a *Your Ariel* Yammer community and an Ariel app.

At the time of writing, the Ariel network is 200-strong. New starters have proved to be particularly enthusiastic, and the network is now promoted at employee induction. The IC and engagement team work hard to keep network members involved and active, come up with interesting ideas and give people opportunities to develop their skills.

Says Eastley, 'We never put pressure on people. They can do as much or as little as they like. They do it as an add-on to their day job, but they might want to get experience of interviewing, being behind or in front of the camera or writing. There are some great opportunities – you can find yourself interviewing some very interesting people at the BBC.'

It's a big contrast to a static print newsletter. And the *Ariel* brand is stronger for it. Heather Wagoner concludes, 'We wanted to reinvent *Ariel* whilst honouring the past. We have a changing BBC and *Ariel* needed to change with it. We are the current custodians of *Ariel*, and we take that responsibility really seriously. And BBC people are delighted the *Ariel* brand has been protected, reinvented, and expanded for a new era.'

Five reasons why employee voice matters

Whether through face-to-face interaction, conversations online or handing over the power of the pen (or keyboard), the tools available to us make it easier than ever to have an ongoing conversation with employees, and give people a voice.[2]

Of course, that doesn't mean it's straightforward. There needs to be a genuine intention to listen to what's said, to be open to different opinions, and to take action. There also needs to be a good level of trust for people to feel safe to speak their minds. Throw Yammer into an organization where communication is mainly top-down and people know there will be unhappy consequences if they say the wrong thing, and things might just be fairly quiet in there.

If employee voice doesn't yet feature in your channels mix, here are five reasons to consider it:

1 MacLeod and Clark (2009) say employee voice is one of four key drivers of employee engagement. Centrica's case study in this chapter is a practical example.

2 Peer-to-peer conversations can help colleagues solve problems and share their experience. A simple example we've heard in several organizations is field engineers posting faults they haven't encountered before and getting a quick solution from someone else who has.

3 People have a basic human need for control over their environment. Being listened to – especially if action follows – can help meet the need.

4 Employees know what other people like them want to read about and talk about, and will draw their colleagues into the conversation.

5 Genuinely listening to employees can be an eye-opener for senior leaders and bring insights into planning and decision-making.

CASE STUDY   Employee reporters at AXA

AXA's employee reporter network started as an experiment. A successful push to improve the credibility of the internal communications team had led to a volume of requests for support the team wasn't able to resource. At the same time, the team wanted to shift the communication style from corporate broadcast to employee-led. So, they looked for an opportunity to try something different.

The opportunity presented itself in the form of a refreshed brand position for the global insurance company. Internal Communications Manager Leanne Taylor says, 'The brand advertising felt a bit distant from our people. So, we decided to invite them to get involved and write about their experience from the inside.'

The team put out a call for employee journalists interested in going behind the scenes at photo shoots and filming of the brand campaigns. They also auctioned off AXA experiences linked to the brand, including an invitation to a red-carpet screening of the film *Orient Express*, at which the new brand ad was screening. Taylor explains: 'Our brand campaign was "restless for a reason". We asked people to share their reasons for being restless. Anyone who shared something was put into a draw, with a chance of winning an experience. In return for their prize, the winners had to do a write-up for the intranet, with photographs.'

The first piece written by an employee journalist got three times the readership of a normal intranet article, and was the most liked and commented upon article of the month. 'It was one of those pieces where you think "I wish I'd written that!" says Taylor. 'Really genuine and emotive.'

The experiment ran throughout the brand campaign, with articles by employee reporters consistently getting over 50 per cent higher readership than average. As a result, the approach was formalized. The team put out a call for more employee writers, photographers and video journalists. Those interested completed a form on the intranet, giving an overview of their experience.

The company now has 70 employee reporters. All are members of an intranet community. When a reporting opportunity arises, it's posted in the network, and reporters step up if they are interested. For example, when a new UK CEO joined the business, an employee reporter interviewed him on camera on his first day.

Anyone in the business can ask for an employee reporter to cover their project, and anyone can volunteer to be a journalist. Whilst reporters are asked to talk to their manager, AXA is supportive of people's development and no managers have objected to the time involved. Taylor comments, 'Reporters range from IT people to claims handlers. We've discovered some incredibly talented people.'

Once a reporter is assigned to a story, one of the communications team calls them. Taylor explains, 'We tell them what we'd like to achieve from the piece and how it fits with the wider picture, but we keep the briefs really loose. There are templates people can use for articles and we give tone of voice and brand guidelines. But we never tell them what to write or how to approach things. Some have started writing photo-articles with captions, rather than stories. We sent a reporting team to a big industry broker event. They created flash cards and filmed each other using the cards to interview our senior leaders there.'

Taylor is filled with enthusiasm about the initiative: 'It's one of the most satisfying things I've ever been involved with. It was a good solution to a problem – more work than our team could handle and not enough employee voice. It's influenced our strategy and the way we communicate. We're building more trust in communication because people's voices are being heard. We're looking at how we can use them even more, such as helping to formulate communication plans.'

Her advice to other communicators? 'Give it a try! Pick one thing to try it with, and see if it works. And don't try and communicate *through* the reporters. Help *them* to communicate. Keep it authentic.'

CASE STUDY   Centrica: Helping leaders listen

Centrica's group Head of Internal Communications Geoff Timblick draws a clear distinction between leadership 'visibility' and 'connection': 'Visibility is about "that person over there is the leader of the business and I know they want these three actions in Q4". With a visibility campaign – while it has some benefits – you end up with a monthly update email and a top 10 things you didn't know about leader X. What I'm looking for is a sense that people know what drives that leader, they feel listened to, and they feel some kind of connection.'

For Timblick, connection might mean a vlog 'where people can look them in the eye, hear the passion in their voice', someone sharing an interesting story about their day on Yammer, or – most importantly – listening, preferably via small group sessions. And when Centrica's 2017 employee survey results showed people wanted to feel listened to, it was time for action.

The communications team organized a programme of leadership listening sessions, publicized via internal social media channels (#wearelistening) and starting with the executive team. Each executive committee (exco) member ran yam jams or face-to-face sessions with 20–30 people. They asked three questions:

1 What can I do to help you feel more valued and included?

2 How can we build trust in senior leadership?

3 What could I do to help you feel more inspired and connected with the strategy?

Since the company's top 250 leaders were about to participate in their own virtual leadership event, they were then asked to hold listening sessions as pre-work. They were given a short toolkit with tips and tricks on good listening and invited to ask the same three questions as the executive team had, or simply start with 'I'm going to an event with the company's top 250 leaders and your feedback is on our agenda. What would you like me to know?'

'Leaders are busy, but even the busiest people ran three or four sessions. Some did it in their own function or team. Others went to a site and said, "I'm here for the afternoon. Who wants to talk?" The leaders shared what they heard on their closed Yammer group, and spent an hour and twenty minutes of their leadership event discussing it.'

The sessions showed people were not focused on actions being taken – they just wanted to be heard. This took the communications team by surprise. 'We underestimated the strength of feeling,' says Timblick. 'When we communicated about the listening sessions, we asked how could we #dothingsdifferently? But people really just wanted to talk and have leaders listen to them.'

The exercise was the start of a journey to build trust and give people a voice. Centrica is using pulse surveys to track people's perceptions moving forward. Actions taken as a result of the conversations are labelled #wearelistening, so people can easily connect them back.

Timblick says the sessions have changed the conversation at a senior level: 'Senior leaders are now making listening a priority. As one example, during the quarter following the sessions, the exco spent two hours in each of their monthly meetings dedicated to what they had heard from staff. That's pretty much unprecedented.'

Leaders' efforts seem to be paying off. Centrica's subsequent annual census survey 'Our Voice' saw increases across the board. Engagement was up three points, despite continuing business transformation, including 'efficiencies'. Two of the organization's focus areas – 'trust in leadership' and 'connection to the strategy' – also increased three points. But most impressive was a 13-point increase in the 'valued, included and listened to' section.

Asked if he would advocate the exercise to other communicators, Timblick is unequivocal: 'Absolutely. We did it as an experiment. We didn't know whether it would work, we thought let's do it and see what happens. There wasn't a lot of structure around it – the first exco member said "I've got a free slot next week" and it all happened quite quickly. We got more feedback and fewer actions than we expected. But it was a worthwhile exercise and created a sense of momentum and passion within the leadership community for their people. I'd definitely do it again.'

Conclusion

The channels landscape is full of possibilities and potential. Steer away from falling into habits, otherwise you'll be guilty of always offering your stakeholders the communication equivalent of the hammer, the screwdriver and the funny pointy thing. At the same time, beware of the 'shiny trap' – don't get carried away with trying something out just because it's the latest thing.

In the end, it comes back to our mantra: outcomes, not outputs. Channels are a means to an end. They exist for the reasons we set out in Chapter 1. The right toolbox should equip you (and your stakeholders) to solve problems. Put the right infrastructure in place, and you'll be able to use your channels in a myriad of ways, impress your employees and make your own job easier and more interesting.

Notes

1 A simple matrix of different channels and their strengths that we produced can be found on the UK Government's IC Hub at https://communication. cabinetoffice.gov.uk/ic-space/wp-content/uploads/2015/01/choosing-a-comms-channel.pdf. The site includes other case studies from a public sector perspective.

2 Emma Bridger (2018) gives a good overview of the topic of employee voice. And the *Engage for Success* website (https://engageforsuccess.org) is a great source of resources and ideas.

References and further reading

Bridger, E (2018) *Employee Engagement: A practical introduction*, Kogan Page

MacLeod, D and Clark, N (2009) *Engaging for Success: Enhancing performance through employee engagement*, Department for Business, Innovation and Skills, London. [Online]: https://dera.ioe.ac.uk/1810/1/file52215.pdf

Quirke, B (1995) *Communicating Change*, McGraw-Hill

Willis Towers Watson (2016) The power of three: Taking engagement to new heights. [Online] http://www.towerswatson.com

Line managers as communicators

07

How to help them add the most value

CHAPTER OBJECTIVES

According to studies, leaders spend 70–90 per cent of their time at work communicating (Mintzberg, 1973; Tengblad, 2006). Of course, 'communicating' could mean anything from answering emails to taking part in yet another conference call – possibly both at the same time! But there's no doubt some proportion of it will relate to employee communication.

Time invested by leaders and line managers (we'll use the terms interchangeably) doesn't show up in communications team budgets, but it's a precious resource. So often, we call on leaders to help communication happen. Shouldn't we occasionally take a step back and reflect on what we're asking of them? How much time are we asking them to invest? Are we helping them make the best use of it? What does good leadership communication look like? How can we help leaders make it happen, through the materials we provide, the processes we use or by developing their skills?

This chapter poses a number of questions about when a line manager is most effective as a communicator, the role we might ask them to play and the techniques we can coach them to adopt.

Seeing it from the leader's perspective

We've often heard communicators despair at line managers for just reading out content they've been sent. (We once watched a briefing in which a manager read out the contents word for word… including the instructions to 'please turn over' at the bottom of a page!) Then there's the scenario of forwarding on the note or PowerPoint presentation, without bothering to talk to people about it at all.

But put yourself in their shoes. Imagine you've been sent a presentation full of carefully crafted bullet points. It's corporate information that isn't directly related to your team. You have no additional context to supplement what's on the slides. You've been given the presentation at short notice and asked to pass on a 'consistent message'. Some of the slides use business jargon. Meanwhile, the same information has been published in a story on the company intranet. The story ends by saying, 'If you have any questions, please ask your line manager.' How would you feel? What would you do? How would you react if anyone asked you a question?

These are real issues, which any communication manager will surely recognize.

How and why were the materials sent? Has anyone talked to the managers themselves about this topic? How is our local leader expected to feel about being asked to explain when they don't have time to prepare and their team can get the information from another source anyway?

But there's something more fundamental to think about here: how we *talk* about communication in our organizations, how we *think* about communication in our organizations, and how we can involve managers in the communication process.

Briefings, cascades and 'getting the message out'

If the way we talk about communication guides the way we use it (Axley, 1984), it's interesting to reflect on the language we use. If we talk about 'briefing teams', 'cascading information' and 'getting messages across', could we be making communication sound easier than it is? Do cascades flow effortlessly like waterfalls? As long as information is passed on, is the job done?

What lies behind this kind of language is a particular view of communication. Traditionally, academics viewed communication as information transmission: sending messages from A to B which, it's assumed, are then received, understood and acted upon. Leadership communication in the spirit of this approach has been described as the 'controlled, purposeful transfer of meaning by which leaders influence a single person, a group, an organization or a community' (Barrett, 2006: 398). Observers suggest this is a common perception in organizations today (Johansson, 2018; Fairhurst, 2005). We provide leaders with carefully crafted materials, perhaps with manager guides and pages of supporting questions and answers, with the aim of ensuring as far as we can that our corporate messages are transferred consistently from A to B.

But what does it mean? And why should I care?

Communication researchers now largely agree (Johansson, 2018; Fairhurst, 2014) that leaders can do more than just pass on information. They can help create meaning.

Where the information transmission view of communication assumes the aim is to pass consistent messages from a sender to a relatively passive receiver, a meaning-centred view assumes people interpret and make sense of situations. They decide whether something is relevant for them and take a view on what it means for them. A leader can influence how their teams interpret issues and help team members make sense of situations in two ways:

- through the way the leader interprets and talks about the issues;
- through encouraging and enabling their teams to discuss the issues themselves.

The way leaders frame subjects, the personal opinions they add and the stories they tell can make the difference between a change being seen as an irrelevant flavour of the month or worth taking seriously. And through dialogue, leaders can help team members draw insights and meaning together. The questions managers ask can direct a conversation one way or another; can open it up or close it down.

Putting theory into practice: How can leaders add the most value?

We were once asked to train frontline managers to use an organization's monthly briefing process. Briefings weren't happening, and the client was concerned managers weren't passing on core messages around the need to reduce costs and increase revenues.

We asked if we could start by talking with some managers. In a number of interviews, people told us they saw it as a poor use of their time to read out bullet points of corporate messages – so they were choosing not to. They, and their teams, were well aware of the high-level priorities. They wanted to talk practically about what they meant, discuss opportunities to take action, and have a route to feed back when there were things they couldn't act on locally. For example, the team leader for the car park bus drivers told us how the payment machines kept breaking, so customers couldn't pay in their money. Surely this wasn't helping to increase revenues, he asked?

We went back to our client and advised this wasn't just a training issue. It was about what managers were being asked to do. If the cascades of corporate messages were changed into dialogue-based problem-solving sessions, teams could talk about how they could play their part in the priorities. The client said no. They just wanted their messages passed on. We politely declined the training work on the grounds we didn't believe it would address the real issues.

Do you see the contrast between the two views about leadership communication? Face-to-face communication is valuable, expensive (just multiply the time spent by the salaries of everyone involved) and sometimes difficult to make happen. In this case, people had to be brought in on overtime or bribed with a free breakfast to arrive before their shift.

There's a common view that face-to-face (or at least virtual) communication from line managers is always best. But is that true? Is it a good use of leaders' time to be human emails or talking posters, passing on information? Are they always the best person to talk about every subject?

Busting a myth: People don't always want to hear it from 'my line manager'

It's commonly assumed employees want to hear everything from their line manager. But, according to measurement expert Angela Sinickas (2004), it's not the case. She says the misunderstanding arises from a flaw in how communication is audited, when employees are asked, of all the available sources of information:

1 Which one of these sources is *currently* your primary source for important company information?

2 Which one of these sources is your *preferred* primary source for important company information?

The most common answer to question one is 'rumours'. The answer to question two? 'My line manager'.

In fact, people typically want to hear from their line manager about certain subjects, but prefer to go elsewhere to hear about others. For example, they might want to hear from a senior leader about a major change, if they don't believe their manager will have all the answers. They might prefer to read detailed or contextual information on the intranet or in print. But the research methodology shown here doesn't allow them to differentiate, because it asks only a single pair of questions about 'important company information'.

The assumption that line managers are always best can lead to leaders being swamped with requests to communicate. Set yourself up a dummy account on a line manager's distribution list or ask a leader if you can shadow them for a day or two. It's a good way to get an impression of how much they're being asked to communicate, and whether some subjects are best handled via another route.

Pause for thought: Talking about communication

How do you talk about communication in your organization? What phrases and terms are commonly used? What names have you given to regular communication methods involving leaders? What signals are you sending? (One organization changed the title of their regular face-to-face from Team Brief to Talkabout, to signal a change from information cascade to leader-led conversation.)

How do materials steer leaders to communicate? Are you providing information to pass on, and if so, how much? Too much information, and there's no time for conversation. Easy-to-read-out, beautifully crafted bullet points lend themselves to... being read out! Are there questions to prompt discussion? Help managers out by suggesting a few good ones.

What demands are you making on leaders' time? From requests to 'please talk to your team about...' to the number of articles ending with 'please ask your manager if you have questions'?

Do you assume line managers are always best? Are some topics better rerouted to the intranet, a consolidated news update or a different person? If you had to decide between spending 20 minutes talking to your team about this subject or addressing a pressing quality or safety issue, which would you choose?

CASE STUDY   Aviva: Helping leaders make strategy meaningful

The *koru* is a Maori symbol of strength and new life. Shaped like an unfurling fern, it was chosen to visualize Aviva's strategy, purpose and values, since their CEO at the time was from New Zealand. Aviva wants its strategy communication to be 'leader-led and dialogue-focused'. Its *Big Koru* Conversations help employees understand how the company is performing and what their team and they personally are doing to help it happen. They're held twice a year, to give people a clearer understanding of their personal goals for the next six months.

Sessions last 60–90 minutes and over 90 per cent of Aviva's 30,000 employees take part. Business areas have a choice about how to run them. In some markets, the CEO might lead a large event. In others, conversations are led by line managers in smaller groups. Aviva's Jon Hawkins comments: 'The sessions can feel really different, because leaders have freedom about how to run them. But they all have the common thread – a pause for people to connect back to "what do we all do here, and what's the role that we play?"'

The sessions contain little information to share, with a focus on managers leading a conversation to get people thinking and exploring. Jon Hawkins explains: 'We used to give people loads of content and reasonably detailed manager guides about how to run the session. But we've learned over time what brings energy to a conversation and what doesn't. For example, in the old days we would have provided a newsletter-style case study and said "Read this out, or get someone from your team to read it out." But it's not a valuable use of time to have someone standing there reading things out. If we provided a detailed overview of the strategy, people weren't doing anything with it. We can publish that kind of content in advance, to give context. For the session itself, less is more – the more content that's in there, the less conversation there is.'

In the run-up to the conversations, the team makes sure leaders know what's planned and gets them thinking about why sessions are so important and how they might run them. They work with HR and local communication colleagues to make sure everyone is clear how conversations will happen in the different markets. 'So, when we push the button and say "Here are your materials", they're not landing cold.'

Simple cue cards have replaced the detailed manager guides. They give prompts for topics that leaders can talk about and suggested conversation starters. Recognition is an important part of the sessions and leaders receive blank postcards to write and hand out, to say thank you. The team often provide a short film that brings out some form of emotion. Hawkins comments: 'The films are important because they can make people feel proud or worried – whatever is right for the time. This year we want people to have the emotion of confidence. The person running the session can play the film, stop it and ask "How did that make you feel?" It's an instant conversation starter.'

There are also activities to take part in beforehand, to prompt conversation. For example, in an online *Game of Growth*, employees made decisions about how to run a business. Jon explains: 'Things would pop up, such as a government policy change you weren't prepared for. If you hadn't been sacked by the end of the game, you were told you were one of four types of CEO. In the session, people talked about what their profile was, and how it was to experience the complexities of running a large business.'

Figure 7.1   Leader prompt cards for Aviva's Big Koru Conversation

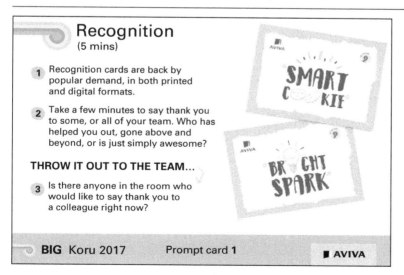

(continued)

Figure 7.1 *(Continued)*

Purpose
(10 mins)

1 Watch the **'Uncertainty: Defied' video** that can be found on the Big Koru Aviva World site.

GET THE CONVERSATION STARTED. YOU COULD ASK...

2 The film shows just a few examples- how does this change your perception about what is possible at Aviva?

3 Can we really prevent things from going wrong?

4 What does this mean for our business?

5 What are the things we're really good at that we can continue to build on?

6 Can you see the role you play in defying uncertainty for customers?

BIG Koru 2017   Prompt card **2**   ▌AVIVA

Commitment
(10 mins)

YOUR TEAM SHOULD HAVE ALREADY PLAYED THE 'GAME OF GROWTH' AS PART OF THE 'BRAIN FOOD'.

1 Discuss game results as a team.

2 Did the game change your view on how difficult or easy it is to grow a business?

GET THE CONVERSATION STARTED. YOU COULD SAY...

3 What do you think are the biggest opportunities for us to grow our business?

4 How confident are you that we can grow? What do we need to do differently?

BIG Koru 2017   Prompt card **4**   ▌AVIVA

SOURCE Reproduced with kind permission of Aviva 2018

Figure 7.2   Screenshots from Aviva's *Game of Growth*

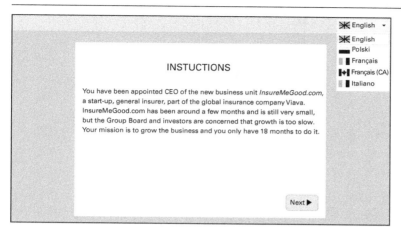

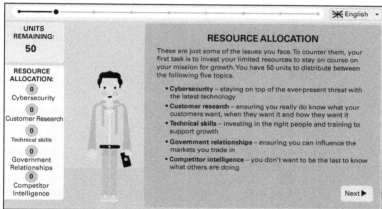

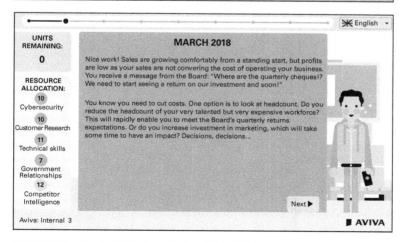

SOURCE Reproduced with kind permission of Aviva 2018

So what do leaders who communicate well do?

Research into the behaviours of communicative leaders has generated some interesting findings. In particular, a group of researchers have looked at best practice and thinking on the subject and defined a communicative leader as 'one who engages employees in dialogue, actively shares and seeks feedback, practices participative decision-making, and is perceived as open and involved' (Johansson *et al*, 2014). They set out eight key principles for communicative leaders:

1 Communicative leaders coach and enable employees to be self-managing.

2 Communicative leaders provide structures that facilitate work. (Authors' note: This includes items such as providing a mission and acting as a role model.)

3 Communicative leaders set clear expectations for quality, productivity and professionalism.

4 Communicative leaders are approachable, respectful and express concern for employees.

5 Communicative leaders actively engage in problem solving, follow up on feedback and advocate for the unit.

6 Communicative leaders convey direction and assist others in achieving their goals.

7 Communicative leaders actively engage in framing of messages and events.

8 Communicative leaders enable and support sense making.

The research also draws out four key behaviours that are the hallmarks of leaders who communicate well:

- **Structuring:** Clarifying goals and expectations, defining mission, planning and allocating tasks, selecting appropriate team members, and providing sense making or interpretations of events.

- **Facilitating:** Coaching and training, providing performance feedback, engaging in problem solving and encouraging self-management.

- **Relating:** Creating openness, demonstrating supportive behaviours and approaching difficult issues in a constructive, respectful, even-handed manner.

- **Representing employees and the unit:** Being able to exert upward influence and being seen as capable of obtaining resources, actively monitoring the environment and networking.

What about cultural variations?

Research suggests certain leadership attributes are seen as positive the world over, whilst others might be seen as helpful in some cultures, neutral in others and unhelpful elsewhere. For example, as part of the GLOBE study Den Hartog *et al* (1999) found a 'charismatic/value-based leadership style' is seen universally as contributing to effective leadership. It includes aiming to inspire people around a vision, creating a passion to perform, setting high standards and being committed to values. Also universally recognized is the 'team-oriented style', which includes developing pride, loyalty and focusing on a common purpose or goals.

However, the study found there's more cultural variation about how the 'participative style' is viewed. This style is about encouraging input into decision-making and implementation, and valuing equality and delegation.

Communicators working in global organizations will recognize this. They know that in many countries people want to feel their opinions are valued and be involved in shaping solutions, giving feedback and building consensus. In other places, leaders seeking input from team members would be seen as weak. Elsewhere, employees wouldn't think of offering a contrary view, out of respect for the organization's hierarchy.

This is not the place to go into the complexities of cultural considerations. Suffice it to say, know your audience. Don't assume that your home country's view of good leadership communication will work everywhere. Make sure you have a good leadership contact or two in each country to test approaches and plans.

Building leaders' communication competence: Training and coaching

Are you sometimes mystified by the 'obvious' communication blunders managers make? Do you find it hard to understand why leaders seem oblivious to 'simple' communication principles? That's because people who find a skill easy often assume others do, too. On the other hand, those who are the *least* competent are the *most* likely to overestimate their skills, whilst the phenomenon of 'illusory superiority' means most people rate themselves as above average in many aspects of life, from driving to job performance (Ghose, 2013). So the next time you're feeling frustrated that everyone thinks they're a communication expert, remember they're being entirely normal!

Training and coaching in communication can make a marked difference in your organization. Apart from the fact that leaders should be better communicators as a result, one head of communications told us their leaders are more self-sufficient and ask for less support from the communications team after training. But be careful how you position it – remember that telling someone their communication skills need improving can feel like questioning their driving ability. It doesn't make people the most open-minded in a training room!

After many years working as trainers and coaches, we advocate approaching a training need in a similar way to how you would a communication strategy. Don't jump straight to tactics. Start by getting clear about objectives. Base your decisions on research and data – what is your employee survey telling you about problem areas, for example? Ask leaders what their challenges are; ask team members what they'd like to see more or less of from their manager. The more your training is built on business needs, data, and by involving the leaders you're targeting, the easier it will be to make a case for it and get buy-in from training participants.

Work together with your HR and training teams. This relationship is rich with potential for politics and turf-guarding, but you have the communications expertise and they are experts in training. They also often have access to funding and administrative resource, and can get your training talked about by HR business partners and in performance management conversations.

Training topics to consider

- Make leaders conscious of how they use communication: Remember, people often think communication is common sense and believe they're pretty good at it. Many assume it's about passing on information. It's only when you get them to step back and think about it that mindsets start to change.

- Show leaders how good communication can help them get business results, if they use it in the right way.

- Preparation and planning: A simplified version of the planning process we use as communicators can work well for leaders. Have them think about communication goals, knowing their audience, choosing key messages and the advantages and disadvantages of different communication methods.

- Feedback and follow-up: Measurement is a tricky topic for many professional communicators, so we're not advocating anything complicated. But once managers realize just sending out messages is no guarantee of a result, they become interested in simple ways to follow up.

- The role of emotions in communication: Feelings matter. But much business communication is based on facts. Try using a bit of neuroscience to explain why leaders need to think about heads *and* hearts to get results.

- Framing and sense-making techniques.

- Dialogue: How to start a conversation, ask effective questions and listen well.

- Communicating at a distance: Communicating via web-, video- and audio-conference.

- Taking the conversation online: Using digital and social media tools.

What are framing and sense-making?

Years ago, an organization Sue worked for was going through a difficult time. There had been redundancies, closures and budget cuts. And now came the hardest cut of all: no more free vend on the coffee machines! Talking points were carefully crafted for leaders and sent out by email. A day later, an email came back. It had been forwarded on down the hierarchy with 'fyi' added at each point... until it reached the front line manager, who had added a comment before forwarding it onto their team: 'Shafted again! Shows how "valued" we are, doesn't it?'

This is an example of *framing* (though a very unwelcome one, from the organization's perspective!): a leader interpreting and positioning an issue in their own way, which then shapes how their team are likely to see it. Used positively, it's a key skill for managers seeking to use communication to create meaning, rather than to give information.

Fairhurst (2005) says many managers struggle with the concept and may see it as being manipulative or inauthentic: one leader once asked us 'Isn't this just spin?' No – it's about helping team members understand 'What does this mean to me?' and 'Why should I care?' When preparing to talk about a corporate message, it would involve deciding which parts of that message to include, which to exclude and which to emphasize, to make it more relevant for the team.

You can help leaders with framing by coaching them to use the 'do, feel, know' technique, so they think about using communication to reach a goal other than 'brief the team'. You can also teach a simple messaging framework, so they learn to choose and emphasize the most relevant points. In addition, consider helping leaders use sense-making techniques to help their teams understand more concretely what those points mean. For example, they might give an example, tell a personal story or use a metaphor.

CASE STUDY   Volvo Group: Developing communicative leaders

In 2013 Volvo Group launched a project to develop a communication training programme for its leaders. The programme is now successfully running worldwide, and has been expanded to include a version for management teams and a train the trainer programme for communicators. As Director of Communicative Leadership, Kennie Kjellström led the programme's development and shares these tips from his experience:

Be clear about your business needs and training objectives. We analysed our employee engagement survey data in detail and also had a communicative leadership index, enabling us to diagnose leaders' capabilities and performance over several years. We were also part of an academic research programme into communicative leadership, so we looked at the research outcomes and compared them with our own data, to identify what we should focus on.

Look for a window of opportunity. There was a business reorganization, which created a good opening to involve different stakeholders, for example HR. The company was also setting up a new internal training structure, and we were in position to hit the ground running as soon as our training partners were recruited.

Develop a good project plan. I was formerly a project manager and these skills were helpful at the start for all the data analysis, setting out and following up plans, mapping and managing stakeholders.

Involve and partner with communication colleagues. I work in headquarters. It was important to involve business divisions early. We held workshops to invite them to input their needs and ideas. I kept an ear to the ground to find individuals who were engaged and willing to take the training forward in their area. This is how it spread, little by little, until it reached a tipping point. When people challenged our ways of working, we listened and were flexible – that's how the train the trainer and management team versions began. It's important to put your ego to one side and be open to new possibilities. Have communicators observe the training or try it themselves. They are your ambassadors and change agents.

Involve leaders who will take the training. We interviewed leaders up front to understand their challenges. We're proud so many leaders comment that the training exercises feel 'real' and relevant to their daily work life. Then they tell colleagues they should attend – sometimes the grapevine is the best way of communicating. We also invited leaders to three pilot sessions to test the concept. When pieces didn't work, they sat with us afterwards to give suggestions. Dare to start before you're 100 per cent sure everything will work – but in a planned way.

Invest time in the relationship with the training function and your supplier. We are very honest and transparent with each other. We have clear roles – I own the training and contracted with our supplier to develop it. Our training function is the provider, and our supplier contracts with them to deliver the course. I don't promote it to leaders – our training teams do that, through their channels and yearly planning process.

Go for it, and be persistent. It felt at one point like standing at the door of an aeroplane, waiting to make a first parachute jump: do it and see what happens. Keep going, even when you keep hitting obstacles. You will run into difficult conversations and resistance. Sometimes it's tough if managers say to you that they already know everything, they don't need training, they don't have time. It's worth it, in the end!

Creating the right environment: Make it easy

As we explain in Chapter 9, people are more likely to change their behaviour if we make it easy for them and take away barriers. If you tell leaders you want them to personalize messages, but keep sending out documents at short notice, it's not going to happen. If you invest two days with your top 120 leaders to discuss the new strategy, then those leaders just forward on the slide deck, you'll see a big drop in understanding of the strategy between senior and middle managers. If the operational schedule in your factories or call centres doesn't allow time for communication, you can train leaders as much as you like, but their hands will be tied. So:

- Find a format for communicating that works for your leaders. Spend time in their workplaces. Ask to watch communication sessions. Talk to them. Build materials accordingly. Test what you've built.

- Allow leaders time to prepare. Don't spring communication on them at short notice or catch them out with a sudden controversial story online.

- Use the well-worn phrase 'If you have any questions, ask your line manager' with care. Don't set them up for endless answers of 'I don't know – I don't know any more than you do.'

- Get to know the operational constraints. If time for communication is limited, either limit the time you're asking leaders to spend communicating, or challenge the constraints. Something has to give.

- Ask senior leaders to role model good communication behaviours. In particular, make sure they discuss important topics with managers reporting to them and help those managers understand the context behind decisions and changes.

- Be realistic. Communication is the only item on your job description. It's one of many things your leaders are responsible for, and it's more than likely not their profession.

Our case studies here are from two organizations that understand the power of their senior leaders to act as communication advocates and role models, paving the way for others to follow their lead.

CASE STUDY   Aviva: The ripple effect of senior leadership communication

In 2017, Aviva did a global review of communication and correlated the results with their employee engagement survey data. A key theme was the crucial role of senior leadership communication. The data showed that for people to trust the organization and its messages, they needed to see their senior leader more regularly. The more visible the senior leader, the higher the level of trust.

The method used by senior leaders also had a big impact. Where leaders were involved in a conversation of some kind, scores went up. The most effective form of interaction was to gather a group of people together for an informal chat. Even a conference call rated well, if it was interactive. On the other hand, the effect of formal larger-scale 'town hall' events was low – they showed up in the data in the same way as an intranet article or video.

What's more, in those areas where senior leaders were perceived as more visible and interactive, there was a ripple effect: people also reported they had more frequent, collaborative and useful team meetings with their immediate line manager. There was a direct correlation between interactive behaviour by senior leaders and more effective, interactive team meetings. And the bottom line: employees in these areas were more engaged with the organization as a whole.

Aviva's Sarah Carr says, 'Now, when we put together a communication plan for a senior leader, it looks very different. Before, we might have relied on their monthly newsletter. Now we'll say "When you travel to this office, let's factor in time in your diary – even half an hour – to chat to people in an informal way, to have a much richer conversation."'

CASE STUDY   Ericsson: The CEO as a communication role model

When Ericsson's VP Internal Communications and Engagement Kirsty Fitzgibbon met new CEO Börje Ekholm, she recognized a great opportunity. 'In conversations with the communications team before he joined, he said his main priorities on starting were employees and customers. It was gold dust!' And so it has proved to be. 'He's been a great advocate for communication. Leaders across the organization think, "If I do what he does, I could get the same impact and engagement." They copy his transparency, his direct style, the way he recognizes people, the way he talks about the bad as well as the good.'

The actions Börje has taken seem simple: a weekly letter to staff, sent by email and posted on the intranet; and meeting employees informally whenever there's an opportunity. So what are the keys to using such simple tools to make a big impact? Fitzgibbon explains:

A personal, consistent commitment from the CEO. Börje told us he wanted to write a weekly letter and open up for everyone to talk to him directly. We pointed out the risks to this – could he, and we, handle that many responses? Would he have the time to keep up weekly letters? But he was passionate and determined that this would be the best way to reach out to 110,000 colleagues. He gets direct emails and there's also feedback through the CEO mailbox. He answers a lot personally. There's a comments section on the intranet, which I monitor. If there's something I think he should see, I tell him and he comments directly or emails the person. He never shies away from a difficult question and sometimes takes feedback to the executive team. He uses employees as a sounding board and gets candid input to the corporate strategy.

His written style. The letters have been hugely important. Börje has made it OK to talk about stuff that doesn't work, to criticize. He's made it unacceptable to be fluffy or use business buzzwords. He started by pushing buttons, giving his views about PowerPoint, culture, behaviours. He can be quite blunt, quite funny. The topics covered in his letters are topical – the aim is to reflect what employees are talking or asking about. The letters are a collaboration between Börje and communicators, but ultimately they are his.

His informal style of interaction. He'll have coffee or breakfast with a group, or walk the floor. He doesn't do big, formal presentations. He'll do 15 minutes with no slides and take questions. He's humble and prefers wearing a casual gilet to suits. And he's an engineer, so he's genuinely interested in talking techie. If there are lots of questions coming at him, he'll stop people and say 'Now let me ask you some questions.'

A weekly planning meeting. There are no boundaries between internal and external communication. Three letters were published in the media and more have been quoted. We know our investors read them. Every week I meet with our heads of IR and PR and our function's senior vice president. We discuss what the letter will be about and what the limits are. Is it too risky? Not risky enough? We try not to censor ourselves so much. We can't talk about things that are confidential but we can have opinions and talk about our internal life. We're not always complimentary about ourselves! Börje is often bolder than we are.

Using the network. Whenever Börje travels, there will be an interaction with employees in some form. If I get a note from his executive assistant to say he's travelling, I contact the local communications team and say, 'What are your plans?' I have a standard briefing document for people to fill in, so we can brief him about local issues. I ask local communicators not to hide tricky issues and to make sure difficult questions are raised. Börje wants to have real conversations and to understand what's really going on.

Why does it matter? Investing time and energy in leadership communication

Good leadership communication is associated with increased trust, employee engagement, health and well-being, effective change and organizational effectiveness (Johansson, 2018). Leadership communication shapes what employees think of their organization, and how they feel about it (Men and Bowen, 2016). But whatever the research says, you've seen it yourself, haven't you? You know from experience the impact of a leader who communicates well. And we're willing to bet there are far more business leaders in your organization than there are professional communicators. Which means you have far more chance of getting results from communication if you're working in partnership

Working with leaders takes time, isn't as visible as 'producing stuff' and the results can take longer to see. But it's an opportunity to leave a powerful legacy. What's more, it can change the way you're viewed as a professional communicator, and the conversations you become involved with. It can develop your skills beyond communication expert into business person, trainer and coach, pull you out of your comfort zone and help you find a new energy and motivation in your work. What are you waiting for?!

CASE STUDY Volvo Construction Equipment (VCE):
Communicators as leadership coaches

In 2012, VCE's Internal Communications Director Tiffany Cheng spotted both a business need and an opportunity for her team. For the first time, the business had chosen leadership as one of three cornerstones of its strategy. Simultaneously, some of her team were feeling frustrated – they were lone communicators on their site, not feeling challenged in their work. Cheng says, 'We thought, why not bring these two pieces together? Instead of being the ones communicating our strategy, why don't we become part of it?'

An external supplier was contracted to develop 'Inspire': a communication development programme for senior leaders consisting of short training sessions, followed by six months of regular meetings with a communication coach from Cheng's team.

Cheng explains, 'There was a lot of initial resistance. Some colleagues believed training should be provided by HR functions, and questioned the capability of mid-level communicators to coach senior leaders. I argued the programme would fill a gap and was a win–win for the organization and the coaches. Also we wouldn't be using a lot of budget by bringing in external support long-term: we use our own coaches and now run the training sessions ourselves, too.'

The same supplier trained communicators in coaching skills. Each person was then assessed, before being accepted as an Inspire coach. Cheng says, 'They had to be great. Coaching is 80 per cent of the programme. I knew leaders would tell their colleagues if they had a good experience. And they would tell them if they didn't! It took two programmes for word to spread and to overcome the initial resistance. Then we had a waiting list of participants. It was crucial not to implement too fast, but to focus on quality.'

Coaches meet leaders weekly or fortnightly, working with real-time challenges. The sessions are non-directive, helping leaders to think through the issues. Cheng comments, 'When we started, the company was entering a downturn. There were lots of difficult messages. It can be lonely for leaders. Sometimes they needed to keep engaging people who were losing their team members or projects' findings, whilst delivering performance. They rarely have others to talk to about the sensitive challenges, except their coach.'

Stepping into a coaching role, initially communicators felt nervous. 'To go to someone's office and start not giving answers but asking questions, people felt challenged. In our day-to-day job our conversations are quite surface level. This required communicators to go much deeper and build the kind of trust they were never able to build before. They gained a whole new insight about what was going on in leaders' minds and what their struggles were.' Whilst time was another challenge, Cheng found the communicators never complained. 'We had several people ask to keep coaching during their maternity leave. It's so rewarding to them.'

Stepping up has helped coaches take a front seat at their management table. 'Before they might have been there, but seen as someone who organized events or wrote newsletters. Now they are respected, invited to more strategic discussions, brought in at the front of changes instead of at the end. Coaching has given them confidence and insight.' The relationship with HR, too, has transformed, 'because they have seen the value of what we're doing. They are now part of the programme – they recommend who should participate, through talent management and succession planning.'

Cheng's advice for anyone wanting to train communicators as coaches is to start by speaking the business language. What does the organization need that you can help with? Next, take the perspective of the communicators. Why would they want to do it? 'Don't say "We're doing some training and you have to give me 20 per cent of your time." I talked to each person, to understand how it might be meaningful for them. You have to be able to sell it to both sides.'

References

Axley, SR (1984) Managerial and organizational communication in terms of the conduit metaphor, *Academy of Management Review*, **9**(3), pp 428–37

Barrett, DJ (2006) Strong communication skills: A must for today's leaders, *Handbook of Business Strategy*, **7**(1) pp 385–90. [Online] www.emeraldinsight.com/doi/abs/10.1108/10775730610619124

Den Hartog, DN, House, RJ, Hanges, PJ, Ruiz-Quintanilla, SA and Dorfman, PW (1999) Culture specific and cross-culturally generalizable implicit leadership theories: Are attributes of charismatic/transformational leadership universally endorsed? *Leadership Quarterly*, **10**(2), p 219

Fairhurst, GT (2005) Reframing the art of framing: Problems and prospects for leadership, *Leadership*, **1**(2), pp 165–85

Fairhurst, GT (2014) Leadership: A communication perspective, *Leadership*, **10**(1), pp 7–35

Ghose, T (2013) Why we're all above average, Live Science, 6 February. [Online] www.livescience.com/26914-why-we-are-all-above-average.html

Johansson, C, Miller, VD, Hamrin, S (2014) Conceptualizing communicative leadership: A framework for analysing and developing leaders' communication competence, *Corporate Communications: An international journal*, **19**(2), pp 147–65. [Online] www.emeraldinsight.com/doi.org/10.1108/CCIJ-02-2013-0007

Johansson, C (2018) Leadership communication, in *Encyclopedia of Strategic Communication*, ed RL Heath and E Johansen, Wiley Online Library

Men, LR and Bowen, SA (2016) *Excellence in Internal Communication Management*, Business Expert Press

Mintzberg, H (1973) *The Nature of Managerial Work*, Harper & Row

Sinickas, A (2004) Supervisors are still not the preferred communicators, *Making Managers Better Communicators*, Melcrum Publishing

Tengblad, S (2006) Is there a 'new managerial work'? A comparison with Henry Mitzberg's classic study 30 years later, *Journal of Management Studies*, 43(7), pp 1437–61

Making it happen

08

Making sure your great ideas
see the light of day

CHAPTER OBJECTIVES

The world of employee communication is full of people with great ideas that they never get to put into action. Are they hopeless dreamers who cannot project manage, or are other forces at work?

This chapter looks at five strategies to improve our chances of outsmarting the challenges that come with the job. Importantly, we want to suggest a thought to bear in mind: overcoming barriers always begins with an open-minded curiosity about where each barrier really comes from – is it them or is it us?

Why is employee communication so difficult (for some of us)?

Some years ago, one of us was asked to support a change project. It was a relief to find when we arrived in the office that there was already a freelancer on the case; we'd actually heard of them from occasional articles and seen their name on conference agendas. Our expectation was that she knew all about change communication and that this gig was going to be easy.

Sadly, things didn't quite turn out that way. Our new colleague was full of great ideas and fun to be around but she never seemed to be able to deliver anything. Content tended to turn up late (if at all), they couldn't organize simple meetings and essential project plans were not updated. And after six months they knew fewer people in the organization than we'd connected with in a few weeks.

Our freelancer friend was actually not that unusual in our world. We've all met people with brilliant ideas who can't seem to do apparently straightforward tasks. When we've researched what skills, knowledge and experience EC professionals need, it seems that making the leap from idea to execution comes up as an important, but often missing, competency.

Being able to push things through really matters for professionals who often find themselves without budget or official authority and surrounded by people with strong opinions about what communication is needed. And then there are the never-ending demands on our time; we love to be involved, but exactly how many meetings can we fit in in a day when our presence is demanded?

But how is it that some people seem to float above it all? What makes the stars align for them and why do some of us live in a personal hell of broken connections, unexpected and insurmountable barriers, uninterested and uncooperative colleagues and have days when just making a coffee feels like an achievement?

What can we do to cut through the sludge that can block our path to adding value?

The big five EC facilitators

We have spent years talking to communications leaders, we've run training courses, developed competency models, carried out audits and overseen change programmes and, from what we see, effective communicators seem to get similar things right on a regular basis:

- They have a clear *focus* – they know what employee communication is for in their organization.
- They translate that focus into the *right role* for themselves and their teams.
- That role is supported by a set of consistently applied *processes*.
- They are connected *networkers* and *collaborators*.
- They take their *professionalism* and *competency* seriously.

Our experience partly echoes a long-running and highly respected study among communications directors in Europe. High-performing communicators clearly partner and collaborate more closely with leaders and other departments, they have strong processes that include research and listening and they focus on strategic issues rather than tactical outputs (Verčič and Zerfass, 2016).

Naturally, at different times and in different organizations other attributes may matter as well, but reflecting on our own observations, these seem to stand out. And, just as our case study from the UK Department for Business, Energy and Industrial Strategy (BEIS) suggests, if we don't know where we want to add value and the role we should play, it is unlikely that we'll ever feel that we're doing the right things, and doing them right.

CASE STUDY   Getting on the front foot with EC at BEIS

'It's *all* about getting on the front foot rather than waiting for the organization to ask for things,' says Penny Mitchell, Head of Internal Communication at BEIS. 'If you hang back, you are lost.'

Penny is charged with helping her 3,500-strong organization, and the 25,000 people in associated public bodies, deliver for the government and the citizens they serve. She explains, 'We help colleagues advocate more effectively for what we do and why, and we get them to work with each other better.'

The organization is quite new, being formed from a merger of two large government departments in mid 2016. Explaining the mission of the new organization gave Penny and her team an early opportunity to demonstrate their value and define their role. 'People wanted to understand more about the purpose of their new department,' she recalls, 'so we set about both explaining the vision and how everyone's work contributes, and driving a conversation about how people want to engage with each other in delivering the vision.'

Penny's team set out to help shape the transformation and highlight day-to-day successes. It's a complicated task, being part of an operation that involves advising government ministers, developing policy and supporting the work of 25,000 people in the network of public agencies working on a wide range of issues ranging from facilitating investment for innovation to developing a strategy for clean growth, from forecasting the weather to bringing in new minimum wage levels.

Providing a strong suite of channels is important for the team. They own and develop an increasingly interactive online digital workplace (replacing an old-style broadcast intranet); install and play creative content through digital screens in lifts, lobbies and meeting areas; run events; and use the physical office environment to communicate and stimulate conversations. For example, they launched the government's flagship industrial strategy by turning the office's central lobby into an exhibition space. The award-winning approach delivered a 70 per cent awareness rating for the new policy. Other projects have included an internal trade fair, involving 40 different teams, spread around the London office so that colleagues could explain their work and priorities to each other.

What you use those channels to talk about matters: 'It's critical to ring-fence resource in your team to develop good-quality communication focused on the impact of your organization,' she says, suggesting that at least half their time should be spent talking about the organization's role in wider society rather than internal 'pay and rations' concerns. 'Any operating model too focused on internal activities and corporate stuff will fail,' she warns.

She also values having strong performers from a variety of backgrounds – not necessarily 'qualified professional communicators' – in her team. 'If you have bright, engaging, capable people, you can train them to hone their writing skills, plan creative campaigns and think strategically,' she says. 'But the key thing is having people with the ability to work effectively at a human level. Excellent interpersonal skills are harder to train and it's these that form the bedrock of our business partnering model where we try to apply a consulting and agency mindset.'

Energy and people skills are also the antidote to the perennial public sector challenge of tight budgets. Penny reflects, 'You can do a lot with a few sharp people who are prepared to roll their sleeves up and can engage with the top of the house.'

Getting out and talking to people is also part of the BEIS EC formula. 'It's essential that you understand the audience,' she says. 'You don't need to rely on extensive external research; just talk to people informally, daily – catch them in the lift; ring them up; go and sit with them – and do light touch polls and surveys that you can run and analyse quickly yourself.'

Having a finger on the organization's pulse is Penny's acid test of being valued and engaged with key business priorities. 'If something comes up unexpectedly we should see it as a reminder to ask ourselves what more we need to do to get "in with the business" so we don't get taken by surprise. It's up to us to earn the right to be involved and consulted early by demonstrating that we add value.'

Proactivity is key for Penny and her team: 'You can't sit back and wait for people to come to you. You have to take the initiative by defining and engaging everyone in the strategic narrative.'

Bringing value into focus

Every organization needs people who are skilled writers, who know how to apply brand guidelines to an internal logo and who can project manage events. But, paradoxically, if you want to get things done you shouldn't start obsessing about the detail; results come to those who start at the 'why'. If what you do is founded on the true needs of the organization and your stakeholders, the detail becomes easier.

In Chapter 1 we talked about the importance of understanding where you added value and we suggested that we are most useful when we facilitate the flow of information, help people get the results and build intangible assets like a positive culture or employee engagement. Clarity about what outcomes we're supporting is the first step towards securing your budget, gaining access and being given a licence to operate. And it helps you decide what role you need to play.

Playing the right communications role

EC professionals are lucky, as we usually have quite a mixed role fulfilling a number of functions, including being a message distributor, a crafter and drafter, and a facilitator or consultant (Quirke, 2002: 205–06). We tend to move between roles, and there are times when even the most strategically focusedi director is writing content and the in-house journalist is advising on messaging and impact.

A word of advice...

Common to all of our roles is advising; we are always exploring with stakeholders what they want and suggesting how to achieve it (Dewhurst and FitzPatrick, 2007: 7). This applies as much to suggesting what to post on Yammer as it does to planning a campaign to explain a new strategy.

This idea of being an advice giver is already very familiar to the world of HR. Since the 1990s writers like Dave Ulrich have been talking about moving HR away from being mainly about services like recruitment, payroll, pensions and training to being a facilitator for business success (Ulrich, 1998). Given that so much of what we do in EC is about getting other people to do things or make sensible management choices (Zerfass and Franke, 2012), it is surprising that we sometimes still lag behind our HR colleagues.

It matters because our roles tend not to come with much power. French *et al* (1959) suggested that power and influence come from position, the ability to offer rewards, expertise, relationships or access to punishments or coercive power. Of these, we generally can only rely on expertise and relationships in order to achieve anything.

As in-house practitioners we can exert influence by exploiting the value we bring in several ways:

- **Capacity to fulfil requests:** Often people come to us because we have time and space to do things that they are unable to do themselves. It's an opportunity to show how we could do something differently or better. Perhaps we can supply some unexpected information about readership or some feedback from our network, highlighting that we know how to get the outcomes or results they want.

- **Access to processes and resources:** Even though technology is loosening our control over many communication processes, there may be channels like the intranet or emailing software that people can only access through us. Maybe we have a roster of freelancers who can help out on projects, or (and this is not to be underestimated) we have the keys to the cupboard where the branded gifts are kept. We can choose to guard all of these jealously or we can use requests as an opportunity to offer advice and help.

- **Knowledge:** There are quite a few areas where we should hold expert knowledge in our organizations – what audiences are thinking, what different projects are doing and when, which channels work for whom, what has worked in the past (and failed) and who are the guys who make things happen in different parts or the organization. If we understand knowledge as an asset, our holding of it can be used to add value to our colleagues.

- **Skills and capability:** As advisers, we can only add value when our advice is worth taking. Growing our expertise is a serious matter and worth investing in. Potential 'customers' should know who we are and what we can do for them and then they should believe you could do a great job for them if the need ever arose.

That means we should think continually about the skills we need to develop. Senior communicators often mention to us coaching and counselling as areas they would like to grow. Working with leaders is profoundly rewarding and exciting and, writing about being a close adviser, Richard Hytner (2014) talks about the joy of making leaders feel liberated, enlightened, authentic and decisive. Achieving these things is not hard, according to crisis PR expert James Lukaszewski, who suggests developing a trusted relationship, thinking like a leader and a strategist (rather than a technician) and helping your boss answer the question 'Does my adviser seem genuinely interested in the problems I have and do they seem to care about my success?' (Lukaszewski 2010).

Our point here is that seeing the world in terms of the needs, both business and personal, of your stakeholders is key to unlocking support, resources and permission to do the job we all know we are capable of doing. Great consultants solve other people's problems – not their own.

Processes that work

Of course, none of this matters if, in the (abridged) words of the familiar English saying, you can't organize a party in a brewery. A lack of organization is the undoing of so many people.

We said in Chapter 2 that we all need a range of processes. Processes help us to be consistent, not miss things and commit the right time and resource to a job. Every professional will have a unique set of processes they need to oversee, and these can be quite fluid over time, but we think great practitioners all have up to five things under control:

- brief taking – collecting requirements in a rigorous and consistent way;
- stakeholder planning – knowing who matters, when and how;
- audience awareness – knowing the audiences and what they think better than anyone else;
- message clarity and consistency – being clear about what they are saying and making sure everyone else is as well;
- grid – organizing the timing and sequencing of communication.

Taking the brief – being clear about the why, the what and the when

Spending time with a stakeholder, exploring what they want and actually need is invaluable. Clarity reduces the risk of an unsatisfied customer and Table 3.1 (page 46) sets out a series of questions that Sue has developed over the years to get people talking about what outcomes they really need.

Stakeholder planning

Sometimes it seems that everyone we work with is very important. They expect us to spend all day looking after them, but if you ever want to do anything productive you have to have a way of deciding which stakeholders need your full and undivided attention and which you can ignore.

Naturally, some of the important ones will be obvious – they control your budget or have job titles like CEO or boss. And equally easy to spot will be the time thieves you want to avoid! However, mostly we'll need ways of analysing who needs attention and what sort of attention is needed for each.

A longstanding model adapted by Johnson *et al* (2008) suggests plotting stakeholders on a grid with interest and power as the two axes. Stakeholders who are seen as having a high level of interest and high power are to be treated a key players and probably closely involved with the project. By contrast, people with lots of interest but little power merely need informing.

The thinking behind this model is reflected in the well-known RACI analysis tool (see box).

Try this: RACI analysis of stakeholders

A popular technique for project communicators is to list all of your potential stakeholders and then classify them according to whether they are:

- **Responsible:** People who have a hand in making things happen, perhaps by doing something specific that appears on the detailed project plan. They should know what is needed of them and by when.

- **Accountable:** Whoever is ultimately responsible for the success of the project. Ideally you will have a single name tagged as accountable and they should definitely be clear that they are accountable.

- **Consulted:** Whose input is needed to make a success of the project? They might be people with an important technical contribution to make, or they could be people with power or resource who could derail everything.

- **Informed:** Not to be confused with consulted stakeholders, these are people who should be aware of the project so they can plan accordingly. They may want to tell the project what to do but unless their contribution is useful it can be politely ignored.

There are slight variations to this model, but the value is in sitting down and identifying people and making a conscious decision about their respective roles.

Although many RACI plans are not revisited after the initial insights have been gained or reviewed in regular project meetings, the exercise has enormous value in the opening stages of a project.

In Chapter 2 we suggested involving important stakeholders in defining the core focus of the communications function and, from time to time, your most important stakeholders should be asked where they think EC should be adding value and how well you are doing it. This should be part of a periodic stakeholder analysis for your communications function. It doesn't need a complicated process and can use a great deal of intuitive input, but it can significantly reshape your strategy and approach.

Being the audience expert

This is the subject of a whole chapter in this book so, for now, we will just repeat a very simple point. In your organization, who knows what employees are thinking and is trusted to give a reliable and unbiased insight? If it is not you then you have two problems.

You have a problem because if you are not the CEO's go-to guru on employee sentiment, you may well not be in the room when how to influence that sentiment is discussed. Whoever is there may lack your expertise in shaping messages or may not understand what approaches work best. They may also neglect to share with you what the boss is planning.

Your second problem is that communication should be shaped to reflect the needs and moods of your audiences. Your content must resonate with them and managers will not be well served if your briefing materials are uninformed or irrelevant. If you are guessing how people see things, your effectiveness will be as damaged as your reputation for getting results.

Message definition and consistency

How people perceive ideas and the craft in expressing them are at the heart of our professionalism as internal communicators. And we need to ensure that messages are delivered consistently and reliably. Our case study from

SAP looks at how their HR community use a platform to ensure communications are planned consistently. In Chapter 5 (page 97) we had another example from Schneider Electric of how they keep their large network on message around the world.

CASE STUDY SAP's online tool for keeping HR communication aligned

The global HR communications team at SAP are responsible for supporting messaging to the firm's 96,000-strong workforce around the world. They face the challenge of managing a digestible flow of information that is consistent and impactful; it's a task that is greatly helped by their SharePoint-based HR Communications HUB.

As with many large organizations, HR in SAP has a complex mission. It is not just responsible for operational items like pay and staffing, but also has an agenda that covers upskilling teams and developing the organization. Chief Human Resources Officer Stefan Ries's goals are to bring HR out from the 'back office', disrupt the norm, provide positive HR experiences and generally punk things up. Their 'HR punks' movement has gone viral, internally and externally, with the HR communications team leading the charge.

Ann Miller-Rauch, Vice President, HR Communications at SAP, explains: 'We are communicating with the entire SAP audience on HR topics that can impact the way managers and employees work and the way they do things. This means that we can often have multiple reviewers and approvers for a single communication and it can be hard to keep track of changes and versions.'

Miller-Rauch adds that they also try to stop the organization being overwhelmed by messages coming from the HR organization. 'In the past we've had so many emails from HR landing in in-boxes it has to impact the effectiveness of our messages, so we need to coordinate the flow and ensure that we have a consistent tone of voice and approach.'

The HR communications team have developed a platform using SharePoint to tackle some of the practical issues. The extended communications team, of nearly 30 colleagues across Global HR, use the tool to create and approve communication content.

The platform includes a dynamic calendar that allows communicators to identify the best timing for campaigns and announcements. As well as including obvious things like national holidays around the world, the calendar allows communicators to negotiate with each other when conflicts are possible.

Figure 8.1 SAP HR communications team's single-page guidelines for creating communications

The Heart of our HR Comms Guide - Cheat Sheet

These guidelines help you plan, create, and execute your HR communication activities

Step 1 - Plan	Step 2 - Draft	Step 3 - Refine	Step 4 - Feedback	Step 5 - Approvals	Launch
1. Create your project and communication and enablement plan	1. Create a draft of your content for communication and enablement	1. Refine your content	1. Check the approval process to see if Q-Gate is required	1. Approval process (L1 & Q-Gate in HUB)	Execute your communication and enablement activities
2. Include **approvals** and key milestones in plan	2. Review the **Writing Style Guide**	2. Put your content into the right template, design, and format	2. Upload your communications materials to HUB and start review and approval workflow.	2. Finalize drafts based on feedback	
3. Review the **communication and enablement checklist**			3. Give all stakeholders 48 hours to review	3. Adapt translations, if required	
			4. Request translations, if required		

Sources to support you

- 'HR experiences' and 'HR punks' materials on the **HR Comma HUB**
- Email templates, etc. also in the **HR Comma HUB**
- Images, pictograms, illustrations are here: **SAP Image Library** (for Total Rewards pictograms, search for 'total rewards')
- Employer brand campaign (EVP) is here: **SAP Jam**

- Create on-brand communication with **Studio SAP**
- **SAP Corporate E-mail templates**
- **SAP Corporate PowerPoint and Word templates**

SOURCE Reproduced with kind permission of SAP 2018

The HR communications team have regular HUB meetings, four days a week, for just 20 minutes. It's an agile approach and gives the global, virtual team a holistic view of communication with key audiences. During these calls, as well as sharing operational updates, the team can call on the expertise and interest from colleagues on particular elements of their communication projects, for example 'Who can help me with a video production?'

Fortnightly, a 'bundling council', an hour-long Skype meeting involving key communication specialists across the broad remit of HR topics, identifies messages that could sensibly be amalgamated to cut down on unhelpful email overload.

The process for coordinating signoffs and approvals is also managed from the HR communications HUB. SharePoint's functionality for multiple reviewers to see each other's comments is very helpful and creating and approving content has been assisted by the provision of standard resources through the platform. Templates for emails, PowerPoint, posters and for standard situations like organization announcements have improved consistency in style and content. Having a clear HR tone of voice matters at SAP where the function seeks to challenge and push the business forward and be mindful of how its message lands with its 'consumers' – the employees and managers.

Guidance on planning communication is set out on a single page 'cheat sheet' which takes colleagues through the steps of planning, drafting, refining, seeking feedback, gaining approval and launching communication. For each step, there are links to specific resources such as a writing style guide, the collection of branded templates and the image library.

The SAP HR communications team is open about the challenge of getting the platform up and running. 'Getting HR colleagues to buy in has taken some work but having senior commitment has been crucial. Our HR leaders are encouraged to use only the platform for all approvals, for example,' said Nicola Murphy, Senior Communications Specialist in Global HR Communications. 'We have had to develop a mindset in HR communications as well that the HUB is the centre of our work flow. We're based around the world and so promoting collaboration and sharing has to be a priority for us; but it's something everyone has to work at.' Although the platform was developed for the HR communications team, the broader communications community across SAP are already interested in its features and functionality.

So what is your preferred way of being clear about the message to be used and does it ensure that everyone can be trusted to stick to it?

Grid – organizing and coordinating communication

Employee communication innovator Bill Quirke (2002: 182–83) said our job includes preventing mid-air collisions between ill-planned and uncoordinated communication. Even in relatively simple organizations with few employees, there is every chance that on the day you announce the new sustainability policy, facilities take away the cycle parking racks. When the dust settles it is hard for communications to avoid some of the blame – no matter how unfair!

Your air traffic control process need not be complex (in fact our experience is that simple is better); you need a mechanism for capturing upcoming initiatives, the messages they will need to deliver, the audiences to which they are aimed and the likely timing when they will be communicated. In our case study about EY, we see how they have a relatively simple process that keeps everyone aligned.

CASE STUDY   Message management in a matrix world

Professional services firm EY has a complex matrix structure. Colleagues could potentially receive multiple communications from different sources, so how does one area of the firm manage internal conversations?

Ben Firth, who heads up engagement for the UK financial services practice, explains that the firm's structure can make life complicated for communicators: 'We're a large global firm with multiple sources of messages from global, EMEIA, the UK and more. There's a lot of information that can easily get lost. Implementing strategy is complex, as we have to translate an overarching direction into practical terms for 4,600 people spread over seven locations working on everything from tax advice to artificial intelligence.

'We'll need to share how the strategy works and what it means for our people, clients and the communities we serve. Take something like diversity and inclusion, for example. Outlining how an inclusive culture benefits everyone in the firm, and therefore our clients, requires actual engagement and not just broadcast communication.'

Firth adds that localizing messaging is especially important. 'We have tried to move away from "tell" and are focusing on enabling people to have those light-bulb moments where they understand the local relevance, feel listened to and can see their thoughts being put into action.' This is not something that can happen without some careful planning and coordination.

'IC professionals need to act as air traffic control,' says Firth, 'with a clear aerial view of how press, marketing and internal communications activity fit together. Having separate approaches for each function or business unit simply doesn't allow you to do that. One of the most effective tools that helped bring real change was introducing a simple communication grid.'

The communications function created the grid using Excel for a day-by-day breakdown of what each audience stream (engagement, marketing, press) is planning, as well as significant external events like religious festivals, diversity and inclusion days or major news events. Each item is a one- or two-word description and, when necessary, a very short additional explanation. The aim is to have something brief and quickly understood.

As well as listing individual strands, the grid identifies programmes that will work across the whole communications function, for example when the managing partner speaks at a major conference and sets out an important position for the firm, and significant publications that EY releases to the financial services sector.

Says Firth, 'Having sight of the external activity means we can plan for our people to hear the message internally first. Press activity can trigger marketing activity and vice versa. Ultimately, we want the organization to know what we're saying and why. We also want to spot the opportunities to really engage people via two-way activity rather than just broadcast information.'

Developing a common process across a communications team is not without its challenges. Initially, selling colleagues on the idea of a unified grid meant asking them to move away slightly from their own individual processes. Firth explains, 'We know as change specialists that it can take a while for people to come around and if you believe that what you are suggesting is right, you need to stick with it. The most important thing is to listen, empower people to help shape the new approach and persevere; people have to see the benefit of doing things differently and that can take time.' He also thinks it was helpful that the resource for developing the approach came from his own area so he didn't need to ask busy colleagues to devote time beyond supplying information.

However, the benefits have been worth the 18-month journey. 'It's been brilliant at creating alignment and we're more coordinated because we get to see the entirety of everything that's going on.' He stresses that the objective is more than capturing information. 'It has shaped how we run the communications function. The grid itself is useful, but needs to be used as a strategic planning tool. So we introduced a monthly meeting for communications managers to review the grid and debate the implications or potential clashes and overlaps. They resolve a lot of the tactical issues and the senior communications leaders can then concentrate on using the grid to think through wider issues about messaging and supporting the business strategy.'

The process has started shaping how leaders in the business are communicating. 'We share with the leaders the view ahead; they can see what is coming, what could be significant and what they might need to get involved with.'

Firth advises other communicators to think about the level of detail they want to capture in their aerial plans. 'It's easy to get drawn in to the minutiae. This isn't about messaging, for instance, which needs to sit elsewhere as part of the detailed communication plan for that activity.' Importantly, the process relies on communicators planning communication with the same rigour. 'Naturally, some things have to be aligned, like a common approach to getting stakeholder approval, but you have to assume that mostly we're all working to similar standards. For example, at EY we're very interested in evaluation and the planning process is forcing us to have more and more conversations about how we track and measure what we're doing.'

On reflection, Firth advises every communications function to invest time in planning. 'It's easy to get stuck in the weeds when the demands to deliver are high. But taking that step back, managing the traffic and having the leverage to say "No – we're doing too much" or "These things clash" will pay dividends longer term. It's a simple process but in a large, complex firm with multiple business units and communication sources it's essential.'

Networking and collaborating

Above, we said that there are five things that successful communicators get right. The ability to develop and work with a network of colleagues could be the most important one. Liam tells the story of the best team member he ever had. She was a very heavy smoker and she worked on a large site with multiple buildings. If she received an email or a message from someone on the other side of the site, she saw an opportunity for a cigarette if she popped over to talk rather than respond online. With luck, she could turn the trip into a two-cigarette errand as she could smoke on the way back. If you bumped into her en route she'd naturally spark up a conversation and another smoke. She knew everyone and she knew everything that was going on. So, when the CEO wanted to know what people were thinking he would check in with her.

A great network isn't just about knowing what the current mood is. Our heavy smoker knew who could get things done for her. If the head of design was being difficult, she knew who could bend the rules to get things printed, her friends in IT ensured that our online survey worked like a dream and her PA buddies on the executive corridors found slots for the senior leaders to visit sites or have lunch with the long service award winners.

Your network should also give you an early warning of events that are coming up. Sometimes that means you can't avoid going to boring meetings but choose the meetings and events where you are likely to bump into colleagues you would not otherwise meet or who are at the centre of other networks.

You don't need to smoke to be a good communicator, but an interest in people and a willingness to make time to get out and about and meet them are essential.

Try this: 10 relationship rules for communications leaders

Everyone has their own approach to growing relationships but here are a few principles that might yield results for you.

1 Act as if you're part of the CEO's or your director's team – know their agenda and their calendar, and anticipate how to free their time, keep them briefed on what you know and protect their authenticity.

2 Never, ever let the boss down – always deliver what you promise, make sure it's always perfect (even your 'rough draft' should inspire confidence that you're a safe pair of hands).

3 Your stakeholders should never have to 'wing it' – when they go out to talk to employees, they need to feel that you've prepared them with a clear message, intelligence and the sense that you're on hand if they need you.

4 No one has better information about your audiences than you, and you should be known for the depth of your insights.

5 Use your interactions with senior stakeholders properly – they're a privilege that needs care – so bring data, talk about their agenda and be ready to grab your chances when they arise, be that in a weekly 1:1 or in an elevator at the end of the day.

6 Look for gate-keepers and information catchers – your network should contain people who decide if the CEO can reschedule their diary or who can make your IT needs a priority. People who sit at the centre of a web of information, such as the programme management office, the strategy team or the head of the staff committee, should be on your radar.

7 Be generous with your network without always expecting something in return – that's just borrowing and possibly manipulative! When you have a reputation as someone who helps, magical things happen.

8 Don't push it; just be around – pretending to be interested or forcing a conversation just makes you seem fake. Be patient and authentic.

9 Pick the meetings you attend with care – go where you can be sure you can have an impact and, ideally, interact with people you don't meet in other places.

10 Lunch eaten at your desk is an opportunity lost; go to the restaurant, sit in the sun or ask a friend on a 'date'. Do anything that breaks the routine and connects you with someone.

Competencies: What it takes to do the job

At the end of an audit, Liam commented that one member of the team seemed to really know her stuff. 'Oh,' smiled the director, 'you must mean "Textbook Tanya" – she can tell you the theory but she never delivers anything!' It seems that knowledge alone is not enough. Recent academic writing is coming to the same conclusion and is dismissing studies that only look at what knowledge a professional needs in order to be effective (Tench *et al*, 2013; Fuller *et al*, 2018). Being good at your job needs a mix of skills, experience and general ability – what HR professionals refer to as competencies. It's an area that has long interested us.

As far back as 2003 we were involved with a small team from the main British professional associations trying to define a competency model and then in 2007 we asked practitioners around the world what it took to be a good employee communicator. Our research over a decade ago (Dewhurst and FitzPatrick, 2007) confirmed that what mattered were certain clear personal traits rather than a long list of traditional skills such as writing, event management or video production.

Since we published that work, the world has moved on and there is little point repeating our findings in detail here. However, now as then, practitioners find that success depends on attributes such as good relationships, a focus on the business, the ability to consult and coach, an interest in helping other people to communicate and an interest in listening. There is still debate about the exact list of competencies but the need for people and personal skills comes over loud and clear. It's a theme that comes out in other research; communications leaders are not talking about specific craft skills, as might have been expected 20 years ago, but rather say we need decisiveness, integrity, empathy, curiosity and courage (Fuller *et al*, 2018).

But where can we find this paragon of excellence who can listen and be trusted to take bold decisions whilst all the while making things happen? Take heart, we're only human and no one can hope to have the full set or develop these attributes at the drop of a hat. Rather, we can set in place strategies to help us be the person who is impactful in their communication. Having superior data and insight reduces uncertainty and makes decision-making easier. Defining our own value proposition and being mindful of our personal values enable integrity. Strong stakeholder relationships make bold conversations easier. Curiosity is a state of mind that we can cultivate (and we find is naturally quite common among our peers), and that just leaves empathy, which comes ready bundled with listening 1.0.

Conclusion

We have consistently argued that we should stake a claim on a particular territory – we are the professionals who know how communication can help our business to get results. That's what we do, it's what we know how to do and it's what people should respect us for. But, that assumes we have made that territory our own and put in place the processes and systems to secure our right to get on with the job.

There are fewer barriers if we know why and what we're trying to achieve, invest in insight and intelligence and we are set up to be effective in the role we have designed for ourselves. Most important of all, a powerful network unlocks many of the problems we experience; get out of the office and get talking.

References

Dewhurst, S and FitzPatrick, L (2007) *How to Develop Outstanding Internal Communicators*, Melcrum

French, JR, Raven, B and Cartwright, D (1959) The bases of social power, *Classics of Organization Theory*, 7, pp 311–20

Fuller, M, Heijne-Penninga, M, Kamans, E, van Vuuren, M, de Jong, M and Wolfensberger, M (2018) Identifying competence characteristics for excellent communication professionals: A work field perspective, *Journal of Communication Management*, 22(2), pp 233–52

Hytner, R (2014) *Consiglieri: Leading from the shadows*, Profile Books

Johnson, G, Scholes, K and Whittington, R (2008) *Exploring Corporate Strategy: Text and cases*, Pearson EducationLukaszewski, JE (2010) *Why Should the Boss Listen to You? The seven disciplines of the trusted strategic adviser*, John Wiley & Sons

Quirke, B (2002) *Making the Connections: Using internal communication to turn strategy into action*, Gower

Tench, R, Zerfass, A, Verhoeven, P, Verčič, D, Moreno, A and Okay, A (2013) *Competencies and Role Requirements of Communication Professionals in Europe: Insights from quantitative and qualitative studies*, ECOPSI Research Report, Leeds Metropolitan University

Ulrich, D (1998) A new mandate for human resources, *Harvard Business Review*, 76, pp 124–35

Verčič, D and Zerfass, A (2016) A comparative excellence framework for communication management, *Journal of Communication Management*, 20(4), pp 270–88

Zerfass, A and Franke, N (2012) Enabling, advising, supporting, executing: A theoretical framework for internal communication consulting within organizations, Institute for Public Relations Top Three Papers Award, presented at the Fifteenth Annual International Public Relations Research Conference

Employee communication planning for change

09

CHAPTER OBJECTIVES

Some years ago, we knew of an organization introducing HR self-service for managers. Amid great fanfare, new IT software was introduced, managers were trained, and responsibility for recruitment, and pay and performance data, was handed over. Managers were warned that if they didn't take on the new tasks, vacant positions wouldn't be filled and their teams wouldn't get paid correctly.

But managers resolutely ignored their new responsibilities. Then, HR staff who had previously carried out the tasks – sympathetic of leaders' workloads, concerned people's pay would be affected, and worried about their own status (and potentially their jobs) – stepped back in. Despite the training, explanations, reminders and exhortations, people carried on working in the same way as before.

People make change happen. (Or they don't.)

Change is just part of the job for most employee communications professionals. That's why the basic ingredients for good change communication – such as clear objectives, audience insights, thoughtful messaging, listening and tracking – are to be found throughout this book.

This chapter will add two more ingredients into the mix – extra spice that can make change challenging, fascinating and frustrating. First, however much organizations urge people to 'embrace change', human beings are often instinctively not too keen on the idea. Second, it's not easy to change behaviours. Hence the intransigent line managers, the worried HR folk, and the software sitting unused.

We're choosing to look through the lens of neuroscience (which studies the nervous system including the brain) and behavioural science (which studies why people do the things they do). We're interested in the perspectives they offer, and there's a wealth of material already available about the classic change models. Although, we would add a word of caution about the importance of keeping up to date. Kotter concluded a few years ago that his popular eight-step framework had become *out* of step with the modern pace of change, and updated his approach (Kotter, 2012). And don't believe everything you read. That much-quoted statistic that '70 per cent of change projects fail'? It turns out that there's no substance behind it (Hughes, 2011).

When a plan comes together

First, we'll look at how the 'basic ingredients' come together in a change scenario. We've broken them down into chapter-sized pieces, but in real life, of course, they are used in combination. We asked a business leader and a communications professional to give their take on what makes change communication work well.

CASE STUDY   Ian Thompson, Zurich Insurance: A leader's viewpoint

Ian Thompson is Group Chief Claims Officer for Zurich Insurance and has over 20 years' experience in strategic change leadership. After many years working with, and learning from, communications professionals, here are his reflections on how the best practitioners help him facilitate change.

They spend time listening and understanding. They don't just jump to solutions. They are inquisitive about the context of the change, the outcomes expected, the behaviour change needed and the practical impact on people.

They help shape a clear purpose. As leaders, we can struggle to articulate the outcome we want from communication. It's easy to direct someone to produce a video or write an email. However, the best communicators help to take a step back and ask 'What is it we're really trying to achieve?' They challenge us – in a positive way, with good coaching questions – to explore things we might not have considered.

They make communication simple and direct. Change programmes are often complex, and it's tempting to include too much detail. Good communications people insist key points are kept simple and relevant. It's important to be reminded that people don't always listen to high-level messages; they want to know what will really be different for themselves and their colleagues – they want an answer to the question 'What does this mean for me?'

They force both the negative and positive impacts of change to be communicated. When talking about why change is needed, leaders often focus on the 'burning platform' – the negative environment the organization needs to move away from. As Napoleon once said, 'the role of the leader is to define reality and give hope'. A good communications professional will help leaders paint a positive picture of the future, not just a negative image of the present.

They understand what 'makes people tick'. A strong communications practitioner has well-developed emotional intelligence and can put themselves in the shoes of the people impacted by the change. They continuously seek feedback and bring new insights, so that leaders can understand not just how people might be feeling about a change, but why they might be feeling the way they do.

They prompt us to pause and reflect. Sometimes, in a programme environment, you're running so fast to deliver the hard benefits, you can miss the criticality of bringing people with you on the journey. It's vital to the overall success of the programme to have someone on the team who will ask difficult questions, challenge preconceptions and force a clear understanding of the people impact of decisions.

They force transparency and authenticity in communication. Too many communications practitioners seem to feel engagement is about always painting a positive picture. However, our teams will see this as spin, and this will undermine both the communication strategy and the success of the programme itself. Our people want honest communication and respect leaders who are authentic and transparent.

My advice to communicators: The most effective communications professionals I have had the privilege to work with have not just 'produced communication', they have actively contributed to the success of the programme. They have achieved this by asking a lot of questions, and have not been afraid to put forward a perspective, even if it was uncomfortable for me to hear it. They have also built trust, and supported their advice with evidence, drawn from talking with our people.

Overall, my advice is to be clear about what type of communicator you want to be. If you choose to focus on high-quality communication outputs, there's absolutely a role to play. But there's a critical role to be played by communications professionals who focus on achieving outcomes. If you're truly committed to the success of the change you're supporting, you will be recognized as an intrinsic part of its programme team.

As well as mentioning (unprompted!) many of our core ingredients, Ian Thompson highlights the temptation for leaders and project teams to focus on 'hard benefits' and forget about 'bringing people with them'. He emphasizes the important role communicators play in speaking up for people during change: acting as a conscience and having the courage to challenge where this perspective is missing. There's also a hint about what earns the licence to do it – a trusted relationship, backed up by evidence and insight.

Let's now take a look at a view from the other side, in a different organization. How does an experienced communications professional work with change?

CASE STUDY   Schneider Electric: Working with stakeholders to deliver change

At Schneider Electric, the multinational energy and automation technology company, communicators get involved early in projects because stakeholders are clear about the value they bring. 'We embed with projects driving change,' explains Simona Radu, Internal Communications Business Partnership Director, 'and we keep asking, "Who do we need to bring with us, why do they have to come and where are they in their current thinking and attitudes?"'

By committing to be involved in initial face-to-face meetings at the beginning of change projects, Simona's network of business partners build a deep understanding of the scope and impact of a project: 'We make sure there's a full briefing from the project team about what is going to happen, what is going to change. That's about more than the PowerPoint presentation; we want to know the practicalities in detail. You have to ask, "How will my life change and how will it affect an average Joe?"'

The ability to tap into a strong local network of communicators who can share expertise and insight brings added value to projects, particularly early on. 'We can easily find someone elsewhere in the company who has worked on a similar project or faced similar challenges; we offer that experience to our stakeholders so you're not starting from zero,' adds Simona.

This early planning stage is when strong relationships are built. 'At the start of the project, you haven't built credibility by delivering yet, so good relationships really matter. It is also useful to get clarity on both objectives and expectations.'

This leads on to a stakeholder mapping exercise where the communicators work with the project team to understand:

- Who is affected?
- What change will they experience?
- What is their anticipated reaction?
- What do we want them to know/feel/do?

As an example of the importance of understanding stakeholder interest, Simona recalls a project to roll out their new social enterprise network across the 140,000-strong company. A previous social tool had been unsatisfactory partly because leaders had not really connected with it. 'We knew that when the company set out to implement the new solution, leadership engagement would be vital.'

The mapping exercise helps the communication team classify stakeholders into broad groups such as

- sponsors – the people who need to make the project a success;
- champions or change agents – the people who will help drive the project forward;
- promoters – friends whose enthusiasm will be helpful;
- neutrals;
- detractors – people who could potentially lose out as a result of the project.

These are not set terms, and Simona encourages a flexible approach. 'You have to be aware that someone might be initially neutral but might change as they learn more or if we adapt the project to deliver some benefit for their business areas.' She also suggests that care is taken in the titles given to these groups as their subjects may not be flattered to discover how they have been labelled.

Schneider Electric has the added dimension of its size; the stakeholder planning process recognizes that change can take some time to spread throughout the company and so leaders' experiences could be very different. Radu adds that applying solutions that work for the whole company can sometimes be hard to explain. 'We have to make things work at scale, so occasionally something might not suit a smaller group; we have to think about how we tell the bigger story and how to get people excited about the destination we aim to reach.'

Identifying promoters is an important part of the process. 'On the social enterprise network roll-out,' she recalls, 'we had one leader who was so enthusiastic and digitally savvy that telling her story about how digital tools were making her area work more efficiently had a great impact.' And an employee 'mirror group', which gathered reactions and first impressions from around the world, gives project teams quick access to useful insights to adapt the approach.

Furthermore, the IC team out on the ground are also instrumental in getting leaders on side. 'The success of this project depended greatly on local leaders adopting and modelling the use of the tool,' explains Simona, 'so local business partners were saying "Hey, we've launched this great tool – how about we use it for our next team meeting?" or "Would you like to post this message for your team?"'

Best practice matters in the communications community, and they have regular sharing sessions; after launching the new social enterprise network they specifically talked about how leadership visibility improved adoption and were able to trade useful experiences around the company. 'Our value lies in what we bring to the table,' says Simona. 'Skills are constantly changing so you have to be always asking "What are my colleagues doing? What can I leverage? What's happening in other companies?"' That flexibility also sits well with Schneider Electric's agile approach to project planning and implementation. Communicators need to be willing to assess risks and to know when something is 'good enough'; the ethos that speed trumps perfection is common to the company's approach to IC.

Simona sees a business partnering approach and concentrating on adding value as being key to the success of change communication. 'It's communications' job to think about how things could be changed, and that works best when we get early involvement with projects during the development phase. That means you are present, and have a well-deserved seat at the table to bring good practice and experience.'

Simona's case shows how important it is to understand from the start who will be impacted by change and, in very practical terms, how. She also shows the valuable role stakeholders can play in helping change happen 'on the ground'.

We've included both these cases as a reminder that the ingredients of good change communication are the same as for *any* employee communication. So, now we have the basic recipe, let's add to it.

Why does change feel difficult?

Of course, not all change *does* feel difficult. It's personal. People respond to situations on the basis of their past experience. What feels scary to one person might seem exciting to another, whilst someone else might just think 'Here we go again.'

Having said that, neuroscience demonstrates that change is often literally a threatening experience. It also offers guidance about how to make the experience (literally again) more rewarding.

Take an imaginary step away from your busy, fast-paced, technology-enabled corporate life for a moment, and think of life in prehistoric times. It can't have been easy, living out in the open, with wild animals on the prowl. The brain's focus was survival. It had two core goals:

1 Avoiding threats (very important! being unable to evade a hungry tiger meant almost certain death).

2 Seeking rewards (finding food and shelter was less urgent than avoiding the tiger, but still important).

Human lives depended on their brain's ability to predict what was around the next corner and react instantly if they encountered something life-threatening.

Fast forward to today, and how our world has changed. But not so the brain. It's still scanning for threats and rewards. Still primed to avoid threats above all else. Still programmed to react instinctively and immediately if it encounters one. And still driven constantly to predict what's coming next.

Threats are not just physical. Rewards aren't only about what's for dinner. Both also relate to our *social* experience. The workplace, for instance. The reason why change can prompt an instinctive response is that our brains view it as a *threat, to be avoided.* Or, more specifically, as Hilary Scarlett explains, 'significant organizational change or layers and layers of small changes' (2016: 30).

How the brain responds to threats

Once the brain senses danger, those primal instincts take over and an almost instant physiological response kicks in. Our field of vision narrows to focus on the scary tiger/impending restructure/new IT system. The 'fight or flight' response is triggered. Adrenalin and cortisol (the stress hormone) are released, putting the body on high alert.

As the brain diverts energy into the places needed to do battle or run, it takes it *away from* the pre-frontal cortex – the more evolved part of our grey matter, responsible for planning and decision-making, considered thinking, and controlling our impulses and emotions. Meanwhile, the brain keeps trying to do something else it's designed to do: predict what's around the corner.

This is why change feels difficult. It's also why we might see people becoming distracted from their day-to-day work, not able to think clearly, responding emotionally, and why the rumour mill becomes rife with speculation. Scarlett describes the adult brain in a threat response as 'much like that of a teenager – quick to get angry and emotional, hard to reason with' (2016: 32).

How does it help us to know all this?

First, it's another explanation for why people are behaving as they are, other than 'they're going through the change curve'. Second, being aware of the threat/reward response can help us plan for change, and understand and respond to what we learn through evaluation and feedback.

There are two key questions to ask:

1 **How could we avoid or minimize a threat/avoid response?** For example:

   o Have we only emphasized the negative: problems, what's not working, the 'burning platform'?

   o Could we build confidence by recalling how we've risen to challenges in the past?

   o Do we really need to make this change sound quite so dramatic?

2 **Where are the opportunities to trigger a reward/towards state?** For example:

   o Set achievable short-term goals.

   o Share progress, recognize successes and small wins, reflect on how far we've come.

   o Ask about what's working, not just what still needs to be fixed.

Scarlett suggests there are six areas of our social experience that can trigger the threat/reward response. They're summarized as SPACES: self-esteem, purpose, autonomy, certainty, equity, social connection (Scarlett, 2016). When you're mapping out how a change will impact people, think about it also in relation to these areas. Look for things you can do to avoid or minimize a threat response, and/or trigger a reward response, in each case. Here are some examples.

Self-esteem

Self-esteem relates to seniority; feeling important, skilled, respected, valued, a sense of achievement, improving yourself.
What you can do:

- Offer opportunities for skills development or special tasks.
- Ask for, listen to and respect opinions.
- Celebrate achievements, past and present. Don't belittle what's gone before.

Purpose

Purpose relates to having hope, meaning and a sense of direction; helping others and feeling your contribution is useful.
What you can do:

- Show how people's roles and skills are important and make a difference.
- Have a clear and compelling story about where the organization is heading.
- See also Chapter 12 on communicating on purpose.

Autonomy

Autonomy relates to having control over our environment, feeling we have choices, and being listened to.
What you can do:

- Involve people.
- Provide options and choices.
- Listen, and act on what people say.

- Share how people's input is used.
- Give people even small opportunities to organize their work and environment.
- Provide opportunities for people to talk and work things through to draw their own insights.
- Be aware that taking even small things away can provoke a threat response. (Jane Sparrow (2017) shares the story of how one organization sparked a mutiny by trying to remove people's individual desk bins and replace them with central bins during a merger.)

Certainty

Certainty relates to being able to predict what will happen in the future, and the need for clarity. The uncertainty of 'not knowing' is harder than the certainty of 'bad news'.

What you can do:

- If you can't give certainty about the impact of change, give certainty about the process. Explain how and when things will happen; when and how information will be shared.
- Provide regular updates, at predictable times, even if there's nothing to say.
- Emphasize what's staying the same, not only what's changing.
- Take time to understand what people are worried might happen – their fears could be unfounded. If they are, put the record straight.
- Explain what change will mean for people in practical terms. Senior leaders may feel 'everything' is changing, and want to 'talk up' the change. However, the practical impact on people's day-to-day jobs might actually be minimal or even non-existent.

Equity

Equity relates to perception of being treated fairly, through process or reward.

What you can do:

- See the section on fairness in Chapter 10 (page 190).

Social connection

Social connection relates to having connections to others, feeling part of a group, a sense of belonging and being amongst friends.

What you can do:

- Use inclusive language, eg 'we', 'us', 'together'.
- Arrange discussions, conversations and activities in smaller groups.
- Make time for face-to-face communication.
- Include informal, social activities.

Some of these things probably seem obvious, and you'll be doing them already. Neuroscience brings a fresh perspective on *why* they are helpful, together with an extra layer of credibility. If you're struggling to take leaders along with your suggestions, now you have the language of science to back you up. Don't just present recommendations on the basis that you think they're a good idea. Preface them with: 'according to neuroscience...'.

CASE STUDY   The Body Shop: Neuroscience, communication and a new owner

In June 2017, communication at The Body Shop was in lockdown. Four months earlier, parent company L'Oréal had announced a 'strategic review', essentially putting The Body Shop up for sale. The press was rife with rumours about interested bidders, but none of it could be discussed and the executive leadership team had signed non-disclosure agreements. Change Communication Manager Emma Ridgeon comments: 'There was so little we could tell people that it felt like we couldn't *say* anything.'

However, as the bidding process started to heat up, a decision was taken to gather the top leaders together, even though there was still no information to share. Ridgeon was familiar with the SPACES model, and knew people needed a sense of autonomy and certainty. She explains: 'We said to our leaders up front, "Here's what we're *not* going to tell you today. But we want to listen, we want to support you, and we'll share what we can."'

Much of the event ran like a giant Q&A session. At round tables, groups of six to eight leaders discussed three topics, noting their 'top three responses' into a template:

1   What is top of mind for your people right now?

2   What specific questions do your teams have?

3   What else do you need in terms of support?

Their input was used to start a company-wide Q&A cycle. Ridgeon says, 'We sorted all the questions into categories and said, "We can't answer these sections yet, but we can answer these ones. We're not ignoring the others because we're secretive, but because either we're bound by confidentiality clauses or we don't yet know the answer." Then we answered all the questions about the process and the timings as far as we could. So people realized the leaders weren't just keeping things hidden. We acknowledged we'd heard people and we knew there were these 10 topics they were concerned about – and for now we could only answer topics 2 and 3, but here are the timescales for when we think we'll be able to answer 4 and 5, and so on.'

Every two weeks, the questions were revisited and more answers populated. When details of the bidding shortlist emerged in the press, Ridgeon explains, 'We'd say "We can't comment on this – but here are some of the headlines of what's being reported." It was a way of communicating without communicating. We couldn't put out a statement, but we could show what others were saying, if the reports were credible.'

At the round table session, leaders had been assured that they would always get first sight of anything that was announced – even if it was only an hour before anyone else. Meanwhile, senior leaders were coached in demonstrating they were listening, and in how to answer questions. This support was part of an aim to address the first S of SPACES: self-esteem. Ridgeon comments, 'We wanted to show our leadership group they were valued and that we were listening and responding to their needs.'

Social connection also became a key focus area. There was a sense that leaders were not visible, and engagement survey results showed a lack of trust in formal communication channels – as part of a large corporate group, the leadership had adopted a more formal communication style. So, leaders were encouraged to be visible and gather people together in huddles to check in, listen and show empathy.

As the sale process started moving to a conclusion and there was more to share, email announcements were complemented by town halls headed by members of the executive team. 'We paired up leaders of different functions,' comments Ridgeon, 'to show them working as a team.'

SPACES has been a useful guide for communication at The Body Shop during its time of change. As well as using it herself, Ridgeon shared it with the HR community, so key elements could be built into related initiatives. Her other guiding light has been a set of communication principles. She comments, 'They seem simple and obvious, but they guide you through when you're sitting at your desk and you can't see the end point – at least you can agree the approach and the principles, and from there the activity plan usually becomes clearer.'

The Body Shop's change communication principles

Our communications will be:

- **Targeted:** They will reflect the needs of our demographic and in particular our disparate groups across worldwide offices, stores, in franchises and at home.

- **Timely:** They will reach global audiences simultaneously as far as possible, so that people worldwide receive consistent and coordinated communications regardless of time zone.

- **Prioritized:** Personally affected teams will be briefed in advance of any broader announcements.

- **Led by leaders:** Leadership communities will be equipped to support teams through the changes.

- **Coordinated:** Messages will be developed centrally for consistency, tailored for local relevance.

- **Sustained:** There will be a regular rhythm of activities and an emphasis on face-to-face where possible, supported by online and written channels for reinforcement of key messages.

- **Two-way:** There will be ongoing opportunities for feedback and discussion.

In the next chapter, we'll focus on scenarios that are particularly likely to prompt a threat response: those involving bad news and crises. For now, let's move onto the second of our thorny questions.

How do we change behaviours?

Whilst leaders and project teams might like to focus on changing 'stuff' – IT systems, processes, organizational designs – changes are often dependent on people *doing* something differently. It's tempting to assume people take action on the basis of rationally thinking things through. Give people a clear explanation of why change is needed, what it means to them, and what they should do differently, and behaviour change will follow. This is why so many questions to stakeholders are answered with 'I need people to *understand*.' It's also why they might think the communications work is finished, once the 'understanding' box is ticked. Unfortunately, human beings are not as rational as we think!

Do they think it's a good idea?

Armenakis and Harris (2009) propose that five key *beliefs* underlie people's motivations to support change. They call them discrepancy, appropriateness, efficacy, principal support and valence. We've translated these into five key questions:

1 Do people believe change is *needed*?

2 Do people believe the solution being proposed is the *right one*?

3 Do people believe that a) they personally and b) the organization are *capable* of implementing this change successfully?

4 Do people believe the organization's *leaders are committed* to the change? Are trusted peer influencers committed, too?

5 Do people believe there's some *personal benefit* in this for them?

Use the questions to guide communication planning and evaluation. If the answer to any of them is 'no', you'll have some clues about where to start work. Possibly with the exception of question 5 – not all changes benefit people. If they don't, it's a bad idea to pretend otherwise.

They believe in it, they're supporting it... but they're still not doing it. Now what?

Understanding + good intentions don't always = action. (Healthy eating, anyone? Exercise? That task you were *definitely* going to finish today?)

Behavioural science shows that:

- People's behaviours are strongly influenced by context and circumstances.

- Behaviours are often unconscious and automatic. What people think they do, and what they *actually* do, may be entirely different. We're much more influenced by emotions, social factors and cognitive biases than we realize (Samson, 2014).

This means we need to dig deep with our questions about what people need to *do* differently. Are we really clear what behaviours need to change? When? Where? What context will people be working in? Who or what might influence whether this behaviour happens?

We also need to turn detective about what's happening now, and why. If there's a behaviour you want to stop or change, is it happening consistently, or only in certain circumstances? What's going on, in those circumstances?

Remember, people won't always be able to describe accurately what they're doing in practice or explain why they're doing it. You might consider going to watch the current behaviours in action and talking to people in context.

CASE STUDY   Siemens and M&C Saatchi: Understanding the know–do gap

Global powerhouse Siemens Wind Power, now Siemens Gamesa Renewable Energy, has a 'zero harm' approach to safety. The company aspires to create a work environment where nobody is hurt, ever. The company asked M&C Saatchi to help bring to life the zero harm concept and raise awareness of key health and safety issues.

However, whilst the brief was clear, what proved more difficult was understanding what these 'key issues' were. Health and safety data couldn't bring to light exactly what was going wrong, or why. M&C Saatchi's Stephen Jolly explains: 'To influence performance, you need to influence behaviours. And to influence behaviours, you need to understand your audience.'

The M&C Saatchi team asked to speak to people working on the front line via a series of telephone interviews, and visited two Siemens Wind Power sites in the United Kingdom and Denmark. It quickly became clear that awareness of health and safety wasn't a problem. Staff were excellently trained, knew the protocols they should follow, and talked at length about how seriously they took safety.

So, what *was* the problem? Employees knew how to be safe, yet they were still getting hurt. Incidents were apparently just 'freak accidents'. Jolly comments: 'Often it's not a question of what people *say* they do or believe. You have to get under their skin, and preferably watch what they do in practice. It's about understanding norms and identifying the motivations for people's behaviours.'

The team revisited the anecdotes they had gathered and got back on the phone with some of the interviewees to understand more about the context in which accidents had happened. It was at this point that two themes emerged:

1   The Wind Power division was founded outside Siemens, as part of a 30-year-old industry in Denmark, with small beginnings. Many employees remembered the 'good old days', when they had the freedom to do the job as they saw fit.

2   There was sometimes huge perceived commercial pressure to meet a strict deadline.

Here lay the answer. A telephone conversation on a relatively calm day was one thing. Being up against an important commercial deadline and making a quick personal decision to jump between a boat and a turbine platform in the North Sea, or quickly weld something so you didn't let people down, was quite another. People believed safety was important, knew the safety protocols, and had the ability to act safely. But in certain situations, the surrounding culture drove behaviours that could lead to unsafe situations.

This realization enabled the team to find the central idea for its campaign: employees are the company's most precious resource, and *nothing* is more important than their safety. They were helped by a policy decision taken by Siemens to make a promise to employees: anyone who missed a deadline because of a concern about health and safety would not be held to account. Critical to the campaign's success was to empower those on the ground; to legitimize the action of questioning an order if there was any concern over safety.

'Just raising awareness of an issue or telling people to behave differently doesn't work,' says Jolly. 'You have to understand why they are doing the things they're doing. My advice to any internal communicator is to get a lot more serious about research. Understand your audience. Get to know the motivations behind their behaviours. Without these insights, you are communicating for communication's sake – and you will be ineffective.'

So, we understand what people are doing and why. How do we change it?

As this case shows, once we understand the motivations behind behaviours, potential messages and strategies start to emerge.

We can also use insights from science to help things along. We said earlier that behaviour is often driven automatically. Our brains are pulling the strings, without us even being aware of it. Insights from behavioural science can help us work *with* the brain, instead of fighting against it. The UK-based Behavioural Insights Team has devised the EAST ® framework,[1] which sets out four principles to apply. It states that to influence behaviour, we should make it *easy, attractive, social* and *timely* (Service *et al*, 2014):

- **Make it easy.** Our brains like to save energy, which makes them inherently lazy. So:

  o Ask for simple actions. If necessary, break things down into easy steps.

  o Be clear about what people should do. Make messages short, simple and concrete. Use everyday language.

  o Make it as quick and easy as possible for people to act. Strip out anything – however small – that could be an obstacle.

- **Make it attractive.** People are more likely to act on messages that stand out. So:

  o Attract attention. One organization got people to complete mundane but important process changes by using humorous celebrity GIFs.

  o Know your audience and what matters to them. Appeal directly with something that's personally relevant. How can you meet a need or address a frustration?

  o Appeal to people's self-image. Could performing this behaviour help them feel or look good?

- **Make it social.** People are more likely to do something if they see others in their group doing it. We like to 'fit in', and copying other people saves mental effort. So:

  o Use social networks to help behaviours spread peer-to-peer.

  o Say and show that 'most people are doing this'.

  o Use personal testimonials, reviews, examples and case studies.

  o Beware inadvertently using social norms *against* your aim. For example, 'We're still waiting for most people to complete the training.'

- **Make it timely.**

  o Communicate with or prompt people when they're most likely to be receptive.

  o Show quick, immediate benefits from taking up the behaviour.

CASE STUDY WTF: Breaking the rules at AXA

'We can't solve problems by using the same kind of thinking we used when we created them.' Albert Einstein's words were the philosophy behind AXA's Write the Future (WTF) day. 'WTF was a deliberate play on words,' laughs Internal Communications Manager Leanne Taylor. 'We wanted to suggest, "You can do more than you think you can – you don't need to ask."'

The initiative came about in response to UK pulse survey results showing employees didn't feel comfortable taking decisions without leadership approval. 'There was a lot of feedback about rules and processes,' explains Taylor. 'People didn't know when it was OK to take a decision. At the same time, we'd been talking about the future. Our brand has a long history and there are lots of start-ups in our industry. We want to be more agile, and have our people help us get there.'

WTF was to be a day focused on helping employees get rid of rules they felt were getting in their way. The communications team's first task was to get people involved. They identified a number of 'rule breakers' across the UK and involved their CEO forum, a network of people covertly peer-nominated as influencers.

Taylor explains: 'We found the rule breakers by talking with the management team – we wanted people that would get involved. The CEO forum had been set up already, through a high-visibility campaign. We'd asked questions like "Who in your office always does the right thing, even if it's not the easy thing?" and "Who's really good at getting people collaborating?" Then we gave out nomination cards and set up online nomination boxes. We found 60–70 people whose names came up over and over again, and we now ask them for help with business problems, testing and feedback.'

The groups helped settle on a format, with the central aim of helping people be more empowered. It was decided to lock the leadership team in a room for a day and give each business site a video conference slot with them, in which anyone could pitch a rule they wanted to break.

To prepare for the sessions, rule breakers and forum reps at each site were tasked with gathering the rules people hated. They had free rein about how they did it, though the communications team provided template emails and posters they could use. Some ran surveys; others held workshops. Around 700 rules were identified, which were prioritized according to how often they came up.

On the day, employees were told 'Today is about breaking rules.' If they wanted to order pizza for breakfast, dress down, or – as one site did, bring their dogs into work – that was fine.

Depending on size, each site had 10–20 minutes to chat with the leadership team. 'We called them "speed-hating" sessions, to keep up the pace,' explains Taylor. The leadership team agreed to break 147 rules – around 80 per cent of those raised. Some were broken immediately; some needed arrangements putting in place; others required checking with the regulators. The communications team live-blogged throughout the day. Since the activity fell within the company's CSR week, AXA donated £5 to charity for each rule broken.

'We got all kinds of requests,' says Taylor. 'From empowering people on the phones to agree cases up to £100 instead of £10, to giving a team manager the go-ahead to trial giving time back as an incentive to people who meet targets. It was the 2018 World Cup, so people asked if they could have TVs on. We reviewed flexible working policies and dress codes. One site wanted to wear colourful wigs one day a month and another wanted the loo roll cupboard unlocked!'

Whilst the team is waiting to see the results of the next pulse check, anecdotal feedback has been positive and some sites have since held their own WTF sessions, keeping the focus on empowerment.

Taylor's advice to anyone considering a similar exercise? 'Don't underestimate how big it can get. If we did it again, I'd be a bit more prescriptive about the type of rules we looked at. And involve IT early on – the logistics were a big thing!'

Whilst they may not have realized it, AXA's approach followed the EAST principles. They made it *easy* for people to act, by giving them access to the senior team. They made it *attractive*, with the attention-grabbing WTF title, the angle of breaking rules people hated, and a fun approach. They made it *social* by using rule breakers and peer influencers, and live-blogging about how other colleagues were getting involved. And they made it *timely* by giving instant answers and getting TVs switched on for the World Cup!

Conclusion

The ingredients of good communication planning also work for change scenarios, as for any other. Insights from the fields of neuro- and behavioural science can build on these foundations. They help us understand why people find change difficult, and how to make the experience easier. They show why rational explanations alone don't change behaviours. They bring insights about what *can* help to change behaviours. And, even where insights might simply confirm things we 'knew' already, or create suggestions that may seem obvious, they bring with them the language of science and the robustness of evidence. Use them to bring weight to your recommendations and credibility to your interventions.

Note

1 EAST is a registered trademark of Behavioural Insights Ltd. ©Behavioural Insights Ltd 2014. Not to be reproduced, copied, distributed or published without the permission of Behavioural Insights Ltd.

References

Armenakis, AA and Harris, SG (2009) Reflections: Our journey in organizational change research and practice, *Journal of Change Management*, **9**(2), pp 127–42

Hughes, M (2011) Do 70 per cent of all organizational change initiatives really fail? *Journal of Change Management*, **11**(4), pp 451–64

Kotter, JP (2012) Accelerate! *Harvard Business Review*. [Online] https://hbr.org/2012/11/accelerate

Samson, A (2014) An introduction to behavioural economics. [Online] https://www.behavioraleconomics.com/resources/introduction-behavioral-economics/

Scarlett, H (2016) *Neuroscience for Organizational Change*, Kogan Page

Service, O, Hallsworth, M, Halpern, D, Algate, F, Gallagher, R, Nguyen, S, Ruda, S and Sanders, M (2014) EAST®: Four simple ways to apply behavioural insights, Behavioural Insights Team. [Online] https://www.bi.team/publications/east-four-simple-ways-to-apply-behavioural-insights/

Sparrow, J (2017) Primeval suits, *The HR Director*, **148**, pp 20–21

Sharing the bad news

10

Communication in tough times

CHAPTER OBJECTIVES

Every day, employee communicators deal with change, but sometimes that change is unwelcome. Every organization faces bad news from time to time and it is our job to make sure that news gets broken fairly, respectfully and clearly. Get it wrong and you can dispirit colleagues, undermine your ability to respond to the bad news or fundamentally rock people's faith in the organization where they work. Get it right and you build loyalty and have a platform for seeing though your recovery plan.

We have talked a lot about change throughout this book, so this chapter is more about the practicalities of breaking bad news. We will explore a little why traditional ideas about crisis communication do not fully apply to internal situations and look at some principles to apply to how you share bad news.

We'll also pick up a couple of the themes that appear elsewhere in this book. Networks and line managers matter – neglect them at your peril.

It's not always sunshine and roses

We first met, too many years ago to remember, when we were both doing almost identical jobs in similar tech businesses that were going through tough times after the dot com bubble burst in the early noughties. Both our companies were effectively bankrupt and fighting to stay alive. Whilst corporate financiers did deals, the management cut costs and closed sites in an effort to rediscover profitability.

We used to call each other up for moral support and share stories. Our daily round included discussing with HR how many jobs were being cut this month, how to explain worsening terms for voluntary severance in the next round of reductions or telling IT that reducing the number of printers couldn't be positioned as a move to make people take more exercise around the office. Liam had the experience of facilities announcing an end to free drinks in vending machines just as details of executive retention bonuses were leaked.

Sometimes we'd laugh at the perversity of our situations, but mostly it was unrelenting crisis after crisis over two years. We'd crave the opportunity to run campaigns about anything, no matter how banal, that weren't about bad news. After a while, we'd both developed a competency we wished we didn't need – being adept at handling bad news.

However, we have to remember that even when we are not facing a challenge like the global financial crisis, bad news is never far away in most organizations. Cost reviews, product cancellations, hostile takeovers, changes in regulatory or government policy mean that no EC professional can produce an unending diet of happiness for their colleagues. We have to be able to manage bad news and support our organizations through tough and good times. And our experience is that survival and success are largely a matter of anticipation, planning, execution and integrity.

Why should an EC professional care about bad news?

Leaders' attitudes to the communications team seem to develop fastest when something goes wrong. A crisis is one of the few moments when our stakeholders pay full attention to us, so we'd better have something sensible to say.

If we get it wrong our leaders can cause real damage to the willingness of employees to support their organization. We know that staff are some of the most potent sources of information for external stakeholders, especially in this age of Twitter, Glassdoor and Facebook (van Zoonen and van der Meer, 2015). Ill-conceived comments by managers or mistimed announcements can easily alarm internal audiences with serious consequences.

Sue tells the story of one CEO who mused in public about the company having more contact centres than it needed, and Liam remembers the chairman of one large agency group making sexist 'jokes' about compliance officers to a room of mostly female staff who advised clients to take compliance seriously. How hard will people work to solve problems when they fear for their own jobs, feel that they are not valued or expect poor treatment? Getting the management of bad news right isn't just important for our sanity; it matters for the health of our organizations.

Let's just tell them it's not as bad as they think

Students of British political history might recognize the headline 'Crisis? What Crisis?' In 1979, with public sector strikes leaving refuse piling up in central London streets and shutdowns at crematoria stopping funerals, the then Prime Minister tried to downplay the extent of the troubles besetting his government. The *Sun* newspaper summarized his ineffective attempt at reframing perceptions of the situation in those three words, and thereby sounded the death knell of his premiership.

People just did not recognize this politician's relaxed interpretation of events. Their experience was of chaos, of inflation at over 10 per cent and of emergency measures in hospitals and local councils. It's a story that should resonate with many EC practitioners who have been asked to explain that job losses are part of a growth strategy, that cuts to staff benefits will mean bigger rewards for people or changes to the pension scheme mean people can now work even longer. Communications folk know all about bad news and crises.

Although in recent decades researchers have spent a lot of time looking at crisis communication and reputation, surprisingly relatively little work has gone into analysing good practice in the areas of employee/internal communication in tough times. There is an irony in that study after study tells us that communications directors say IC and crisis are their two most significant concerns, but so little work has been done at looking at the two together (Johansen *et al*, 2012). This might be because of how we tend to think of bad news and crises.

Bad news – crisis or just a nasty shock?

For internal communicators, bad news or crises are not synonymous with a loss of control or unexpected events in the way it might be for our external PR colleagues. Not all crises are bad news, nor is all bad news a crisis. Workers in a water or power company might want to celebrate their response to extreme weather; customers might see a loss of power or flooding as a crisis, the workers could see it as an opportunity to step up and excel. Bad news about the planned run-down of production at a factory over many years is a worrying development but may not feel at all like a crisis to some people.

It's about the meaning – not the event

Very often, our bad news is fully intended and for some sections of our organization actually welcomed. We need to deal with the big unexpected issues that have external causes or are the result of failures internally, but we also have to manage communications around deliberate decisions taken by our leaders. These decisions, such as closing a site or cancelling a product line, will be perfectly legitimate and intended to ensure survival and a return for investors. It's bad news, but not for everyone.

Academics who look at bad news inside organizations suggest we think about crises[1] in terms of events that could damage our fundamental understanding of what the organization is about (Heide and Simonsson, 2013). How might employees of a wholefood chain react if their company chose to sell heavily processed junk food? What would happen in a public hospital if they refused to treat patients on low incomes? If police forces decide they will no longer arrest burglars, how might committed officers feel about it?

These would all be bad news that has significance beyond its impact on operations or individuals. We're interested in protecting the fundamental trust that people have in the organizations for which they work. Our colleagues have a unique relationship with the organization and the stakes are always higher for them than for a journalist or financial analyst who has other companies to track and write about. This means that we have to think beyond the factual detail of the news we're sharing and advise senior leaders about how people will interpret what we are telling them. What might seem straightforward to a leader could have profound implications for trust and engagement among the workforce.

Pause for thought: What could possibly go wrong here?

Writers on communication and bad news are increasingly encouraging us to think about how events or developments could undermine our core beliefs about what an organization exists for.

What, in your organization, are the fundamental values that matter to your colleagues? Could it be a service that you offer? Maybe there is a brand that everyone cares about or a level of quality in the goods you produce? Perhaps there are a set of beliefs about the culture or the history of the organization.

And what is your evidence for that? How do you really *know* what people actually think – have you spoken to them or are you guessing why people keep coming back to work for your organization? Do you speak often enough to regular colleagues? Have you gone 'back to the floor' recently and worked alongside customer-facing staff recently to see what really matters to them?

If you were asked to communicate something difficult, would you know enough to help you advise senior leaders on the real impact of their decision?

Fearing the worst

Much of the advice that exists about managing bad news revolves around planning, and it begins with a simple risk analysis which involves thinking about:

- What could happen?
- What is the likelihood of it happening?
- What impact will it have if does come about?

(Yaxley, 2016: 179)

Potential sources of bad news may include unpopular decisions and change, unexpected internal events or unexpected or unwelcome external events. It can be helpful to start by reviewing the overall business strategy, the business continuity plan and the external PR crisis plan. And we have found it useful to invite a cross-section of colleagues from your networks across the main functions in the business to a workshop and ask them to nominate potential issues which could come from, for instance, business change, acts of God, bad behaviour, market changes or external forces. It is easy to create a very long list that could become unmanageable, so prioritize by identifying those items that could threaten trust in the organization or understanding of its core purpose.

Subsequent stages of the workshop would then turn to likelihood and then impact. You will want to return to our continuing themes:

- How could business continuity be impacted?
- What damage will be done to people's belief and faith in the organization?

The results of this exercise will point in several directions. It will tell you which areas of the organization you need to be close to so that you can better understand where bad news could come from and to develop relationships ahead of anything blowing up. You might decide that you need a tracking process and specific contingency plans. You will also be clearer about which facts and data you need to have to hand; trying to pull information together when you suddenly need it to support an announcement is always a challenge. And you will have an insight into the context you need to be setting now to remove the element of surprise from later announcements.

Finally, do you understand how your audiences might react? You might assume a negative response but do you really know? Deepening your understanding of the workforce and how it sees the world is always useful, as your insight can help you avoid misunderstandings and an unnecessarily negative reaction.

Are we telling our people the whole story?

Employees will be quick to notice if they are not being told the whole story or be suspicious if they see things differently to how leaders want to explain it. We can be caught in the middle if we're not careful, being pulled between promoting a management version of events that lacks credibility and a workforce that doesn't get why things are happening.

To protect our organization from losing the trust of its people we have to ask difficult questions about all the causes and remedies for the current situation. If an initial conversation doesn't reassure you that you know the truth, your Q&A drafting process is your last chance to find out. And having to hand data about what people really think is going on puts you in a better position to discuss the most productive way to explain bad news.

Thinking about breaking bad news – some principles

Few people like breaking bad news to people they've worked alongside for a long time. However, we have found that people are generally better at receiving tough news than you might expect, as long as it is done with respect and intelligence. We have found the following principles to be invaluable.

It's always emotional – keep it human

When we discussed change we talked about the physiological reasons why our brains are not the reliable rational machines we'd like to think that they are. We know from the study of how brains work that emotion plays a role in deciding how we interpret information, or indeed deciding which facts we actually hear (Lu and Huang, 2018). It's not the facts we hear that dictate our feeling, it's our feelings that dictate what facts we are going to hear. We might therefore suggest dropping the 25-slide PowerPoint pack and making space for people to meet in person whoever made the decision and hear their story about why it matters.

Do, feel, know – action oriented

People respond better, they remember more and feel more engaged if they have a specific task to do. Action is an antidote to feelings of helplessness and powerlessness (which we know derail change). As local managers are instrumental in translating high-level messages into to-do lists, be sure to get them fully briefed to identify tasks of short-term improvement projects.

You're the expert on employee communication

It wasn't long ago that we heard the head of a large UK PR agency dismissively telling an audience of EC professionals at a conference that 'when a crisis hits, the CEO is far too busy sorting things out to talk to staff; you have to let the PR guys advise him; staff will appreciate why they can't see the boss...'.

Heaven help any CEO taking employee communication advice from that PR! Sadly, it is typical of the problem faced by many IC professionals who have to push to get access to the important conversations when there's bad news to deliver. Leaders can be easily distracted by concerns about the media or investors and may not notice that unqualified professionals are volunteering advice about your audience groups.

It is sometimes easier to be bolder in stating our case when we can bring evidence to support our advice. Data or insights that clarify how people are feeling, their historic response to similar news or the advantages of different communications channels protect your leaders from uninformed amateurs when they most need it.

Honest... but always open?

In a company where Liam worked, the head of the US division stood up at a town hall meeting and told staff that within days they were about to clinch a deal with the government for a game-changing product; it would be a sale that would secure their prosperity for decades to come. It was a lie.

Within minutes, news of this lie got back the UK and everyone was furious. When staff in the States didn't see this massive Federal contract turn up, what were they going to think? They certainly would never again trust anything they heard from the US boss or the company. One manager singlehandedly had caused lasting damage. Only a fool thinks they can lie to, deceive or misdirect their staff. You will be found out and you may never be forgiven.

However, to be clear, honesty and openness are not the same thing or interchangeable terms. There might be legal issues relating to consultation processes, regulatory restrictions or rules about telling financial markets or works councils that make it impossible or inadvisable to share everything. There is very little you can do except have slick processes for telling your own people as soon as legal embargos are lifted and act in good faith to tell people what you can, as fully as you can and as soon as you can.

There are also times when leaders can share information that is just unhelpful – like publicly speculating how many contact centres a company will eventually need or saying what they really think about the head of the German works council. As a rule of thumb, it is acceptable to decline to speculate or make promises about the future that can't be guaranteed.

Know the rules

You must know the rules governing things like consultation, regulatory disclosure or works councils in the places where you operate; do not rely on other people and their potentially limited understanding to guide you. It cuts out the need to spend time getting guidance when you are trying to get out communication in a hurry and, as you are often the last person to hit the send button it allows you to be the final check that your organization is following the rules.

Surprises are not always nice – be timely

If you don't want to have to educate people from first principles when things start going wrong, invest ahead of time in providing context about your markets, customers, stakeholders, competitors and the world outside the front door. Senior leaders might have seen your bad news coming for ages but a workforce that is unprepared just won't understand.

Quick is usually good

Turn up anywhere with bad news and you'll be asked, 'When did you find out?' We all hate discovering that we've been kept in the dark: it creates suspicion that more information is being held back. There is no point in delaying bad news in the hope that the problem will go away; bad news rarely improves with age. Even if you have to say the picture is incomplete, or there are legal constraints on sharing more, it is normally better to say so than to keep mum.

Always give them something to read

People absorb information at their own pace. It seems that, no matter how simple the message, tough news takes time to sink in. At the start of your communication process you will set emotional context and talk in headlines, but you should either give people material they can take away and digest or tell them where to find it.

Keep it as clear as possible and consider producing a short Q&A document that people can take home and discuss with partners. We have also had some success with question sites or platforms like Yammer as long as you can respond quickly and factually, and avoid reacting to frustrated colleagues.

Show you have a plan

When we talked about change, we said that people ask whether it's needed, if you have the right solution, is the plan possible, whether leaders are committed and how they will be impacted. Our job is to help them find the answers to those questions. Often, spending time with the boss and sensing their confidence and command is a pretty good substitute for an actual plan because, as we said a couple of pages back, we're emotional first and rational second. A leader who is confident, appears to know the facts, understands what staff and stakeholders are thinking will be judged competent.

Our role is to both show that there is a plan and that leaders are 'planful'. We do this by making sure the plan and the planners are visible and credible. Opportunities for conversation with leaders, content about the operating environment, information about customers, service users and competitors and clarity about goals all help and are within our gift.

Is it really fair?

In Chapter 9 we mentioned the SPACES model to understand what makes people respond negatively or positively to change. The 'E' of SPACES stands for equity. When things are going badly people expect fairness and equity in how decisions are taken and implemented. 'Procedural fairness' helps colleagues accept unwelcome decisions and removes a reasonable objection to whatever leaders are proposing.

Follow this checklist to make sure your communications are highlighting procedural fairness in your organization:

- **Consistency counts.** Workers will want to know if you are acting the same way as in the past. If redundancy terms are not the same as in previous severance rounds expect to explain why.

- **Be unbiased.** Will individuals get the same treatment regardless of who they are or groups to which they belong? Do HR procedures unwittingly penalize people because of their age, function, gender or ethnicity? Might some people appear favoured because they have access to privileged communication channels?

- **Ensure information fairness.** Do people trust that decisions will be made on the basis of complete information? If your HR database is out of date, site records patchy or there are differences between parts of the organization in how data is recorded, can fair decisions be made?

- **Who is listening to me?** Will people feel that they are going to be listened to or is 'consultation' a complete sham with no attempt to share information or hear concerns? Failing to give people a voice stores up frustration and makes any change process more painful for our colleagues and the organization.

- **Show a little respect.** When you have run multiple rounds of job cuts and closed several sites, it can all become routine. But our colleagues may often pour their lives into our organization, the workplace may be the scene of their greatest personal triumphs and moments of great joy and comradeship; shoving them out the door without respect is both wrong and a message to existing staff that their contributions will never be truly valued. Show respect in the tone of your communications, the seniority of your spokespeople and by acknowledging the achievements of the people who are affected.

- **Train managers to deliver bad news.** People value hearing bad news from a boss who understands their situation; a manager who can deliver it with good grace, respect and compassion will be perceived as fair. Investing in training to help supervisors with this most difficult of tasks pays dividends (Richter *et al*, 2016).

It's how you say it...

How you say something impacts what people hear. Don't be one of those organizations that sack people by text message, with a fast car waiting to whisk the CEO away after delivering bad news, or that stops communicating when things are tough. Having processes in place that maintain a steady flow of information, allowing staff to check their understanding and exemplifying a commitment to fairness and transparency, is vital. But most importantly, ensure that local managers are supported and able to translate what is being said globally into a local context. They're your defence against staff having to invent their own version of events because no one is around to answer their questions (Strandberg and Vigsø, 2016).

Decide some principles about how you handle bad news well in advance; the middle of a storm is a bad place to start inventing boundaries. What works for you may be obvious, but, drawing on points we have made throughout the book, we have ten golden rules to consider:

1 **Human:** People want to hear from people, not read a memo that sounds like it's been lifted from a legal textbook.

2 **Action oriented:** Show people what they can do next.

3 **Honest:** Make sure what you say is truthful, never mislead.

4 Legal: Don't neglect your responsibilities.

5 Timely: Don't leave people hanging to hear news that is already known externally or spreading around internal networks.

6 Informative: Provide clear useful information not corporate platitudes or overcautious doublespeak.

7 Planful: Build confidence that your leaders will fix it.

8 Respectful: Your tone, speed and responsiveness should show that you have thought about people fairly and with care.

9 Local: Make sure that local leaders are supported and can confidently explain how their teams could be impacted.

10 Listening: People must see that their views are being heard by leaders, and leaders need to know that someone – you – has their finger on the pulse of what staff are saying.

The announcement

We have found it useful to develop specific packs to support announcements. The process of developing the pack is as important as the final product itself as it helps refine the message and ensure that key players are aligned.

Packs usually contain the following elements.

- **The announcement schedule:** These normally have a cover sheet and include a clear timeline of who is doing what and when. Everyone who receives the package should be clear about their role and responsibilities. It should include items like when a press release might be issued and the name of the person doing it, when an announcement is to be posted on the employee portal or when the CEO's all-hands call will be held. If relevant, it will also explain how you will manage the announcement across time zones. This will also include an instruction for how employee feedback and reaction should be shared.

- **Contact list:** Have the most up-to-date contact list of all of the key parties in the announcement process, including colleagues in press or investor relations or the team in HR who might be handling technical matters.

- **Background:** Provide a few lines about the background to the current issue.

- **What is happening:** As clearly and as briefly as possible, describe what is happening or the news that is being announced. This will be repeated and said aloud, so write it in everyday language and avoid words that obscure or over-qualify; we're aiming to inform and not write a binding legal document.

- **Our message:** This should be a simple expression of the message we need to get over to colleagues, written in plain language (remember what we said when we talked about change and how our brains like to save energy on processing things).

- **Announcement texts:** Include copies of announcements to staff, customers, the press and other relevant stakeholders (along with instructions about who will be contacting each group).

- **Q&A:** Avoid drafting a massive document that attempts to answer every possible question; it will drive you mad, eat up valuable time arguing with senior colleagues and be out of date with days of publication. As a general rule, three pages of questions is the limit of usefulness. It is not a script to be delivered verbatim, but it should include suggested clarifications to likely questions. Keep the document manageable by concentrating on a few important areas based on your core message:

  o What is happening, when and why?

  o Who be affected and how?

  o How was/will any decision (be) made?

  o How are customers/clients/suppliers/significant stakeholders affected?

  o What happens next?

  o Where do I find out more?

Preparing leaders and managers

Time invested in preparing managers is never wasted, especially if you can give leaders as much time as possible to digest the information you are sharing and prepare to communicate with their own teams.

In Chapter 9 on change, we included a case study from The Body Shop that described the steps they took to keep leaders up to speed during a major change. It's an inspiring example and might give you ideas for developing your own approach, which could include:

- **A briefing from the CEO or the most senior leader:** This will include a request for help and a specific ask for managers to communicate. Give as much background as possible about the proposed changes and the actions to be taken. Core messages will be introduced at this point.

- **Question time:** Attendees should be given time to discuss what they have heard and consider what questions their teams will have. This underlines the message that they are expected to communicate, that they need to see things from the perspective of the audience and not be embarrassed to ask 'obvious' questions. The questions should be answered as fully as possible and any follow-up clarification noted and put into action. The managers must know that nothing is being held back from them; where there are sensitivities and any no-go areas these should be clearly and openly explained.

- **Messaging preparation:** Managers should have time to practise delivering the key messages and be shown how to bridge between an answer and the core message.

- **Announcement practicalities:** There should be a final briefing on the logistics surrounding announcements and a chance for managers to point out any flaws in the process. There should also be a briefing on the process for gathering feedback such as a catch-up conference call at the end of announcement day or a social media request for reactions. The gathering of feedback is significant as it underlines the senior leaders' concern for the difficult task being undertaken by supervisors, reinforces the expectation that they will communicate and gives them the ability to reassure their teams that concerns and feedback will be heard.

Any questions?

The CEO has just made a presentation that contained a bombshell. Jobs are going, a site is closing or a well-loved product has reached the end of its life.

'So,' she says, 'any questions?'

And she is met with silence. Well, almost. After a few moments of embarrassment another senior leader can stand no more and so asks something barely relevant. The CEO mumbles a reply and finishes on a sad note of failure by saying 'Well, if that's all the questions we'll close it there...' and everyone shuffles out.

In a face-to-face meeting avoid this situation by stopping at the end of the presentation and inviting people to discuss it amongst themselves for five minutes after which you'll take questions. Tell people that you'll welcome points of clarification as much as anything else.

The short discussion helps people process what they have just heard and confirm their own understanding. It always generates questions, the answers to which should be noted and circulated to underline your willingness to listen.

For large teleconferences, consider having a host to act as compere. Before the conference tell people that they are welcome to pre-submit questions. Try to persuade your CEO not to present for more than a couple of minutes and then open up questions. Do this by reminding staff that they can submit questions, but before taking the first question ask the boss a question of your own that you know people will be itching to ask. Ideally it should be tough enough to show the audience that hard questions are accepted. If your CEO has prepared their messaging they won't need prior notice, which would in any case undermine the authenticity of their reply.

Have a couple of back-up questions ready in case the flow of questions flags and to avoid closing the conference because your audience sounds like its either too horrified or bored to ask any further questions.

Building your bad news muscles

We explained earlier some processes for anticipating issues, but they do rely on us finding time to plan for something that we hope will be unnecessary. Yet, trouble will probably find you at some stage, especially if you work in a large organization or (as most of us do these days) you are in a volatile sector. Make the time, not least because it provides a valuable learning exercise for your team and you will be glad you did when things get rough.

Remember that your most vital resource is your network. Your contacts around the organization will give you early warning of impending issues, will smooth your approvals processes, provide intelligence about sentiment and help you solve problems in difficult times. Your network comes into its own as an asset during turbulent times and helps you support senior leaders with insight and the ability to make things happen on the ground when normal channels are in turmoil. If you only have capacity for one contingency preparation it should be in developing your network.

Look after yourself

Communicating tough news is tough. In fact, few of us would want it to become easy or routine. As well as caring about the people we're breaking bad news to, we're dealing with stressed senior leaders who don't always behave well in private. And many of our anxious colleagues will suspect us of holding back information or potentially being part of a conspiracy; some can forget their manners and direct their frustration at the communications team.

We therefore have to find space for ourselves and be ready to create boundaries that protect us and our teams. It is worth considering issues like placing limits on your availability during times of crisis (especially if you are in an organization that works around the clock), who will listen to your feelings and what you will and won't hold yourself accountable for. Working during crises can be exciting, intense and exhausting but in order to thrive in that environment you need strategies to preserve your compassion, equanimity, distance and ability to celebrate your own and others' successes. How you do that is a personal matter, but a sensible professional who cares for themselves and their colleagues will do it before life gets out of control.

Conclusion

To paraphrase an old saying, for an employee communicator, few things in life are certain except change and bad news. We might as well get ready for them.

There are a number of practical things we can do, such as develop our networks and anticipate the types of issues that could come our way. We can invest time in building our understanding of how our audiences think and what they value and we can make sure that leaders know we're the people who can help them when the going gets tough.

And we need to decide for ourselves some essential principles about how we manage bad news in our organization. The best boundaries are defined well before they are needed, so find time soon to decide how you would want to do things. What principles will you apply to protect the organization, your team and yourself?

Note

1 Johansen *et al* (2012) mention Weick's work on crises, which looks at how we make sense of the world around us. Anyone who wants to understand the theoretical aspects of crisis communications should find this interesting.

References

Heide, M and Simonsson, C (2013) Cross-fertilizing change and crisis research: Towards a better understanding of internal crisis communication, 3rd International Conference on Crisis Communication in the 21st Century

Johansen, W, Aggerholm, HK and Frandsen, F (2012) Entering new territory: A study of internal crisis management and crisis communication in organizations, *Public Relations Review*, **38**(2), pp 270–79

Lu, Y and Huang, YHC (2018) Getting emotional: An emotion–cognition dual-factor model of crisis communication, *Public Relations Review*, **44**(1), pp 98–107

Richter, M, König, CJ, Koppermann, C and Schilling, M (2016) Displaying fairness while delivering bad news: Testing the effectiveness of organizational bad news training in the layoff context, *Journal of Applied Psychology*, **101**(6), p 779

Strandberg, JM and Vigsø, O (2016) Internal crisis communication: An employee perspective on narrative, culture, and sensemaking, *Corporate Communications: An international journal*, **21**(1), pp 89–102

van Zoonen, W and van der Meer, T (2015) The importance of source and credibility perception in times of crisis: Crisis communication in a socially mediated era, *Journal of Public Relations Research*, **27**(5), pp 371–88

Yaxley, H (2016) Risk, issues and crisis management, in *The Public Relations Handbook*, pp 172– 196, Routledge

Is it working? 11
Employee communication evaluation and measurement that adds value

CHAPTER OBJECTIVES

Organizations run on data; without it, you're just someone with an opinion and there's no shortage of those when it comes to employee communication. This chapter builds on what we said about auditing and looks at the value of applying data to your work and the range of things that you can track. Of course, evaluation and measurement also includes listening to employees.

At the heart of our message is a powerful idea. Measurement is about action; we track because we want to help decision-making, find improvements or increase impact. If our motivation is to justify our existence, we're probably missing the point. Our aim is to help our organization achieve its goals, so as professionals we take the initiative in measuring to ensure we're making a positive difference in our work.

Why should we bother with communication evidence?

A few years ago, Liam was working on a change project and was asked to come to the monthly programme meeting attended by the CEO. Liam turned up with a presentation detailing all the activities that the communications team had planned, and some discussion points about potential issues. He never got to make the presentation. HR was ahead of communications on the agenda and the hour-long meeting was dominated by the HR director being told off about a range of failings, most of which seemed to relate to his vagueness about how the processes for which he was accountable were working and his inability to be precise about some key numbers. The CEO clearly liked data and was very unhappy; it wasn't pretty to witness. The next month, the communications team turned up with facts; they had numbers for attitude change, they found figures to explain how many colleagues had seen a video, and they managed to back up opinions with some representative verbatim comments. The HR director didn't turn up – he no longer worked for the organization.

Modern organizations run on data and facts; the data may be unreliable and the facts flimsy, but woe betide anyone walking into a leadership meeting without some evidence to support a decision or some intelligence to inform a debate. Communicators are not immune, although how some people get away with their statistical sloth is a mystery. A fact-based approach is partly what has secured our colleagues in marketing a strategic voice, but many communicators still rely on their experience or gut feel to guide leaders to do the right thing.

Let's not forget that we don't have a monopoly on opinion. Our fellow leaders are as capable as us of extrapolating a single conversation in the car park into an insight about the whole organization, or asserting a point of view based on a combination of many years' experience and a bit of personal prejudice. Why bother asking us to come to the meeting if our judgement is no better researched than their own?

Communicators need data to help organizations make better communications decisions, but the need for evaluation and tracking goes deeper than that. Securing budgets, assessing team efficiency, getting away from obsessing about tactics and moving the conversation onto strategy and helping drive improvement all need information and facts. In Chapter 2 about auditing we argued that professional communications managers need to identify what are the right things to do and then ensure that they are doing them as efficiently as possible. Both of these will certainly benefit from evidence.

However, studies seem to suggest a mixed approach to gathering data amongst communications. The long-running European Communications Monitor (Zerfass *et al*, 2018) tells us that external communications practitioners are well used to gathering data and reporting insights on media or reputational issues. Yet we hear from employee communications reports and our own experience that evaluation remains stuck on the 'to do' list for many EC practitioners. We know we should do it, but somehow never get around to it!

We suspect that people may neglect tracking and evaluation because they think its main purpose is to justify their existence, that it's too difficult, too time-consuming or that counting hit rates on the intranet is enough. When we don't pay enough attention to evaluation, we miss the opportunity to help leaders understand how better to make the most of communication.

Assuming you are not tracking and monitoring to appease an unappreciative boss, who are you hoping to engage? Do you want to help the CEO think through their messaging approach? Perhaps you would like to help a project team to understand the limits of communication and explore what else might change behaviours? Defining this part of the mix will influence the data you choose to look at and how you analyse and report it.

This is clearly a central issue at HSBC, as we can see in the next case study. The bank has made a strategic investment in communication and engagement data, and expends a lot of effort helping senior leaders apply the data to their operations across the global organization.

CASE STUDY HSBC: Insight-driven communication

At global bank HSBC, employee insight sits at the heart of the communications function. 'Research and insights are an essential part of our strategic toolkit,' says Pierre Goad, HSBC Group's most senior communicator. 'We're interested in how employees feel and act, and the role of communications in that. Over time, we've developed a reliable approach that is valued by our colleagues across the business.'

Internal communication at the bank ensures that strategy and purpose are well understood and executed. It's a role that includes helping senior stakeholders understand sentiment and how it varies across the very diverse 250,000-strong organization. 'There is so much scope for confusion and misunderstanding in the modern world; a global organization needs a mechanism to understand its true self and be faithful to its purpose,' adds Goad, who stresses the importance of evidence and facts to shape strategy.

Sitting within Goad's global communications function is a dedicated research unit led by insight specialist Marielle Clarke Price. She explains, 'When you understand what people feel and believe you can make a judgement about how people will behave. For example, if people think ethics matter, we should expect better compliance to group standards. If people believe they have the tools they need to do their job, then our corporate strategy is more likely to be implemented.'

That communications host a research function is perhaps unsurprising in a data-rational organization. Clarke Price says, 'In a time-pressured world it's good to explain things to leaders in their terms; having a consistent set of metrics enables us to have a conversation about what's changing and what action is needed, rather than explaining new data and insights every quarter.'

HSBC use insight to inform strategic decision-making, so do not use a traditional employee engagement survey approach. Rather, they use a bespoke survey to look at a range of issues, including:

- Employer advocacy – would people recommend HSBC as a place to work?
- Confidence in the organization and understanding of the strategy.
- Whether people feel equipped to do their job and be effective.
- Do people feel comfortable speaking up and voicing an opinion (especially around preventing financial crime)?
- Collaboration – how well can people navigate the complex matrix of the bank?
- Do customers feel the bank treats them fairly, can staff answer their questions, do we use their feedback?
- Employee well-being – are people being supported in the right way?
- Organizational culture – are people experiencing positive behaviours at work?

'We're interested in knowing how people feel about the bank, and most of the issues we look at serve as barometers for wider organizational health,' says Clarke Price. 'Although we are hearing things that relate to engagement in the traditional sense, like whether people feel equipped to do their jobs or their willingness to recommend HSBC as a place to work, we're aiming for a deeper insight into what it feels like to work here and what it will take for communication to be effective.'

Currently, the frequency of surveys is changing so that all staff will be surveyed twice a year (previously there was a mix of an annual staff survey and quarterly sample studies). There are eight language options that set out a number of statements in the first person. Respondents are asked how strongly they agree with the statements on a five- or ten-point scale. Clarke Price says, 'For more emotive questions we use a ten-point scale for responses as that gives a sense of the richness and subtlety of the sentiment across the bank.' The survey also has ample space for open text responses, allowing deeper insight into topics of particular interest. The survey attracts a response rate in the range of 30–40 per cent, which reflects the lack of pressure put on managers to drive completion rates. The insight team feel that not campaigning to drive up participation rates actually adds to the credibility and honesty of the responses.

The team also oversee ad hoc qualitative and quantitative research and, to balance the hard data in the survey, there is a global listening forum called Exchange. It's a bank-wide methodology that involves managers holding a frank and open discussion with their teams.

Typically, Exchange is run without an agenda as an opportunity for employees to speak freely on the topics they care about. However, in some instances Exchange is used to support employee insight by capturing feedback on themes of particular interest to senior leaders. Managers can upload a summary of these conversations to a central site and the collated results can be shared with senior leaders and inform wider insight work.

HSBC's Group Management Board gets a first view of the survey results, but this is not a data swamping exercise. 'I take the opportunity to discuss an issue with my peers on the executive rather than run through a schedule of figures,' says Goad. 'Of course, we'll share some key tracked metrics each time – we're very concerned about confidence in the organization and understanding of the strategy, for example – but it's also helpful periodically to draw out an issue like the drivers of advocacy or what makes a great people manager.' The aim is to talk about opportunities for change rather than producing tokenistic communication. Says Clarke Price, 'We want to talk about things that will lead to real movement in the data because actual change is happening.'

Dashboards and datasheets are more widely available for groups with a current minimum of 125 people (that being the level below which the margin of error could have a misleading impact). The local communications network is a core part of the process. Clarke Price explains, 'Around 30 functional and regional reports are distributed via communications business partners. They get briefed on what the data means and how to explain it.' Those business partners also have a relationship manager in the insight team to ensure they are comfortable with the report deck and how to handle the questions that are likely to come up. This is supported by ongoing training to help communicators work with the insights received and to connect to the needs of the business.

Pierre Goad stresses: 'Leaders at HSBC see insight as important and it's the job of communicators to make the connections for them between data and business goals.'

Your evaluation journey starts with deciding why you are tracking, and who needs to be involved in the conversation. You can start making choices about methodology when you have thought out the role of monitoring in:

- identifying improvements;
- helping leaders consider strategy and messages;
- understanding risk areas;
- informing project teams;
- spotting non-communications issues;
- understanding what colleagues are really thinking;
- shaping your content.

This list isn't exhaustive and you can't pick them all. We're just saying that you need to sit down and prioritize why you are evaluating. Your answer to this will shape your approach so it's best to decide at the very beginning. And, most importantly, it gets you thinking about what you are going to do with the data – you want facts that you can act upon.

What specifically should a communicator look at?

Communicators might value the online advice that the UK government provides to its professionals through its IC Space.[1] In particular, it highlights the role of evaluation in the public sector in improving performance, but there are other important reasons why you should do it.

Broadly speaking, Figure 11.1 illustrates five areas we think communication should be interested in qualifying:

- inputs;
- satisfaction;
- outputs;
- out-takes;
- outcomes.

Figure 11.1 Five areas for communication measurement

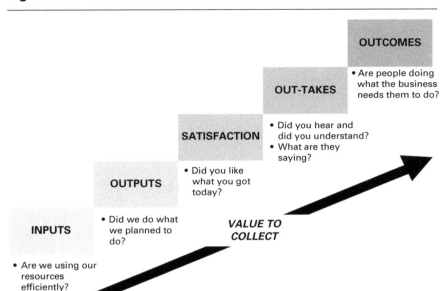

Inputs: What it takes to run communications

Sooner or later we all find ourselves having a budgeting conversation or explaining to a project director that they'll have to find the resource for their communications team or sitting in a meeting with a finance director who wants cost savings and expects everyone to make a sacrifice! We suggest two approaches to consider.

The first is to ask what value internal communication contributes to the organization and what would seem a good investment to secure the communications team's contribution. Of course, it's hard to claim exclusive credit for making something happen, but if our involvement is an essential part of the plan to deliver $10 million in cost savings or to achieve a €1 million jump in revenue we have the starting point for a conversation about how much resource is needed.

The second approach is to think about where you add value across the range of your activities. The questions we raise in Chapter 2 on auditing should help here, but essentially you need to think about how much of your effort goes into:

- gathering and sharing intelligence;

- planning and coordination;

- ensuring messages align with business needs;

- running channels;

- supporting line managers;

- supporting leaders;

- supporting projects.

You might have a longer list of core activities, but once you have decided what proportion of your staff time or budget is going into each you can ask if the split is appropriate considering the usefulness of each activity to the organization.

Sadly, there is no reliable reference point for how much time, effort and money is needed to run communications. Attempts to benchmark the size of employee communications departments, for example, might notice similarities within sectors but then issues of country, history, culture or profitability might muddy the waters. We might attempt to compare the cost of running an intranet or introducing Office 365, but again organizational complexity, the differing needs of stakeholders and the geographic spread of the workforce might make it impossible to draw parallels between entities.

Our view is that your judgement and a sense of the value you intend to create are your guide.

Outputs

Throughout this book we have distinguished between the things we produce, such as content or events, and the results we achieve in terms of understanding or behaviours. Whilst we have stressed the importance of asking about the intended effect of our activity we must never neglect to think about the outputs we produce.

Closely allied to understanding whether we have the right inputs or resources is the question of whether we are using them efficiently and the need to understand what is working smoothly and what is not. We are therefore likely to be interested in the following:

- **Activity against plan**: Did we do the things we planned to, and why is there a variation? Perhaps we set out to update the news pages on the staff portal twice a week but only managed it once a fortnight on average; was that because we were short staffed or there's a failure in how we collect news? Maybe we need a more realistic plan next year?

- **Quality:** Subjectively, is the content we produced good enough? Is it full of mistakes or unimaginative? Are we producing the same boring stuff and could it be time to find some new formats?

- **Participation and reach:** How many people looked at the item on the intranet, downloaded the video, attended the town hall? We should have a pretty good idea of the overall reach of each channel and for typical content types. We should also have a sense of which segments of our workforce are seeing what. For example, producing beautiful material about safety is a waste of time if people in high-risk jobs can't see it because it is only available online and they don't have access. If we are missing out sections of the workforce, what are we going to do about it?

- **Reaction:** Did our communication interest people enough for them to respond at the simplest levels? Do we have the facility for people to 'like' content on the intranet? How many people opened the email and clicked through to the web link? Which conversations generated the widest involvement on the social platform? How many people took part in the competition? If we routinely don't get any reaction is it because we are boring people rigid or is there something we're missing?

- **On message:** What proportion of our content reflects the defined messages? Is the popular material actually about the things we want to talk about and if not, how are we going to make our messages more sticky?

We need to be careful about the volume of data we collect across the whole realm of measurement and evaluation, but it is in the area of considering outputs that we need to be especially wary. Web usage statistics and email tracking, for example, can give you a ton of information and leave you struggling for useful insight. Unless you have the resources for a full-time data scientist you will want to pick a few meaningful indicators and follow them. Leave the fuller data sets for an annual deep dive.

Concentrate on data that helps you draw actionable conclusions. Is it really useful to know which videos were most viewed unless there are lessons you can apply to the least-viewed films? If your news pages exist only to publish on-message material, is there any value in knowing that 98 per cent of content month-on-month is on message?[2]

Satisfaction

Employee communication does not exist solely for the benefit of senior leadership and their desire to charm the workforce. Our agenda as internal communications reflects the needs of our colleagues at all levels of the organization. They want to talk to each other and share problems and solutions, and being listened to is one of the main drivers of engagement.

The extent to which employees feel satisfied with communication matters for us. The indicators of satisfaction can be quite simple. It might be asking people leaving a town hall meeting whether the information they received was helpful or we can look for online comments about the availability or completeness of information.

If you needed more robust data, a focus group or a survey might ask about:

- Timeliness: Did you hear in time or is it too late?
- Volume: Did we share enough?
- Interest: Is what we're sharing interesting?
- Clarity: Is it understandable?
- Usefulness: Does the information address your need?
- Credibility: Do you believe it?
- Did you get a chance to have your say?

Remember that satisfaction is actually made up of expectation and experience, and be sure to understand both parts. Consider asking specific questions about whether the speed, volume, clarity, etc of what they received lived up to expectations.

It is our mission to build dialogue and mutual understanding inside our organization and reporting satisfaction is an opportunity to raise awareness among senior leaders of how staff see things. We find it useful to use verbatim quotations in our reports to bring the voice of the employee to life and to highlight how good communication helps people work better.

Out-takes

We're in the business for communicating with a purpose; outcomes matter. And now we're going to make a small distinction between the organizational results we want to support, called outcomes (which we look at in the next section), and out-takes – whether people actually hear and understand the messages we're trying to put over.

There are a number of ways to do this. One of the simplest we've come across was for a fast food chain that routinely ended intranet stories with an easy and fun multiple-choice quiz, the answers to which were contained in the story. As long as the prize was attractive (and we discovered monetary value didn't actually matter) you would have a crude but useful indicator of how many people actually got the message.

We probably wouldn't want to use this approach for complex or difficult messages but surveying people to establish whether they had heard, understood or retained information is straightforward. Measurement expert Angela Sinickas has written widely on the subject of techniques and provides excellent resources on her website[3] and practitioners might also be interested to read Susan Walker on the subject of designing your questionnaire (Walker, 2012: 71–77).

Outcomes

In Chapter 3 we talked about do/feel/know in the context of planning objectives. What people should know is the out-take part of the objective. We also need to consider how we'll measure the do (the desired behaviour) and feel (the desired belief or sentiment we would like to encourage).

We've said elsewhere that driving behaviour is not just about communication and can depend on a complex mix of factors, such the availability of training, resources to do the job, a supportive manager or anything else you care to imagine. Attributing behaviour to communication is a big challenge and a reliable methodology for demonstrating return on investment in communication is still a dream.

However, we can go a long way towards testing if our communication had the intended effect. Naturally, it starts with our objective-setting and being clear what result we wanted from our communication. Do we have a defined set of behaviours we're trying to promote or is our mission to share a positive frame of reference about the organization, its customers or processes? Without clarity about why we are communicating we will struggle to evaluate whether we have achieved anything.

Actually there may be rare occasions when we can directly link behaviours to our communication. For example, we might have two groups who get different communication and we can see different behaviours. Imagine you have two factories and you run a quality campaign in one of them. Can we see improvements in the factory where we ran the campaign that are significantly different to the factory where we didn't? Perhaps we know that our message didn't reach a certain segment of the population for technical reasons; we could compare the behaviour of this 'control group' to the rest of the workforce. However, these opportunities are rare and typically we have to look for proxy indicators – signs that something is changing.

Often, we use survey questions that explore:

- Intention to act – how far do people agree with the statements:

    'I see the need to do XYZ.'

    'I will do XYZ at the next opportunity.'

- Reporting behaviours – what level of agreement is there to statements such as:

    'I see people doing ABC in my workplace.'

    'I am doing ABC.'

    'Doing ABC has been useful...'

If your objective has been to build a culture or a common frame of reference, attitudinal questions in a survey will be useful.

One of the benefits of surveying is that you can repeat the questionnaire over time, and assuming your population doesn't change or your samples are similar you can see trends. Often on change programmes we ask whether people:

- are aware of a change;
- understand what the change means;
- think the change is a good idea;
- are able to make the change themselves;
- are seeing change happen around them;
- are actually changing themselves;
- are seeing benefits from change.

In the early stage of the change we can hope to get positive responses to the awareness question and later in the change process we expect people to begin to say they are seeing change happen. The trend over the different moments when we survey will give us a good feel for whether our communication is having an impact, especially if we make sure to ask whether people have the tools, resources or training they need to act differently.

Finally, you may enjoy greater success with your tracking if you can break down your desired behaviours into small elements. For example, we worked on a project to improve performance management for one organization.

As well as tracking HR data about completed and recorded performance reviews we also looked at very specific things like the numbers of manager packs downloaded from the HR homepage and the dates when review records were updated. These could be cross-referenced to the dates when our communications went live and usefully told us which messages were not working.

Owning your own data

In many organizations we have found a concern that researching attitudes could be disruptive or somehow undermine the validity of the employee engagement survey. IT functions might dislike the use of survey software or feel uncomfortable about whitelisting a specific survey package's URL. Some organizations claim that the handful of generic communication satisfaction questions in the engagement survey should provide ample insight about internal communication, even if the survey only happens every two years.

This is something we should always push against. We're professionals expected to do a professional job and that involves gathering metrics to inform our work. Try telling an engineer that they can't have their gauges or an accountant that they're not allowed to know how quickly cash is being collected and you'd get some odd reactions. Our colleagues need to get used to the fact that employee communicators use data.

Thankfully, many of the data gathering tactics that are available to us do not need permission from other people. Large-scale surveys might step on the toes of whoever is running the annual survey, but smaller sample polls or working with panels may well give us as much quantitative data as we need. There are some excellent resources available for the communicator who wants to learn more about conducting their quantitative study[4] and developing the capability within your team is always a smart move.

Specifically, we can recommend:

- **A simple team call out:** On a regular basis, the whole team takes a couple of hours to call a set number of colleagues and asks a small number of questions. The responses are entered directly into a tool like Survey Monkey or Google Forms. This approach can also be deployed very quickly during a crisis or if senior leaders need a response on a key issue.

- **The regular panel:** Recruit a body of a couple of hundred people from around the organization and periodically ask them to complete a short questionnaire. We do this often with change programmes and, if chosen with care, the group can provide a good sounding board for sentiment and awareness of communication messages. Panel members need incentivizing, but that can be little more than evidence that the CEO is hearing their thoughts or a regular thank-you event. Over time, you need to switch out a proportion of the members and recruit new people on a rolling basis to keep the group fresh.

- **The sample survey:** As consultants with limited networks in the organizations we support during change we need a quick and effective mechanism to understand what messages are landing and where penetration is weak. We mentioned earlier a simple sample survey that works with just a few hundred respondents. We deliberately segment the sample as little as possible – perhaps only making sure that the numbers polled for different regions or divisions are in proportion to the overall demographic of the organization. This approach means we can move quickly and enable actions to be focused on large groups. Whilst this approach overlooks some of the subtlety of how different groups are thinking, its simplicity makes it practical. Even small amounts of insight are powerful during change.

- **Focus groups:** Organizing and facilitating focus groups is a skilled job but not difficult. Unless there are sensitivities about using an internal member of the team, every employee communications function does well to develop the capability to lead qualitative research. A communicator who has run discussions with their colleagues is always much more influential in conversations with stakeholders because they have an authentic understanding of what people are thinking and feeling. We also find that the quality of our content or the material we produce for leaders is greatly enhanced by actually hearing the voices of the people we work with and who will be reading what we have written.

In our case study from Mubadala we see how the company used a variety of research approaches to reach its 66,000 employees. Even a single simple approach will pay dividends, but exploring different ways to listen will help you develop your audience awareness and messaging but most importantly add real value to your organization.

CASE STUDY   Mubadala: Listening during change

When the Mubadala investment company merged with the International Petroleum Investment Company (IPIC), it created a global powerhouse for Abu Dhabi, with over 68,000 employees. During the change and integration process, Head of Internal Corporate Relations Umayma Abubakar saw it as a key role of her team to be a conduit between employees and the leadership team: 'Our leaders are the voice of the company. People need to hear from them, not us. We see ourselves as the facilitators of a conversation, making sure leaders are sensitive to how people are feeling and pay attention to the right things.'

Abubakar was initially conscious of differences in culture between the two merging organizations: 'We were nervous about what it would mean to bring together two very different types of population. We wanted to make sure everyone had a chance to be heard and could participate in shaping the new company.'

One of the first things the team did was a series of walk-arounds of the two head offices. Team members took a list of criteria to observe on their visits. Abubakar explains, 'They had a log to capture everything they saw and heard, from how it was to walk into reception, to the layout and atmosphere of the office, to what it was like to take part in a meeting. They would note things such as "I walked in and I was welcomed", or "It was very quiet"; "meetings were taking place behind closed doors in offices" or "people were gathering for collaborative conversations in open spaces".'

The team took their observations into focus groups, to find out what people liked or disliked. Findings were used to help leaders be mindful of people's concerns and preferred way of doing things, and keep them top of mind in their daily communication. 'We wouldn't give leaders a script,' says Abubakar. 'But we would say, "Take time to acknowledge the gorilla in the room." Or, "Be aware that if you're in this building, people can find it harder to have open conversations – try bringing them together in small huddles."'

Findings also led to practical actions, such as giving out office maps. Sometimes they led to larger changes: 'Eventually we changed the layout of one of the offices to make both offices feel the same.'

In addition, the team established a network of 20 engagement champions who met face-to-face for 90 minutes each month. Their role was to be informed about colleagues' views, give feedback, and test forward plans. The agenda was driven by the communications team, but others could also request a slot.

Clear expectations are set about what is needed from the champions, and what support they will receive in return. Their contributions have been formalized into key performance indicators, and are included in their performance objectives. Abubakar explains, 'Our mutual agreement is that they attend a certain number of meetings, that they stay well informed about views in their part of the organization and gather and provide feedback, when asked.'

The final route available to the team is a quarterly pulse survey. It asks 15 questions. Five questions are consistent; the remaining 10 are used to seek views about whatever is most important for the organization during the quarter, such as introducing shared values or a new performance management system.

Data from all sources of formal and informal feedback, with recommendations for action, is compiled into a quarterly engagement report. Abubakar comments, 'We don't communicate it out. It's sent to the executive team as an aide to help leaders be more effective, and to feed back potential problem areas to the organization.'

Abubakar's advice to others is to make sure employees have a voice. 'Listening is a big part of change management. Leaders should know about the issues, as they walk around the corridors. Often you don't need scripts or campaigns. You just need to remind leaders to keep talking, be visible, and be sensitive to people's emotions and needs.'

(The above represents the individual opinion of Umayma Abubakar and is not to be construed in any manner as the opinion of the Mubadala Investment Company.)

Analysis and insight

For most of the data we collect, the conclusions are obvious. If only 100 people in a 100,000-strong organization viewed a video aimed at all staff we can safely say the video didn't achieve its objective. And most of the time we can work out what we need to do to fix the problem; perhaps the video needs to appear on the front page of the intranet, or we should find a way to get people talking about it on Yammer. If we need more insight from a survey we might consider holding a few focus groups to ask people what they didn't understand about a key message or why they are dissatisfied with communications.

We can also give some thought to doing some deeper statistical analysis on our data, assuming we have it in enough detail or quantity. With access to raw survey data we can look for correlations between how people answered questions such as whether people who think we are a good employer are also heavy users of the intranet. Do people who are dissatisfied with the CEO's communications also think that change is handled unfairly?

In Chapter 4 we mentioned other processes that will enable you to segment your audiences according to their attitudes. A conversation with a data scientist will uncover whether insights about communication behaviours can be extracted from your other data sources such as web statistics and combined with your surveying. Naturally, the results will be more useful for larger organizations or where the data is very rich. However, any statistical review will throw up insights that were not immediately obvious and will be worthy of consideration.

Reporting for action

The point about evaluation is to act on the results. If you only want to justify your budget, facts alone will not help and you have probably already lost the argument if producing statistics is the only way you can be taken seriously. But engaging colleagues in a conversation about improvement will build on the shared understanding of the value of communication and engage leaders in better communication.

When you think about reporting you need to be clear about what you are not going to include. Your boss probably doesn't care about how many people saw the video, how many people had a team briefing and how many stories you published this quarter. You should therefore provide this sort of information sparingly and think about the story you would like to tell around it. For example, if only 25 per cent of people opened the CEO's email do you have additional insights to suggest why and how you get a different result next month? You are more likely to engage leaders if you can talk about whether people change behaviour, if they are excited or what colleagues are talking about.

We have developed an approach to reporting that uses a single page divided into six sections. Figure 11.2 sets out the format, which is easily translated in to an infographic. It works well as a conversation plan, working through each section in sequence and engaging your audience in a discussion about the steps we need to take next.

The exact content of your scorecard will reflect your needs and the problems facing your organization. However, the key point is to focus the discussion on actions and improvements. If you have performed well this format says it loud and clear and you do not need to discuss it further.

Figure 11.2   Standard report format

A	B	C
GENERAL FEEDBACK THIS PERIOD	**ATTITUDINAL SCORES AGAINST BUSINESS OBJECTIVES**	**ACTIVITY COMPLETED THIS PERIOD**
• In general what are people saying or thinking about? • Are these things the boss should care about?	• How well are our messages being understood? • Are people planning on acting on our messages? • Are these results what we wanted?	• What did we do and how successful were our outputs? • Is our activity delivering the outcomes we are seeking?

D	E	F
WHAT WE'RE PLANNING TO DO NEXT PERIOD	**ISSUES THAT ARE COMING AND HOW THEY'LL BE MANAGED**	**HOT SPOT PROBLEMS**
• Here's a list of what is planned. • Is this going to move the needles in boxes A and B? • Is this better than box C?	• Big events are coming for which we need to plan.	• The issues that are not going away.

Conclusion

We're professionals. Collecting data and bringing evidence-based insights says it powerfully and clearly. And as professionals we are interested in doing our jobs better and achieving real results for our organization. What we measure says what is important in our world. So although many of us struggle to find the time, amid competing demands, when we can set priorities through measurement and reporting we are better placed to add the value that we think matters to our organization. That's what professionals do.

Notes

1 The Government Communication Service sponsors a best practice site covering employee communications called the IC Space – its section on evaluation contains some useful case studies and advice: https://communication.cabinetoffice.gov.uk/ic-space/evaluation/

2 The UK's Chartered Institute of Public Relations has produced a useful one-page guide to measurement processes and is particularly interesting in this area. See the CIPR measurement matrix here: http://ciprinside.co.uk/wp-content/uploads/2012/07/Measurement-Matrix-FINAL.pdf

3 Angeal Sinickas' website is https://www.sinicom.com/resources/publications/

4 Susan Walker's 2012 book *Employee Engagement and Communication Research* and Angela Sinickas' website are good guides, as is Liam FitzPatrick and Klavs Valskov's *Internal Communications* (2014).

References

Bolman, LG and Deal, TE (2017) *Reframing Organizations: Artistry, choice, and leadership*, John Wiley & Sons

FitzPatrick, L and Valskov, K (2014) *Internal Communications: A manual for practitioners*, Kogan Page

Walker, S (2012) *Employee Engagement and Communication Research: Measurement, strategy and action*, Kogan Page

Zerfass, A, Tench, R, Verhoeven, P, Verčič, D and Moreno, A (2018) European Communication Monitor 2018: Strategic communication and the challenges of fake news, trust, leadership, work stress and job satisfaction – Results of a survey in 48 Countries. [Online] http://www.communicationmonitor.eu/2018/06/13/ecm-european-communication-monitor-2018/

Communicating on purpose   12

Helping employees find meaning in the modern workplace

CHAPTER OBJECTIVES

As we were sitting down to write this, we came across an online news report about a retailer that had recently gone out of business, leaving hundreds of people without jobs. One of the reader comments caught our eye. It was from a former employee. They said that people had had the potential to be part of something fantastic, if only the company had taken the time to establish what it was really about. Instead, the sole focus had been on making money. And now people had been left with nothing.

It was a sad and sobering read. A story of hopes dashed, of employees who had wanted to be part of something, but whose experience of work revolved instead around going in every day to earn a pay cheque and chase sales targets, to help a company earn money for its owners.

Shouldn't work be about more than that?

This chapter will explore the role communicators can play in helping people find meaning at work, through connecting them to a bigger purpose – the 'something fantastic' this former employee had hoped for. It will explain why purpose matters to people, explore why it has emerged as a hot topic for organizations, and share four examples of how companies are working with purpose in practice.

Why does purpose matter, for people and organizations?

Having 'meaningful purpose' makes our lives more satisfying and fulfilling. A meaningful life is one of positive psychologist Martin Seligman's three paths to happiness. He describes it as 'using your signature strengths in the service of something larger than you are' (Seligman, 2002: 249). Likewise, Dan Pink (2018) explains that it's in our nature to seek purpose, describing those who strive for something bigger than themselves as the most deeply motivated, most productive and satisfied at work. And people are, increasingly, seeking purpose in the workplace, particularly the newest generation of employees.

From a business perspective, the EY Beacon Institute (2016) describes an environment in which the rules of the game are changing, and suggests that focusing on short-term profits is not enough. Across the world, social inequality is rising and within companies the pay gap between top and bottom has grown. Big business is viewed with suspicion and mistrust, especially by younger generations. People increasingly expect companies to think long term, work in environmentally sustainable ways and address social challenges. If they are not happy with what they see, hear or experience, they have the power to spread the word about it via social media.

In short, stakeholders – whether customers, employees, investors or communities – are asking fundamental questions about society, and organizations' role within it. In the past, companies may have responded with change based on a fear-based rhetoric of 'standing on a burning platform'. This time, many companies are responding by seeking to bring people together around something fulfilling – a sense of meaning and purpose (EY Beacon Institute, 2016).

What exactly *is* a purpose?

Purpose in the workplace is the same as in the rest of our lives – it's about contributing to something bigger than ourselves. Essentially it's about the *why*. As Simon Sinek puts it: '*Why* does your company exist? *Why* do you get out of bed every morning? And *why* should anyone care?' (2009: 39).

A good purpose should be meaningful to those who hear it, connecting to emotions, crossing boundaries and appealing to employees, customers, communities and investors alike. The EY Beacon Institute suggest it should 'be grounded in humanity and inspire a call to action' (2014: 10).

You may be wondering what the difference is between the purpose, the vision and the mission. Good question. Visions and missions are about the *what*. A vision inspirationally sets out what the company wants to be several years ahead, whilst the mission factually describes what business the organization is in (Kenny, 2014). According to Sinek (2009) a company's purpose is found by looking back, to the reason the company exists. Every company, he points out, starts out as an idea from someone (or a group) who wanted to strive for something bigger than themselves. There lies the clue to the 'why'.

It's certainly true for our case study organizations. So let's pause here, and take a step back in time with MSD.

CASE STUDY   MSD: 'What gets me out of bed in the morning'

Global pharmaceutical company MSD is also known as Merck & Co Inc of Kenilworth, New Jersey, USA in the United States and Canada. In 1950, the company's then president George W Merck said, 'We try never to forget that medicine is for the people. It is not for the profits. The profits follow, and if we have remembered that, they have never failed to appear.' Internal Communication Manager Clare Warren says this quote still resonates with employees. 'If you asked people, they'd know it. We're a business, but we always link back to putting patients at the heart of what we do.'

Over three years, the company have focused on connecting their people to the company's purpose, setting out to help them 'build our story, know our story, tell our story', and feel proud of the role they play in patient care. Warren explains, 'It can be difficult for employees when your company isn't a household name, and you're in a heavily regulated industry, so they can't talk about your products. Building our story was about looking at who we are, what we do and why we do it above and beyond our brands and products.'

MSD's purpose is 'inventing for life'. Building the story meant holding fact-finding workshops, focus groups and competitions, asking employees what this phrase meant for them and collecting their stories. Warren says, 'We talk about working with our people, through our partnerships, for our patients. Our corporate narrative starts with our people and shows how they are the ones who make things happen. We've focused on getting to know them and asking "What gets you out of bed in the morning?"'

For the first time, the company's external communications put its people in the spotlight. A UK corporate video shows a ficticious day in the life of a young girl, Joanna, and her father. It's punctuated by employees talking about why they feel proud to be part of MSD. As the last employee asks 'What gets me out of bed in the morning?' the video ends by sharing that Joanna's father has been in remission from his illness for six months.

Another video and poster campaign is about getting to know more about MSD's people. Warren comments, 'One of our reps emailed to say a doctor said they'd seen her in her climbing gear. She's a mountain rescue person in her spare time. All full-time employees get 40 paid volunteering hours per year, and she brought this into her story. Other people have told me they showed the videos to their family and friends. It raises esteem internally, and builds trust externally.'

Other more light-hearted tactics have cost nothing. A Yammer campaign asking 'What gets you out of bed in the morning?' led some people to post videos or comments about the difference they make, whilst others put up photos of their dog or cat! A pyjama day was another fun way of keeping the phrase in people's minds.

An annual 'inventing for life' week celebrates the purpose and what's being achieved. It's split into three sections: people, partners and patients. In 2018, the 'people' section focused on well-being at work and included a talk from a well-known mental health campaigner. 'Partners' featured case studies, as well as a panel discussion featuring a digital start-up company MSD has supported. Warren comments: 'We have a saying – "Brave enough to want to change the world, but smart enough to know we can't do it alone". Our partners look to us, but in turn we can learn from them about new ways of doing things.' The 'patients' section always includes a patient sharing their story.

So, is it working? 'From focus groups, we know "What gets me out of bed in the morning?" is resonating strongly. We use it to frame activities, and people are using it themselves – it's popping up in employee videos and was used in business planning round discussions.'

And what's been different about this approach for the communications team? Warren says, 'We've never been so closely aligned with our external communications; it's been one plan to reach all audiences – and it's really helped. We showcase employees all the time now on Twitter and LinkedIn. We've also gone much more bottom-up. Senior leaders have got involved, but we haven't asked them to. We have great internal networks that we tap into, and they've supported us with everything from helping us understand how things might land in the field to getting conversations started on Yammer.

'Above all, what I've loved doing is putting our people at the heart of what we do.'

How can communicators work with purpose?

MSD's case study gives some great examples of how communicators can work with purpose. They have:

- communicated the purpose and helped people connect with it, by asking employees what it means to them and collecting their stories;
- showed the impact employees have on people's lives, through sharing the stories of patients, and showing how people's different roles contributed to them;
- worked with their external communications colleagues to align the purpose message internally and externally;
- used the purpose to frame other projects and activities, so it serves as a 'north star', guiding decision-making and action;
- celebrated successes and progress, within the context of the purpose;
- used the power of the network to get people involved and talking about it.

When we talked about framing in Chapter 5 we shared the idea that people use a model or frame to explain the world around them. Bolman and Deal (2017) argue that leaders tend to talk about change in task- or goal-focused terms but that this 'structural' frame is just one of four models available to them to explain plans and engage people:

- structural: task-orientated and focused on strategy, setting goals, clarifying tasks, systems, procedures and metrics;
- HR: focused on people's needs for personal growth and job satisfaction;
- political: related to coalition-building and power bases at times of difficult choices;
- symbolic: focused on purpose and meaning.

Do you see how you could potentially talk about the same issue or scenario from any one of these four perspectives? Pink (2018) reminds us that the language of business often involves words such as 'efficiency', 'value' and 'differentiation'. Rational, factual, corporate words. The language of purpose is human and emotional. If you're in the 'purpose' space, make sure you and your leaders are talking the language of purpose. Aim to connect to people's hearts, not their heads.

Our next case study illustrates two more ways communicators can work with purpose:

- helping to draft and define the purpose statement;
- helping leaders to work with and articulate the purpose in their own way.

CASE STUDY   The Body Shop: Revitalizing the company's purpose

At the beginning of 2018, The Body Shop had a new CEO, a new parent company and a transformation programme comprising 17 workstreams. First on the list, in workstream one, was revitalizing the company's purpose.

Founded in 1976 by Dame Anita Roddick, The Body Shop had gained a reputation as an ethical pioneer through its sourcing of natural ingredients, sustainable practices and cruelty-free stance against animal testing. Thirty years later, Roddick sold the business to beauty giant L'Oréal, a move that surprised many. As a retail business, The Body Shop was not a natural fit within the global cosmetics group, financial performance suffered and in 2017 the company was sold to Brazilian cosmetics company Natura.

Change Communications Manager Emma Ridgeon explains, 'In fact, Anita Roddick had met with Natura's co-founders in Brazil some years earlier to discuss community trade as they share a similar heritage and ethical stance with The Body Shop. After the sale to Natura was completed in September 2017, the co-founders wrote to employees about how they had admired the company from afar for many years. The tone was very warm and personal, quite romantic, using the analogy of courtship and a marriage.'

It was clear the values of the two companies were aligned. Ridgeon continues, 'When Natura's co-founders came to the UK as our new parents, one of the first things they did was sign our petition against animal testing in cosmetics. It felt symbolic. All their scheduled visits took longer than planned because they wanted to meet and talk with everyone. They also planted a Brazilian tree in the grounds of The Body Shop offices in Littlehampton. People warmed to them immediately, they said it felt like we'd come home.

'The project to revitalize The Body Shop's purpose is about reconnecting with the company's core DNA in a way that's also forward-looking. So many of the causes that Anita Roddick was passionate about are highly relevant today: seeing nature as a source of inspiration, reducing plastics and packaging, celebrating beauty without cruelty and championing equality.

'We didn't need to create our purpose, it already existed. We needed to redefine it, in a way that would resonate for the 21st century.'

The team enlisted the help of a specialist agency who pored over Roddick's writing and archives, and interviewed employees and franchise partners around the globe. Four working groups were established to focus on specific aspects of developing the purpose, and a company-wide survey asked all employees three questions:

- What do you believe The Body Shop stood for in the past?
- What do you believe The Body Shop stands for today?
- What are your hopes for the future?

After months of conversations, analysis, drafting and testing, The Body Shop's purpose was defined and ready for internal roll-out. It was set out in a Little Book of Purpose for leaders, with a set of underpinning principles and guidance about how the purpose should be brought to life, internally at first but ultimately through product launches, campaigns and in-store experiences.

For the remainder of 2018 the company focused on helping its leaders understand, explore and connect with the purpose, starting with a two-day leadership event in September. This began with a scripted conversation between two of the company's executive directors, taking leaders on a journey from the opening of the first shop in Brighton, through the highs and lows of the company's history, to the present-day market challenges and opportunities. The purpose and guiding principles were explained and articulated within this context.

With the purpose focusing on core themes of fairness and beauty, leaders then split into small groups to experience what can happen when the world is neither fair nor beautiful, through the harrowing personal stories of people from different walks of life who had experienced this first-hand. Ridgeon comments, 'We heard powerful accounts from people who'd been trafficked, abused, or discriminated against. There were tears. The aim was to jolt people out of their everyday lives and show that these things are not happening to "someone else, somewhere else".'

Throughout the event, leaders were prompted to reflect on what they saw and heard, and their emotional response to it: 'How was I feeling when I heard this?', 'Why might this topic matter to me?' and 'How do I connect this to our purpose?' Leaders used personal workbooks in facilitated sessions to unpack key themes, and to reflect on their own sense of purpose.

A follow-up session for leaders then focused on storytelling. Ridgeon explains, 'The point is not that we all have to tell the same story, but that we each have to find our own way of connecting with the purpose. It's not about 'learning the lines'. It's about telling your story of what makes *you* proud and where you can take action to make positive lasting change.'

The need for authenticity: Working with purpose for the right reasons

The Body Shop case demonstrates a point made by the EY Beacon Institute (2016) that defining an organization's future is often about going 'back to the future'. It's about revelation rather than invention, rediscovering what a business originally set out to do. As the years pass, *what* exactly the organization does – the products it offers, for example, may change. But the original *why* remains, waiting to be revealed.

The timing was right for The Body Shop to revitalize its purpose. The company invested many months of time in poring over company archives, talking with people to draft and test the words, and then working through how the purpose would be embedded into the business.

Of course, there are also not-so-good reasons to work with purpose. Quinn and Thakor (2018) note that purpose has become such a popular topic that even leaders who don't personally believe in it may feel pressured to step on board and start crafting statements. It's not a good starting point. On a slightly different topic, surely many of us have experienced organizations that placed framed copies of their values around the place and then took not a blind bit of notice of them in reality?

Similarly, purpose is not – or shouldn't be – a superficial branding exercise. Rather, it should be a genuine intention to focus the way an organization works around a more meaningful intention than short-term profits. That means that whilst we have a key role to play in communicating the purpose, there is a much bigger job to be done, in making it real. If the words say one thing and leaders' actions and decisions say something else, the whole exercise will cause more harm than good. Pink (in Stewart, 2017) calls it 'window dressing' and says 'It's worse to have fake purpose than no purpose.' As Quinn and Thakor (2018) put it, 'If your purpose is authentic, people know, because it drives every decision and you do things other companies would not.'

Our next case study looks to a business that is well known in the UK for its ways of working. It's a company in which communication and purpose go hand in hand... but in quite different ways to how we've seen so far.

CASE STUDY John Lewis Partnership: Sharing the responsibilities and rewards of ownership

For Rory Campbell, Partnership Registrar at UK retailer The John Lewis Partnership, purpose is about helping people feel a sense of meaning. This makes communication essential. 'Every Monday morning we talk together in teams about the previous week's sales performance and what we'll do about it in the next week. In detail. I have never worked in an organization where people know their business as well as they do here.'

Campbell explains, 'We talk a lot about two-way communication and sharing knowledge, because it's consistent with what we stand for. It's based on the philosophy that we're not employees as you'd find in any other PLC. We call ourselves Partners. We want people to feel like owners of this business. To make choices and use their judgement to know where best to place their effort.'

The philosophy dates back to the vision and ideals of the Partnership's founder, John Spedan Lewis. The eldest of two sons whose father opened the first John Lewis store, he learned that he, his father and brother between them were earning more than the combined wage bill of the company's then 300 employees. This didn't sit comfortably with him, and he began introducing practices to improve working conditions, including shorter working days, staff committees, and an in-house magazine, *The Gazette*. For their time (1914–18) these were radical ideas indeed.

Later, he handed the company over to a trust on behalf of the people working in it. The company doesn't answer to shareholders. It answers to its 83,000 Partners. Each receives an annual share of profits, via a bonus. The same percentage is paid to every Partner Campbell explains, 'It wasn't purely about being philanthropic. John Spedan Lewis believed if people shared in the rewards of the business, they would be more willing to share in its challenges.' This belief forms the basis of Principle 1 in the company's constitution: 'The Partnership's ultimate purpose is the happiness of all its members, through their worthwhile and satisfying employment in a successful business. Because the Partnership is owned in trust for its members, they share the responsibilities of ownership as well as its rewards – profit, knowledge and power.'

Campbell comments, 'It's not a purpose in a way most people would think of one. If I'm critical of the way some companies approach purpose, that's because it can become a branding exercise. Often what's lacking is the organizational substance behind it. In our case, the purpose statement isn't the point. The point is everything we do that makes it real.'

One important way of sharing knowledge and power is the company's system of operating on democratic principles. In 1919, John Spedan Lewis introduced a Partnership council, an elected body representing the company's Partners. 'It's a way of giving Partners a meaningful voice in their business, sharing responsibility and providing a 'check and balance' to the executive,' explains Campbell. Today, the Council still plays an important part in influencing company policy, and is replicated at different levels of the organization, through to store level. Each forum brings Partners together with a manager who can make decisions. Campbell explains, 'It goes back to the founder saying the people best placed to understand customers are those serving them every day. For example, it's common for teams to influence resourcing levels by sharing their insight about quality of service and operational control, whilst understanding the financial implications.'

Another key mechanism is *The Gazette*. Whilst the humble company newsletter may seem insignificant in some organizations, for the John Lewis Partnership it's an important connection to its founder. Campbell explains, 'Its purpose is to tell the owners of this business what they want and need to know about their business. It's not there to be a management mouthpiece.' Published weekly, *The Gazette* includes Partner letters and management replies. Anyone can write a letter. Unless it's commercially sensitive or defamatory, it must be published on the intranet or in *The Gazette*, and management must answer.

Says Campbell, 'Again, it's about sharing knowledge and power. If communication were only one way, people would not be taking their share of responsibility for delivering the business. If we create mechanisms for sharing responsibility and holding management to account, we close the gap between top and bottom.' He concludes, 'I believe the most energized, resilient businesses are those with a clear sense of purpose. And communication has an essential role in helping organizations to clarify, leverage and deliver it.'

Making purpose personal

So far, we've looked at purpose from the company-wide view. In our final case study, things get personal. Unilever helps each person discover their own purpose. It helps teams discover their team 'why'. And all within the bigger context of the company's overarching purpose. We were fascinated to hear about the stories people bring with them to Unilever's workshops. The topics are set out in this case study. Why not find your own stories, and see where they take you?

CASE STUDY   Unilever: Purposeful people

'People with purpose thrive.' So says Tim Munden, Chief Learning Officer for fast-moving consumer goods company Unilever, describing why the business has invested in helping thousands of employees discover their purpose.

Munden sets the context: 'Purpose runs through Unilever. Our purpose is to make sustainable living commonplace, and we do that through our Unilever Sustainable Living Plan, which sets out three big goals for the business on improving health and well-being, reducing environmental impact and enhancing livelihoods. We know that purpose-driven companies create long-term value. We also know that consumers are increasingly drawn to brands and products with an evident sense of social or environmental purpose that goes well beyond basic function. Similarly, brands with purpose grow. And if you want a purpose-driven business, you need purpose-driven people.'

The company's 160,000 people turn these plans into reality. Munden continues: 'The learning team's work in this area follows two paths: developing purposeful leaders and helping everyone in the business discover their purpose. We started helping our senior leaders discover their purpose back in 2010. In 2017 we opened that across our business, and by the end of 2018, 30,000 employees had attended a 'discover your purpose' workshop. Our ambition is to have reached 50,000 by the end of 2019.'

The 'discover your purpose' workshops are based on asking participants to reflect on their life experiences and bring them to life through sharing stories. Beforehand, participants are asked to prepare personal stories around four themes:

- When I was young.
- The challenge that shaped me.
- Sparking my interest.
- My success story.

During the workshop, each person shares their stories in small groups, and receives feedback from others about what they hear in relation to this person's strengths, passions and values. As a common theme through all four stories emerges, the individual comes closer to discovering their purpose. They then work alone and in small groups to craft their purpose statement.

Munden observes, 'Two things are important. First, making sure deep individual reflection takes place. Second, encouraging people to be brave in their sharing, and generous in giving feedback and helping others. We work hard to create the right energy in the groups. The facilitator participates and shares their own story, as well as managing the process. It's particularly powerful when we run it with people who work together. They really get to know each other, and it takes out hierarchy. Everyone realizes we have the same experiences in life.'

Impact measurement is impressive. Employees who discover their purpose:

- are 9 per cent more likely to know the unique contribution they can make in their work;
- are 11 per cent more likely to find their current role fulfilling;
- spend time 5 per cent more often on things that matter for them;
- are 3 per cent more likely to feel inspired to go the extra mile in their job.

Creating the purpose statement is the first step. After the workshop, participants are asked to share their purpose with others. Teams are supported with materials to talk about their team purpose. What is the 'why' of the team? What is the legacy they want to leave? Says Munden, 'In our language, it's where purpose meets the situation you're in. It helps teams connect back to Unilever's Sustainable Living Plan, and to each person's individual purpose.'

In conclusion, Munden comes back to the importance of context: 'Being purpose-driven is about more than just workshops; you have to create the right environment. Otherwise it risks being superficial. When we start the workshop, people aren't asking "What do you mean by purpose?" The Unilever Sustainable Living Plan has been in place for eight years. We talk about purpose in many different contexts and have embedded it in as many areas as possible. For example, it's embedded in our Standards of Leadership and in our approach to well-being. There should be a perfect flow, from the individual through to their impact on our brands, into what we do in the world.'

Conclusion

Purpose matters. It matters for people, because it means that when they come to work each day, they come knowing that they make a difference, that their work means something, and that they are contributing to something bigger than just making money for shareholders. It matters for organizations, because their stakeholders increasingly expect more from them than just chasing profits, because brands with purpose grow, and because people with purpose go the extra mile. And it matters for communicators, because we can help all this happen. We stand in the middle, with the potential to influence people's experience at work for good, and to help our organizations thrive. *Our* work means something. *We* can make a difference.

Over many years, we have collaborated and worked with internal communicators in many different roles, in countless organizations, around the world. What strikes us about so many of them is that they care about the people they work with, they are passionate about their profession, and endlessly eager to learn how they can make an even bigger difference. They are people with purpose. We've learned from them and been inspired by them. We hope you, too, will be inspired by the experience we have shared in this book. It is thanks to a great many people.

References

Bolman, LG and Deal, TE (2017) *Reframing Organizations: Artistry, choice, and leadership*, John Wiley & Sons

EY Beacon Institute (2016) The state of the debate on purpose in business. [Online] www.ey.com/

Kenny, G (2014) Your company's purpose is not its vision, mission or values, *Harvard Business Review*. [Online] https://hbr.org/2014/09/your-companys-purpose-is-not-its-vision-mission-or-values

Pink, DH (2018) *Drive*, Canongate Books

Quinn, RE and Thakor, AV (2018) Creating a purpose-driven organization, *Harvard Business Review*. [Online] https://hbr.org/2018/07/creating-a-purpose-driven-organization

Seligman, MEP (2002) *Authentic Happiness*, Free Press

Sinek, S (2009) *Start With Why*, Penguin Random House

Stewart, H (2017) Dan Pink: How Drive would be different if I wrote it now. [Online] www.linkedin.com/pulse/dan-pink-how-drive-would-different-i-wrote-now-henry-stewart/

ACKNOWLEDGEMENTS

Writing a book is only possible with the help and encouragement of a lot of people. We owe a massive debt to the people who helped us with case studies who are named in the body of the book (and to their colleagues, who might not be named, but who supported us as well). Additionally, there is a vast regiment of people who have provided advice, insight and understanding when we have cancelled meetings or been preoccupied. There are too many to mention but we would especially like to acknowledge the support or inspiration we have had from:

Brian Bannister, David Beck, Shirley Beresford, Rob Briggs, Torben Bundgård, Jon Chandler, Jenny Clark, Sue Clemenson, Chris Crofts, Chris Cudmore, Mark Darby, Paul Diggins, Graeme Domm, Annabel Dunstan, Nicky Garsten, Russell Grossman, Bob Hammond, Katy Hemmings, Lachean Humphries, Neil Jenkins, Catrin Johansson, Claudia Johnson, Amy Kendrick, Maxine Kohn, Ioannis Kostopoulos, Joss Mathieson, Sue Matzen, Lise Michaud, Jane Mitchell, Aline Moura, Daphne Oliveros, Charlotte Owen, Tim Payne, Adele Pickerill, Caroline Rhodes, Angela Sinickas, Victoria Talbot, Ralph Tench, Fionnuala Tennyson, Rudiger Theilmann, Klavs Valskov, Susan Walker, Stephen Welch, Liz Yeomans and our friends at Leeds Beckett University.

And of course, none of this would be possible without the encouragement of our families. Barry, Jean, Alan, Juliet, Dan and Laura – thank you.

INDEX

CPSIA information can be obtained
at www.ICGtesting.com
Printed in the USA
LVHW071906230620
658433LV00001BA/4